This is a great book. It brir  nt-
ary voices from experier are
thoroughly committed to C000125826 Its
strength and freshness dep 1ot
so much a book for studer 'or,
reading a chapter or two, then a few weeks later another chapter
or two, and so on, so as to refresh your vision and practice.

D. A. Carson
Research Professor of New Testament
Trinity Evangelical Divinity School
Deerfield, Illinois

What a privilege pastors have in preaching the living Word
of God each week. And here is a book to encourage us in that
responsibility. Whether the reader is a pastor fresh out of
seminary or a seasoned veteran of the pulpit, he will find these
pages to be remarkably helpful and practical. Prepare to be
inspired, challenged and exhorted.

Jason Helopoulos
Assistant Pastor, University Reformed Church
Author of *A Neglected Grace*, East Lansing, Michigan

In this valuable contribution to the art and science of preaching,
Rhett Dodson has assembled a team of world-class expositors,
each providing a sample sermon together with a fascinating fly-
on-the-wall look at the preparation methods that produced them.
While sometimes revealing the methodological idiosyncrasies
of the preacher, the different approaches to sermon preparation
nevertheless display a reassuring degree of overlap, driving
home the point that, though personality, cultural context, and
stylistic preferences may vary widely, faithful exposition will
always aim at common goals (faithfulness to the text in its
context, the nurture of believers, the conversion of the lost, the
exaltation of God). Practical and encouraging, this volume will
undoubtedly further the development of faithful preachers and
faithful preaching, all to the glory and praise of the Lord.

David Strain
Senior Minister
First Presbyterian Church, Jackson, Mississippi

I love touring the workshops of craftsmen, examining the tools, the sights, the sounds, the materials and the procedures that result in works of beauty and utility. Dodson gives us just such a tour of the workshops of talented preachers, enabling us to look over the shoulders of these master craftsmen of proclaimed truth in order to learn how we might produce messages reflecting the beauty and utility of their sermons.

Bryan Chapell
Pastor, Grace Presbyterian Church, Peoria, Illinois

I have frequently attended Bible conferences to hear an accomplished expositor and, after my soul was fed by his preaching, I wanted to sit with him and have a conversation about *how* he did it. To what extent does he consult commentaries? How much does he think about illustrations? If the text has three common interpretations, does he tell the congregation all three, or just the one he thinks correct? And how much of what he does relies on creativity as opposed to merely restating the text? Is application necessary in the sermon?

Unashamed Workmen is like looking into the mind and over the shoulder of ten master expositors as they prepare, and then sitting in the audience as they deliver the fruits of their labors. The beauty of this project is that the reader can get answers, clearly noticing the differences of style and approach between the authors and yet also the one thing they hold in common: the primacy of the text.

Hershael W. York
Victor & Louise Lester Professor of Preaching
The Southern Baptist Theological Serminary
Senior Pastor, Buck Run Baptist Church
Frankfort, Kentucky

UNASHAMED WORKMEN

HOW EXPOSITORS
PREPARE AND PREACH

EDITED BY
RHETT DODSON

MENTOR

All Scripture quotations, unless otherwise indicated, are from *The Holy Bible, English Standard Version*, copyright © 2001 by Crossway Bibles, a division of Good News Publishers. Used by permission. All rights reserved. ESV Text Edition: 2007.

Scripture quotations marked "NIV" are taken from *The Holy Bible, New International Version*®. NIV®. Copyright©1973, 1978, 1984 by International Bible Society. Used by permission of Zondervan. All rights reserved.

Scripture quotations marked "NKJV" are taken from *The New King James Version*. Copyright © 1982 by Thomas Nelson, Inc. Used by permission. All rights reserved.

Copyright © Rhett Dodson

paperback ISBN 978-1-78191-319-2
epub ISBN 978-1-78191-516-5
Mobi ISBN 978-1-78191-517-2

10 9 8 7 6 5 4 3 2 1

Published in 2014
in the Mentor Imprint
by
Christian Focus Publications,
Geanies House, Fearn, Ross-shire,
IV20 1TW, Scotland, Great Britain.

www.christianfocus.com

Cover design by
Daniel van Straaten

Printed by
Bell and Bain, Glasgow

All rights reserved. No part of this publication may be reproduced, stored in a retrieval system, or transmitted, in any form, by any means, electronic, mechanical, photocopying, recording or otherwise without the prior permission of the publisher or a licence permitting restricted copying. In the U.K. such licences are issued by the Copyright Licensing Agency, Saffron House, 6-10 Kirby Street, London, EC1 8TS. www.cla.co.uk

CONTENTS

This book is dedicated to
The Rev. Dr. Hughes Oliphant Old,
Preacher of the Word of God
and Chronicler of the History of Preaching
with appreciation for his encouragement to extend my pulpit
ministry through writing

and

To all my brothers who stand each week
and proclaim the unsearchable riches of Christ

CONTRIBUTORS

Peter Adam was born in Melbourne, Australia, and studied classical music. He then trained for the ministry at Ridley College Melbourne. Peter gained his MTh from King's College London, and his PhD from Durham University. His major ministries have included lecturing at St. John's College Durham, UK, serving in Melbourne as Vicar of St. Jude's Carlton and then as Principal of Ridley Melbourne. He has also served as Chaplain of Melbourne University, Archdeacon for Parish Development, and Canon of St. Paul's Cathedral. Peter is currently Vicar Emeritus of St. Jude's Carlton. Peter's publications include *Walking in God's Words: Reading Ezra and Nehemiah Today*, *The Message of Malachi*, *Written for Us: Receiving God's Words in the Bible*, *Hearing God's Words: Biblical Spirituality*, *The Majestic Son: A Commentary on Hebrews*, and *Speaking God's Words: A Practical Theology of Preaching*. Peter continues his ministry of writing, encouraging people in ministry, speaking at conferences, preaching in churches, lecturing, supervising research students, and training preachers.

Rhett Dodson is the Senior Pastor of Grace Presbyterian Church (PCA) in Hudson, Ohio. After completing BA and MA degrees in Bible, he earned a PhD in Old Testament Interpretation. Rhett previously served as an associate pastor and seminary professor.

In addition to articles and book reviews, he is the author of *This Brief Journey: Loving and Living the Psalms of Ascents* and *To Be a Pilgrim: Further Reflections on the Psalms of Ascents*. Originally from Pickens, South Carolina, Rhett and his wife, Theresa, live in Hudson.

Iain Duguid trained as an Electrical Engineer at Edinburgh University and served as a missionary in Liberia, West Africa, before studying for the ministry at Westminster Theological Seminary in Philadelphia. He completed a PhD in Old Testament at Cambridge University, and now teaches Old Testament and Hebrew at Grove City College in Pennsylvania. He also planted Christ Presbyterian Church (ARP), where he continues to serve on the pastoral staff.

Ajith Fernando served for thirty-five years as National Director of Youth for Christ, Sri Lanka, and now serves as its Teaching Director. His primary work includes mentoring, discipling, and counseling Youth for Christ leaders and pastors, and preaching and teaching mainly in gatherings of youth and Christian leaders. He serves as a visiting lecturer at Colombo Theological Seminary. He and his wife are also active in a Methodist Church, almost all of whose members are originally from other faiths. Ajith has written fifteen books, and his books have been translated into twenty languages.

David Jackman is a graduate in English literature from Cambridge University and studied theology at Trinity College, Bristol. After working for InterVarsity (UK) for six years, he served as Minister of Above Bar Church, Southampton (UK) through the late 1970s and 1980s, before becoming the founder/director of the Cornhill Training Course in London, in 1991. He served within the Proclamation Trust for many years in this capacity and ultimately as its President. Now retired, he remains active in preaching, writing, and training ministries around the world. He is married to Heather, and they have two married children and four grandchildren.

Simon Manchester trained at Moore College in Sydney Australia and served as assistant pastor in London before taking up his position at St.Thomas, North Sydney in 1990. He has been privileged to speak at conferences at home and overseas and his weekly sermons are heard on Sydney radio. Married to Kathy, he has three grown up children.

David Meredith is senior minister at Smithton Church, Inverness, Scotland, a congregation of the Free Church of Scotland where he has served for thirty years. The church began as a plant and has grown to be one of the most influential in the denomination and in Scotland. David served as Moderator of the Free Church of Scotland in 2010 and is a frequent preacher at churches and conferences on both sides of the Atlantic. He names among his interests: motorcycles, travel, visiting graveyards and SEC football!

Josh Moody earned his PhD at Cambridge University and is Senior Pastor of College Church in Wheaton, Illinois. His books include *Journey to Joy*, *No Other Gospel*, and *The God-Centered Life*. More information may be found at www.college-church.org and www.godcenteredlife.com.

Douglas Sean O'Donnell is Senior Lecturer at Queensland Theological College, Brisbane, Australia, and formerly senior pastor of New Covenant Church in Naperville, Illinois. He earned MA degrees at both Trinity Evangelical Divinity School and Wheaton College. In addition to serving as an instructor for the Charles Simeon Trust, O'Donnell is a member of the North American Patristics Society, the US Board of the Irish Bible Institute, and the Society for the Advancement of Ecclesial Theology. He is the author of five books, including commentaries on the Song of Solomon, Ecclesiastes, and the Gospel of Matthew.

Richard D. Phillips is senior minister of Second Presbyterian Church in Greenville, SC. He is the author of over thirty books, including most recently a two-volume commentary on the Gospel of John. He is series co-editor of the Reformed Expository Commentary series, is chairman of the Philadelphia Conference on Reformed Theology, and serves as a trustee of Westminster Theological Seminary. Dr. Phillips holds degrees from the University of Michigan (BA), University of Pennsylvania

(MBA), Westminster Theological Seminary (MDiv), and Greenville Presbyterian Theological Seminary (DD). He and his wife Sharon have five children.

PREFACE

As a young Christian, one of the first Bible verses I memorized was 2 Timothy 2:15, "Study to shew thyself approved unto God, a workman that needeth not to be ashamed, rightly dividing the word of truth" (KJV). I took Paul's admonition seriously and tried diligently to learn all that I could about the Bible. I knew it was important to study God's Word in order to grow in my faith. Little did I know at the time that the Lord would call me to a life devoted to the study and proclamation of Scripture.

Paul's injunction to Timothy sets the agenda for every pastor devoted to proclaiming the whole counsel of God. Preaching presupposes study, and diligent study is nothing if not the exertion of deliberate effort to understand the meaning and purpose of every passage of Scripture in its context. Sermons don't just happen. They are the result of hard work in order to understand, explain, and apply a passage or passages to the people to whom you minister.

Such effort implies discipline. When Peter declared that he and the other apostles would devote themselves to prayer and the ministry of the Word (Acts 6:4), he understood that such devotion would require planned diligence. And planned diligence requires, well, a plan.

Soon after I began to sense a call to preach, I purchased Warren Wiersbe's *Walking with the Giants: A Minister's Guide to*

Good Reading and Great Preaching (still one of my favorite books) and began to learn about the great preachers of the past. "How did they do it?" I wondered. How does one get from a passage in the Bible to a full-fledged sermon in the pulpit? Wiersbe's vignettes of the great preachers were helpful. G. Campbell Morgan's early morning diligence inspired me to work hard. D. Martyn Lloyd-Jones's robust, Reformed, consecutive exposition moved me to make preaching primary in my ministry. And a single quotation from John Hall's 1874–75 Yale Lectures on Preaching has remained with me as a motto, indeed a *vade mecum* of proclamation in two clauses: "We are not, gentlemen, heathen philosophers finding out things; we are expositors of a revelation that settled things."

But the "how?" question remained. I asked questions, read what I could find, and headed off to university to pursue a degree in Biblical studies. Along the way, I found helpful examples in many of the preachers I got to know, in books on preaching, and a course in homiletics. My first efforts at preaching were dubious at best, and my method of sermon preparation was worse—I had no method. But eventually the pieces started to come together, and I developed a more systematic approach that has worked for me. You'll find it described later in the book.

Through the years I've remained interested in the "how?" question. And I've discovered that I'm not alone. Preachers and would-be preachers are often interested in the way that others go about the process. Homiletics textbooks can be very helpful in taking you through the various parts of a sermon, but it can often be difficult to know just how to start and work through the homiletic principles and put them into practice in a regular, week in, week out preaching ministry.

My interest in the "how?" question has led to the book you hold in your hands. Several years ago it occurred to me that it would be very helpful to assemble a team of men to explain the way they go about preparing their sermons, what tools they use, and the questions that remain uppermost in their minds as they work from text to talk. I also thought it would be helpful to include an example of an expository sermon so that one might follow the process from the study to the pulpit. With that idea in mind, I began to seek out contributors, and the end result is before you.

The plan of the book is simple. Each author contributes two chapters in which he describes his regular method of preparing to preach and then provides you with a sample sermon. You will find here a variety of approaches in the way men prepare to preach and a variety of styles in the way they preach, but the overriding concern of each is that the Word of God be explained and applied clearly so that Jesus Christ is exalted. In the preparation chapters, some men will walk you through a typical week of study while others focus more on asking key questions or the use of certain tools. The sermons cover a variety of biblical passages. Several authors chose Old Testament texts, while three messages are from the Gospels. And Josh Moody chose a compelling passage from Revelation. The sermon I've included has a decided evangelistic thrust to demonstrate that evangelism can be done through exposition. While it was impossible to cover all of the genres that occur in the Bible, the diversity found here should prove helpful.

Each author expresses his own method and his own opinions about preaching. You may find that you agree, disagree, or aren't quite sure. But what you will find is a wealth of experience to glean from, debate with, and, hopefully, grow through as a herald of God's Word so that your progress becomes evident to all (1 Tim. 4:15).

If you haven't yet developed a method of sermon preparation, my prayer is that these chapters will inspire you to cultivate a systematic way to pursue your studies. "Ministerial study is a *sine qua non* of success. It is absurdly useless to talk of methods of preaching, where there is no method of preparation."[1] If you already have a fairly set way that you go about getting from a passage to the sermon, I hope that you will find ways here to improve your preparation process or, at the very least, be inspired to work harder at the task. The Rev. Dr. William Fitch, sometime pastor of Knox Presbyterian Church in Toronto, wrote, "There is a craftsmanship in preaching that fully repays the study we give to it."[2]

---

1. J. W. Alexander, *Thoughts on Preaching* (1864; repr., Edinburgh: Banner of Truth, 1988), 167.

2. "The Glory of Preaching" in *Christianity Today*, January 20, 1967.

My desire is that you will find in this book a personable companion to the standard homiletics texts that will encourage you to work hard, pray hard, and preach with all the strength God gives you. I also hope that professors of preaching will find this volume helpful supplemental reading for their courses. These chapters will put flesh on the bones—the principles of homiletics—and encourage students that these bones can indeed live in the pulpit ministry of the church!

Each of the men who have contributed to this volume is engaged in a full-time preaching ministry, and some of them carry out this ministry internationally. I am thankful that they have thought this task worthy to take time out of their busy schedules to contribute to this volume. I also want to thank the Rev. Dr. Malcolm Maclean and the good folks of Christian Focus Publications for their belief in this book and the diligent effort they have extended to publish it.

The challenge that lies before us is to preach the Word (2 Tim. 4:2). May the Lord use this book in your life and ministry so that you do so as an unashamed workman who rightly handles the Word of truth.

Should you have any questions or comments, please feel free to contact me at unashamedworkmen@gmail.com.

Rhett Dodson
Hudson, Ohio
February 2014

1 What is God's Word for these people?

PETER ADAM

I work on my sermons by asking questions, because they get my mind working. What does God say in this text to these people? What does He want them to learn, to remember, to know? How does He want them to change, and what does He want them to do? What impact does God intend today for this congregation from these words?

As we begin, there are two things you should know. First, as will become evident throughout this chapter, the part of the Bible that has influenced me most in thinking about preaching is 2 Timothy 3:15–4:2.[1] Second, I think of sermon preparation in three stages:

- Preparation for preaching,
- Working on the sermon, and
- Reviewing the sermon

Preparation for Preaching
The first set of questions has to do with the preliminary work to prepare to preach. Answering these questions calls for personal discipline and pastoral wisdom.

---

1. For more ideas on 2 Timothy for preachers, see my "The Pastor as Preacher" in Melvin Tinker, ed., *The Renewed Pastor: Essays on the Pastoral Ministry in Honour of Philip Hacking* (Fearn, Ross-shire: Christian Focus Publications: Mentor, 2011), 67-82.

1. How is God currently changing me to make me into a preacher?
Being a preacher requires ever-increasing Biblical intelligence, emotional intelligence, theological intelligence, and pastoral intelligence. Of course, by intelligence I mean alert and perceptive wisdom. I don't mean cleverness but depth of understanding and wisdom.

I need to be growing all the time in knowing and understanding the Bible. I need to know my Bible more and more, and not think to myself, "Well, I know it all now." And I need to be continually reformed and changed by the Bible.

I need to be growing all the time in emotional intelligence. God wants to transform people, and I want my sermons to aid that process. God understands our emotional complexities, and I need to do the same. Most people are governed by their emotions. Just as emotions can be barriers to transforming grace, so also emotions can fuel our transformation. To be an effective preacher, I need a pastor's heart. I need to love the people I am preaching to and to understand them and the things that shape them: personality, experience, family, work, and social and political context. I must serve people, love them, rejoice with them and weep with them. Preaching is ministry, not performance.

I need to be growing all the time in theological intelligence. I need to understand the deep structures of Christianity, and the deep intellectual structures of society. I need to be alert to the theological meaning of Scripture, and the theological significance of society's current ideas, assumptions, practices, strengths, sins, and trends. I need to be able to do theological analysis, not just sociological analysis, psychological analysis, or political analysis.

I need to be growing all the time in pastoral intelligence. Pastoral intelligence is a combination of Biblical, emotional, and theological intelligence. All Christians need pastoral intelligence to care for each other and love their neighbors. Preachers need pastoral intelligence, not just about individuals, but also about groups. Preachers need wisdom to understand how people function as members of churches, the dynamics of their relationships and relational structures. Our aim is not just to transform individuals, but to transform churches.

We need to be Biblically, emotionally, theologically, and pastorally wise to understand the Bible, to understand people, and to serve people in our sermons.[2]

2. How will I set time and energy aside to focus on sermon preparation?

I need to set aside time and energy for the creative act of preparing and preaching a sermon. Routine tasks take less energy. Creative tasks like preparation and preaching take lots of energy.

People may want us to preach great sermons, but may underestimate the time needed to prepare great sermons! Or they may want us to spend all our time doing administration, being constantly available, and constantly visiting! If we want to preach, we need to find time to prepare.

I need uninterrupted time, so I clear the diary, turn off the phones and email, and clear the desk of all other material. Of course the moment I start preparing, I think of many other things I should be doing, so I keep a list on the desk, and as soon as one of these comes into my mind I put it on the list, and get back to work!

And I need to be self-disciplined so that I don't waste time in preparation, by following up interesting by-ways that will not help the sermon, or by sitting there achieving nothing!

I find that if I spend ten hours in sermon preparation, it is best to do that in three or four blocks on successive days, rather than spending a whole day at a time on this task. This keeps me fresher, and helps me make good use of my subconscious, which keeps on working on the problems and challenges of the sermon when I am doing other things. I have my best ideas when I am not at my desk! And if I meet a particular problem, I leave my desk and go for a walk, and the solution will often come to me as I do so.

For each sermon, I allocate half of the preparation time to the Scripture passage, and half of the time to the people. My natural tendency is to spend all the time studying the Scripture, and no

---

2. My first and last questions are about my readiness for ministry, because who we are as people is fundamental to the ministry we do. For more, see my *Speaking God's Words: A Practical Theology of Preaching* (Vancouver: Regent, 2004), 157-72.

time on the people. Those sermons always end with the words, "And may God show us how to put this into practice in our own lives," which is code for, "I have no idea."

And I pray. I pray that God will help me understand this Bible passage, and I pray for the people who will hear it. I pray that God will help me to shape the sermon so that the people I am preaching to will be able to receive it, understand it, and make good use of it. I pray that God will increase my love for the Bible passage, and my love for the people to whom I will preach. For I know that it is not enough to love preaching: I must love God's words and love God's people. And I ask God to help me to preach for His glory, not to meet my own needs, or to win approval from the people.[3]

By the way, if some preachers do not do enough preparation, others do too much! This may happen because they are perfectionists, because they don't use their time efficiently, or because they have absorbed the idea that ministers should spend all their time in the study, after the example of the great Jonathan Edwards.[4]

3. Am I preaching the full range of Scripture?

When we plan our preaching program, it is important that we preach the Old Testament as well as the New. In His wisdom, God has kindly provided twice as much Old Testament as New Testament, because He knows we need it. People can't understand the New Testament without the Old Testament, and they can't fully understand Christ without the Old Testament. The basic buildings blocks of Christianity are taught in the Old Testament. There we learn that there is one God, the creator, who rules the world; that everyone is made in God's image; that everyone is under God's judgment. We learn that God is a God of promise, that God pours out His electing and covenant love, and provides us with instruction, law, and wisdom. We learn that

---

3. Of course, I sometimes preach to people and congregations I do not know. I always ask the minister what the people need in terms of the Scripture to preach from, and their current needs. I pray for them, ignorant of who they are, but trusting that God will give me pastoral insight.

4. For people of modest intellectual ability like ourselves, this would be an indulgence. See my *Speaking God's Words*, 160-65.

we should not worship other gods, nor should we worship the creation. We hear God's call to honor Him in every part of our lives. We see that God rules the nations, and plans to bring the nations to know and serve Him. These things are clearly taught in the Old Testament, and assumed in the New. Believers today need to know the Old Testament.

We should also choose to preach unfamiliar and difficult books of the Bible. If we don't preach these books, our people will be nervous about reading them. We should be stretching our congregations, as well as showing them how to tackle new or difficult parts of the Bible. One advantage of preaching unfamiliar books is that people say, "I never heard that before", rather than, "I know all that already"!

4. What book of the Bible does this congregation need?

We choose which books of the Bible to preach in the light of educational strategy and pastoral need. Our educational strategy is to teach the congregation the breadth and depth of the Bible, God's syllabus for the human race. We need to ask ourselves such things as: What parts of the Bible do they need to know? What balance of Old and New Testaments? How can I show them the inner connections of the Bible and its developing themes (for example linking Leviticus and Hebrews, or Ezekiel and John, or Exodus with Isaiah and with Mark, or Exodus with Revelation)? We need an overall educational strategy for our church, remembering that our church will include enquirers and unbelievers.

We should also keep in mind pastoral needs. If our people need a good dose of creation theology and teaching on the providence and promises of God, then preach Genesis. If they need encouragement under pressure, preach Job. If they need wisdom for daily life, preach Proverbs, Ecclesiastes, or James. If they are facing heresy, then preach Jeremiah, Galatians, or Jude. If they need to know the person and work of Christ, then preach a Gospel or Colossians.

Our preaching should be intentional, not just in individual sermons, but in our overall plan. My plan for the year would often include one Old Testament book, one gospel, and one other New Testament book, including one difficult book. I also include a topical series. This could be theological topics, to give a theological overview of Biblical teaching, or topics from daily life. I do the latter, because I want to train people to be useful in daily conversation, and to be able to answer questions like, "What do Christians think about divorce?" "What do you think about social inequality?" "What do you believe about the new Atheism?" "Do dogs go to heaven?" We need to model how to answer these questions if we want our people to be well equipped to talk with their neighbors and friends.[5]

5. *What is the message of the whole book of the Bible in which this passage occurs?*

I try to do this as I prepare for my next year's ministry. My usual practice is to spend a year with a book of the Bible, to soak myself in it, prepare it, and then preach it. If not, I will need to spend a whole week immersed in a book. Finding the *central ministry purpose* of a book of the Bible is essential preparation for all the sermons.

The central ministry purpose of the book is its ministry aim, its pastoral intention. It is the answer to the question that we could ask of the author of the book: "In one sentence, why did you write this book?" Or the answer to the question we could ask of God: "Why did you cause this book to be written?" A statement of the central ministry purpose should include not only the central theme, but also how and why readers should act in response. It uses the language of action, not analysis.

The *text* is the book. It is odd to refer to isolated verses of Scripture as *texts*. The real texts of Scripture are of course the complete books that make up the Scriptures. Preaching books of the Bible takes the God-given book and the God-chosen method of revelation seriously. It respects the human author of the book and is culturally appropriate, because most people naturally read books from beginning to end. It also models a good way to read the Bible.

A big investment of time in working on the message and content of a whole book of the Bible is really worth it, not least

---

5.   For more on the role of the Bible in preaching see my *Speaking God's Words*, 13-56, 87-124.

because when I have done this work, each individual sermon is much easier and quicker to prepare.

Some Bible books make it easy for us, because they tell us clearly and succinctly why they were written, for example in John 20:30-31; Colossians 2:6-7; 1 Timothy 3:14-15, and Jude 4. In other books we have to look for common themes, common words, common ideas. We expect to find the main ministry purpose of a book of the Bible in each of the main sections of the book, and at the natural climaxes of the book.[6] It is often hard work, but it is always well worth it.[7]

You can begin an expository sermon series by preaching on the main purpose of the book, basing the sermon on the key passage which expresses that purpose. This helps people know what to expect, and gives them an overview of the book. Over the following weeks you can then go to the beginning of the book, and begin the consecutive exposition.

6. *How will I divide this book into preachable units?*

We need literary, educational, and pastoral wisdom to make this decision. It is possible to preach a whole book in one sermon. I have done so with Jude; I have even done it with Job! As I divide up the book into the passages to preach, I keep the following issues in mind:

- I don't want to go so slowly through the text that I lose momentum and meaning, and lose the impact of the whole book, or end up giving a Biblical theology of every word in the text.

- I don't want to use a style of exegesis and preaching that suits a densely-argued epistle when the literary style of the book demands larger units such as chapters.

---

6. See my "Finding the Central Ministry Purpose of a Book of the Bible" at http://www.niministryassembly.org.uk/docs/NIMA-2008-02-Handout-Peter-Adam.pdf (accessed Feb. 10, 2014).

7. Some commentaries are helpful, but many are not. Those that are not are those that focus on the words, but not the meaning, those that neglect theology, or those that tackle the theology, but not the pastoral purpose of the theology, the pastoral purpose of the book.

- I don't want to provoke the congregation by demanding from them more than they can manage. I once preached for nine months on Hebrews, but did it in three three-month segments with a break between the segments. Parents should not provoke their children, and preachers should not provoke their people! We should challenge our people to grow but not discourage them by setting unbearable standards!

- I do want to vary my expository speed so that each year I will include one slow and detailed exposition (of a dense passage), one medium speed exposition, and one overview exposition, such as the book of Revelation in six sermons.

- I don't want passages that are too short to make full sense or too long to be manageable.

- If the book is so long that it is not easily preached, then either I take it in two or three segments, and do one segment each year. Or else I preach some chapters, and provide studies on the other chapters for home groups and individuals.

Working on the Sermon

After asking and answering these initial, preparatory questions, it is time to begin work on the actual sermon. This work involves a number of additional questions.

1. Am I making my two journeys, the first to the text, and the second to the people who will be present?

During my preparation I need to take two journeys. I have to travel back to the passage in its original context. Commentaries are helpful in this process. Studying the passages in the original languages emphasizes that these are not contemporary documents. What did this passage mean originally? I have to set aside what I want to find and set aside contemporary issues. I must enter the world of the writer and those who received the writing to find the message.

Then I have to travel to the world of the congregation, remembering that this could include enquirers and unbelievers. What should I do with the message of this text for this people? How can I help them to travel back with me to the world of the text, and then return to their own lives and their life as a congregation, with the message of this text?

Sometimes I find these journeys difficult, but both journeys are necessary. Without the first, my preaching will be superficial, because it will not be based on the Bible. Without the second, my preaching will be superficial, because it will be information, not transformation.

2. *What insights can I get from the three contexts of the passage?*

The three contexts of the passage are the following:

First, the immediate context of the passage. I need to keep in mind the flow and progression of the book, and especially the immediate context of the passage. I will have a clearer idea about the message of the passage if I know its context. Why does it begin where it does? What happens next?

Second, the context of the book of the Bible. I have already covered this exercise above, but I need to keep referring back to the pastoral purpose of the whole book to understand this part of it. A book of the Bible is like a sentence, and each part of the sentence has its meaning in the context of the whole sentence. This is often a neglected context, so you must keep it in mind.

Third, the context of the whole Bible. This context shows us how the passage relates to Biblical Theology, the unfolding verbal revelation of God. By employing Biblical Theology, we can see how each part fits into the larger picture of the whole Bible and how God's self-revelation moves from promise to fulfillment. I make good use of cross-references, and I read one new book on Biblical Theology a year, to keep this perspective fresh in my mind.

If I am getting stuck on a passage, I often find that looking at these three contexts sparks my imagination!

3. *What did this passage mean for the people to whom it was written?*

Some books of the Bible were written as letters, and the question is simply what did the writer of the letter intend for the people to whom it was written. Other books of the Bible are different, in that they contain words for people other than those for whom the book was written, such as the disciples and the crowds to whom Jesus spoke His words, or the people of God on the plains of Moab who heard Moses's sermons in Deuteronomy.

I find it very useful to ask, "What did this mean for the people for whom it was *written*?" "What did Matthew, Mark, Luke, and John intend when they recounted Jesus's words?" "What was the purpose of Deuteronomy, or Judges, or Ruth for the people for whom they were *written*?" If I am struggling with application, then the "Why was it *written*?" question is very productive.

4. How does this passage apply to this congregation?
All of Scripture is relevant and important for God's people. I need, however, to think clearly about how this passage applies to these people today. It may be immediately relevant or generally relevant.

Consider, for example, Malachi 3:8: "Will man rob God? Yet you are robbing me." That may be immediately relevant, because the congregation is casual and negligent in their giving to God. If so, I preach it directly to them. But if the congregation is actually generous and self-sacrificial (like the church at Macedonia in 2 Corinthians 8:1-7), then it would be wrong to say that they were robbing God when they were not. So why is it worth preaching Malachi 3 to this godly congregation? To warn them of the danger of drifting into this pattern of behavior; to challenge any individuals who are not generous to God; to train people to know how to help stingy Christians they meet; and train them to know what to pray for churches which are stingy.

This is why preaching takes pastoral intelligence, because we have to know how immediately the passage applies to my congregation. So, from another perspective, if there is conflict in the church, which passage of Scripture applies most immediately? Is it Galatians 1? This passage tackles the life and death issue of gospel clarity. Is it Romans 14 and 15? This deals with issues about which Christians may differ, reminding them that they must welcome each other and not judge each other. Is it Philippians 4:2? This is about getting along with others. It would be wrong to apply Romans 14 in a Galatians 1 situation, as it would be wrong to apply Galatians 1 in a Philippians 4 situation.

We need the same pastoral intelligence in one-to-one ministry. Imagine you are taking a new Christian through John's Gospel, and the person is ill. You would need to think carefully when you reach John 5:14 (the man had been paralyzed because of his sin), and again when you reach John 9:3 (the man's blindness was not the result of his sin). Which applies to the person? The book of Job is a great warning that a general truth (people suffer because of their sin) does not apply directly in every situation! Preachers need the pastoral intelligence that Job's friends lacked!

To apply Scripture incorrectly is a failure in *pastoral intelligence*. It may also be an example of an inadequate understanding of the whole of Scripture. Preachers often practice *inappropriate universalization*. This is when we take what a passage says and apply it as though it was the only teaching of the Bible on this subject. But the whole Bible may give a variety of messages. Take suffering as an example. Believers may suffer because of their sin (John 5:14); because God wants to prove their endurance (Job); because Satan is attacking them (1 Pet. 5); because Satan is attacking them and God uses that attack to teach them of strength perfected in weakness (2 Cor. 12); for the sake of gospel growth (Acts 9:16); because they are godly (2 Tim. 3:12); because of the sin of others (Gen. 37); or so that they are able to share God's consolation with others (2 Cor. 1). Make sure you hear all that the Bible has to say on a topic so that you don't universalize the passage you are preaching.

5. *What does this passage mean for the people of God?*

Most books in the Bible were addressed to the people of God, not to individuals. We in the Western world have been brainwashed into individualism. We think and feel as individuals, we regard individuals as the most important form of human life, we privilege individuals over communities, and so we read and preach the Bible as if it was addressed to individuals.

Most books of the Bible address the people of God. Deuteronomy comprises sermons to Israel as a nation. Paul wrote most of his letters to churches. Paul's letters to Timothy and Titus are primarily about the life of the churches, and his letter to Philemon was also addressed to "the church in your house" (Philem. 2). Although Luke and Acts were written for Theophilus (Luke 1:1-4; Acts 1:1), it was common practice to dedicate writings to an important person, while keeping a wider audience in mind.

"Scripture is God preaching,"[8] and in the Bible God is mainly preaching to His people. We should follow what God has done, and address the book we are preaching to the church of our day. Our first question should be, "What is God saying to us?" Not, "What is God saying to me?" or "What is God saying to individuals in the congregation?" So rather than looking for individual application, we should work for corporate application. *Corporate* here does not mean big business, it means *body*, as in "the body of Christ." We should train ourselves to look for the shared values of our churches, our shared godliness, our shared sins, our shared blind spots, our shared weaknesses, our shared strengths.

This kind of preaching does not diminish individual responsibility; in fact, it increases it. So if the text says, "We should love one another" (1 John 3:11), then it is not enough for me as an individual to love others in the church. I must also work, pray and encourage until all the members of the church love one another! And I must also work, pray, and encourage the leadership of the church to demonstrate that love, to model it to the church, to encourage members of the church to love one another, and to challenge those who don't love one another to repent and change their ways.

This way of thinking about the Bible and the sermon also means that we must be patient enough to learn things that we don't need ourselves, but which God teaches us so that we are ready to teach, help, or train someone else, or answer the questions that they ask.

6. *Am I making the most of the passage of Scripture I am preaching?*

Finding the *meaning* of the Bible passage is worth doing, but it is also worth asking, "How does this Bible passage convey this message?" What methods, what ingredients are here, and how can I use them in my preaching? These include the following key ingredients: structure, images, stories or illustrative language, motivations, emotions, key words, arguments, evidence, and contrasts. Looking for all of these alerts me to what is in the

---

8. J.I. Packer, *God Has Spoken* (Grand Rapids: Baker, 1979), 97.

passage and how its message is communicated. I want to pick up all the clues I can for my sermon. I find commentaries useful here and also the original languages.[9]

- I look for structure, because I want the congregation to engage with the beginning of the passage and follow the journey of the passage to its conclusion.

- I look for images, stories, or illustrative language because these provide useful illustrations for the sermon. They project the meaning of the passage and should work well in the sermon.

- I look for motivations, because I want to avoid the default motivation beloved of evangelical preachers, that of obeying instructions (unless it is present in the passage!). The Bible uses many other motivations, such as seeing the danger, pleasing God, making sensible decisions, avoiding looking foolish, making wise long-term decisions. Find them, and use them!

- I look for emotions, because they will tell me what style of preaching I should use and help me engage the congregation.

- I look for key words in the passage, so that I can use them in the sermon. This reinforces the power of the sermon and helps people see that the Bible and the sermon connect.

- I look for arguments and evidence because I want the congregation to know why they should do what the passage urges them to do.

- I look for contrasts. These contrasts are those within the passage, and also the contrasts between what the passage says and what I think or expect, or between what the passage says and what the congregation thinks or expects.

My aim is to include the content and style of the passage, as well as its message: or rather, to use the content and style of the

---

9. Useful commentaries have three characteristics: they focus on the text of the Bible, not on the comments of other commentators; they tackle the theological issues of the text, not just the linguistics; and they are not too detailed or too long! I make good use of one-volume Bible commentaries, because they often give a concise overview of the book and the passage.

passage in order to convey its message. And I want to avoid the default evangelical application, which is that we should read the Bible more and do what it says. This is satisfactory if it is the message of the passage of Scripture, but otherwise it obscures what God intends to achieve through this particular part of the Bible.

I try to avoid expression like "preach a sermon", or "teach the Bible." I want to use the Bible to "reprove, rebuke, and exhort" (2 Tim. 4:2).

7. Am I rightly serving the two purposes of Scripture: one, to make us wise for salvation through faith in Christ Jesus, and two, to teach, reprove, correct, and train in righteousness?
These two purposes are based on Paul's words in 2 Timothy 3:15-17. What God joins together, we should not separate. It is useful to distinguish between these two uses but not to separate them. Some preachers focus on one and neglect the other. I want to achieve both purposes.

First, the Scriptures make us wise for salvation through Christ. "And he said to them, 'O foolish ones, and slow of heart to believe all that the prophets have spoken! Was it not necessary that the Christ should suffer these things and enter into his glory?' And beginning with Moses and all the Prophets, he interpreted to them in all the Scriptures the things concerning himself" (Luke 24:25-27).

Second, the Scriptures teach us how to live in response to Christ. When Paul wrote to the Corinthians he warned them from the history of God's people in their wilderness wanderings. "Now these things … were written down for our instruction, on whom the end of the ages has come" (1 Cor. 10:11).

And again, "For whatever was written in former days was written for our instruction, that through endurance and through the encouragement of the Scriptures we might have hope" (Rom. 15:4).

Indeed, Scripture shows us how a saving act may also serve as an example for us to follow. In 1 Peter 2:18-25, Christ through His sufferings provided a unique act of atonement. "He himself bore our sins in his body on the tree, that we might die to sin

and live to righteousness. By his wounds you have been healed."
(v. 24). But these same sufferings are also an example to follow.
"For to this you have been called, because Christ also suffered
for you, leaving you an example, so that you might follow in his
steps" (v. 21).

We need to distinguish between these two uses of the sufferings
of Christ, but not separate them. They are distinguishable,
but not mutually contradictory. Of course imitating Christ's
sufferings does not save us, but saved people should follow
Christ's example!

We should use the Bible to preach the gospel to unbelievers
and believers, and also to teach people how to live.

8. Have I pruned and shaped my sermon to make it more effective, and how will I engage the people in this sermon?

Too many words, too many ideas, too little structure, and too
little purpose make sermons difficult to listen to. If the sermon
is not focused and intentional, it will have little impact. I need
to prune away good ideas (often two-thirds of the good things
I have found!) to sharpen the sermon. I find it useful near the
end of my preparation to say to myself, "What I really want to
tell them is...." and then sharpen the sermon for that purpose.

It is my job to engage the congregation, to help them listen,
understand, and pay attention. I must use language that is
designed to be heard, not read, with more clarity, and with
more emphasis of the important points. I need to think about
my listeners and how they may need help at challenging or
difficult moments in the sermon, by using an illustration, an
application, a memorable phrase, a self-disclosure, or arresting
language. In particular, I find applicatory illustrations, that is
illustrations that show what it is like to put this passage into
practice, most useful. For the main point of a sermon, I might
use three applications: one to clarify, one to motivate, and one
to apply. I also need to decide when to give the application: at
the end, scattered through the sermon, or at the beginning.[10]
I try not to follow the same outline each week, but to vary my
approach as much as I can.

---

10. See my *Speaking God's Words*, 97-102.

As I shape my sermon, I ensure that I think through the range of people who will be present; from unbelievers to mature saints, from the ignorant to the edified, from the lapsed to the mature. I want to make sure that I engage them all.

Reviewing the sermon

Before I preach, I need to review the sermon. Here are the two questions I ask at that point.

1. Have I succeeded in the nine engagements necessary for good preaching?

We learn to preach by learning from good examples. I have learned much from studying John Calvin's sermons. Calvin helped to refashion expository preaching, and he provides a great example for us. His preaching involved nine deep engagements.[11] Any one of these is demanding; to combine all nine engagements is very demanding. But this provides a standard I set myself in my preaching, and also provides nine useful questions to ask about any sermon that I preach. Will this sermon:

- Help the congregation engage with God?

- Engage with the Bible?

- Engage in theology?

- Engage my own humanity in my preaching?

- Engage with the congregation?

- Engage the congregation as hearers?

- Engage in training the congregation in holiness and usefulness?

- Engage in training them to support God's gospel plan?

- Engage in training up future preachers?

---

11. See my "'Preaching of a Lively Kind': Calvin's engaged expository preaching" in *Engaging With Calvin: Aspects of the Reformer's Legacy for Today,* ed. Mark D. Thompson, (Nottingham: Apollos, 2009) and also "Calvin's Preaching and Homiletic: Nine Engagements, Part 1", *Churchman*, 124:3, 2010 and "Calvin's Preaching and Homiletic: Nine Engagements, Part 2", *Churchman*, 124:4, 2010.

2. Am I ready to preach this sermon?

Again, I must ask myself questions.

Do I love the part of the Bible I am to preach? Do I love the people, and am I ready to serve them? Am I ready to "reprove, rebuke, and exhort, with complete patience and teaching" (2 Tim. 4:2)? Have I prayed that God will help me understand and teach the Bible rightly? Have I prayed for the people who will hear, that God will use this passage of the Bible and my sermon to convert, transform, build up, and equip them for life and ministry?

Have I preached this sermon to myself? Are there sins I need to confess before I preach it to others? Do I trust that God will use His Spirit-inspired words of the Bible to do His gracious work? Do I trust that God will use my words for His glory? Am I ready to honor God in my ministry and preach before Him (2 Tim. 4:1)? Am I ready to "preach the Word" (2 Tim. 4:2)?

2   If I perish, I perish

(Esther 4)

PETER ADAM

It was the worst of times. Esther and her people were the people of God, but they had been left behind in the capital of the Persian empire when many of God's people had returned to Jerusalem after their exile in Babylon. The Persians were sympathetic to people of many faiths within their empire, but God seemed far away. He is not even mentioned by name in this book! Persia was a great empire, but the picture we have of its court in the book of Esther is that of conspicuous power, conspicuous wealth, conspicuous luxury, conspicuous consumption, and conspicuous moral corruption, including sexual abuse.

The Persian empire had all that our societies around the world value: power, wealth, luxury, and consumption. But the corruption and sexual abuse at its center showed its moral bankruptcy.

Esther herself had suffered from the sexual abuse, in that appalling beauty pageant by which King Ahasuerus found his new queen, discarding women he had abused until he found his new bride. And Esther, though queen of a great empire, was tarnished by what she had endured, and by marriage to an idolater, King Ahasuerus. Her people were in exile, away from God. Perhaps she too felt in a personal exile, trapped in marriage to a pagan.

With the rise to power of Haman, sworn opponent of the Jews, storm-clouds are on the horizon. Haman has the power, opportunity and plan to destroy all the Jews in the Persian empire. This included the Jews who lived in Jerusalem and Judah, as they too were part of the empire. So this genocide may well have included all the Jews in the world. God's people are in mortal danger, and if God's people are in danger, so is God's gospel plan for the world. If God's people are destroyed, there will be no Messiah, for "from their race, according to the flesh, is the Christ, who is God over all, blessed forever" (Rom. 9:5). And if no Messiah, then no Savior for Jew or Gentile, no atoning death, no resurrection, no church, no forgiveness, no eternal life!

Mordecai, therefore, challenges Esther to act to save her people, by appealing to the king. He wanted her "to go to the king to beg his favor and plead with him on behalf of her people"(4:8). Esther is reluctant, because she risks death if she approaches the king without an invitation, as we see in the next three verses. Mordecai is confident that God will somehow save his people from genocide (4:12-14), but challenges her: "Who knows whether you have not come to the kingdom for such a time as this?" (4:14).

It is all very well to plan to be brave when we feel in control. It is quite different to be brave when we feel cornered. Listen to Esther's words: "Go, gather all the Jews to be found in Susa, and hold a fast on my behalf, and do not eat or drink for three days, night or day. I and my young women will also fast as you do. Then I will go to the king, though it is against the law, and if I perish, I perish" (4:16).

Turn to God

Esther asks for prayer support, for she knows that it is only if God acts that His people will be rescued. And Esther decides to act, to go to the king to plead for her people, even though she may die in the attempt. Notice that Esther knew that without God's work, what she did would be of no value, so she called her fellow-believers to pray.

And I want you to turn to God first, not last. Our first instinct should be to turn to God, and to ask others to turn to God in times of crisis. We should never think, let alone say, "Well, all we can do is pray"!

I want you to put together two powerful sayings from this chapter: Mordecai's challenge, "for such a time as this", and Esther's response, "If I perish, I perish."

You see, it is all very well for us to create opportunities for us to serve God. Praise God when we can do so, and praise God when He blesses us and uses our strategy and work. But so often, we don't choose opportunities, they choose us! Or rather, God gives us opportunities to serve when we least expect them, and in the most unpromising of circumstances.

Once I was serving as an expert witness in a court case, and my ideas were not very popular. I was being interrogated by a lawyer, and the judge intervened with some of her own questions. I had referred to helping someone become a Christian. The judge asked, "How would you do that?" What a great opportunity, but not one that I planned. I quickly thanked God (silently), and then gave as full an answer as I could! I did not choose the moment, the moment chose me, or rather, God chose the moment.

But Esther's moment, Esther's time, Esther's opportunity, was a costly one. She might die in the attempt, and if she died she would fail. Here was the opportunity: "for such a time as this." And here was her response, "If I perish, I perish." Better to serve God even if I fail, than to fail to serve God.

Notice that Esther recognized that God had brought her to this place, this time, and this opportunity. She trusted the hidden hand of God, His providential rule and the care of God in her own life. She knew that nothing happens by accident, that all our times are in the hands of God.

Notice also how isolated Esther was when she made this decision. She was cut off from Mordecai, her uncle and protector, because under Persian law he was not able to enter the queen's apartments, as we see in Esther 4:1-8. And she was cut off from her husband, King Ahasuerus, as we see in Esther 4:11, because under Persian law no one could approach the king without being summoned, on pain of death. How alone she was! And yet, she still trusted God.

I want you to trust the God of Esther, and trust that God rules your life and cares for you in everything. You are always perfectly safe in God's hands, in the hands of the good shepherd, the Lord Jesus Christ. Trust God's hidden hand.

Risk

We like God's providential care when He rescues us from trouble, and rightly so! But here, God's providential care has placed Esther in trouble, and opens the opportunity for more trouble! Yet she was willing to serve God who had brought her to this place, this time, and this opportunity, and to serve Him by risking her life to protect her people.

I want you to learn to follow Esther in her willingness to suffer and die for the sake of God's people, the church of Jesus Christ. I want you to learn to lay down your life for your brothers and sisters, in big ways and in small ways.

Here is what faith feels like ... wobbly at the knees. It might not work. She might die in the attempt. Her death might achieve nothing at all. But better to serve God even if I fail, than to fail to serve God. Her gravestone might read, "She died for nothing", but even if it did, it should also read, "She died serving God."

A good friend of mine had Esther 4:16 as his *favorite* Bible verse: "If I perish, I perish." When I think of him, I always think of those words on his lips. For him it meant that he would do worthwhile things whatever the personal cost. "If I perish, I perish."

We might think that these are extraordinary words. Yet the Bible tells us that Esther's willingness to die to save the people is just part of the normal Christian life. We read in 1 John, "By this we know love, that he laid down his life for us, and we ought to lay down our lives for the brothers. But if anyone has the world's goods and sees his brother in need, yet closes his heart against him, how does God's love abide in him? Little children, let us not love in word or talk but in deed and in truth" (3:16-18).

Is this not remarkable? We ought to lay down our lives for our brothers and sisters, as Esther decided to do! We should have the same commitment, the same self-sacrificing love, as Esther had. We are called to the same personal cost, the same sacrifice. Well, not quite the same, because all John wants us to do is to give to fellow-believers in need, to have pity on them, to love them in deeds and in truth. And even more remarkably, if we follow Esther's example, we will be following the example of the Lord Jesus Christ: "By this we know love, that he laid down his life for us, and we ought to lay down our lives for the brothers."

I remember reading of a sermon preached at the funeral of a Christian leader who had died in an attempt to save a child who was drowning. The preacher pointed out that we naturally think of this as tragedy, but we should think of it as a triumph. For, as the preacher pointed out, Jesus said, "This is my commandment, that you love one another as I have loved you. Greater love has no one than this, that someone lay down his life for his friends" (John 15:12-13). The preacher went on to say that we naturally think of this as extraordinary, but in fact it ought to be ordinary, as we show our love for each other in self-sacrifice and service.

Ordinary opportunities

You might think, "Well, Esther had an extraordinary opportunity. If I had that kind of opportunity, it would be worth doing. But what does it matter what I do?"

You miss the point. All believers are called to lay down their lives in love for other believers every day. We do that by honoring others, by serving others, by setting aside our own preferences in favor of others, by giving practical help to those in need, by welcoming those who are not like us, by praying for others, by encouraging others, by not insisting on our own way in our churches, by giving others time and attention, by showing welcoming hospitality, by supporting others in ministry, and by supporting brothers and sisters under persecution or in great need around the world. If we follow Esther, we will find that we are following Jesus Christ, who laid down his life for his friends.

Why is it so difficult to love people? Why is it so difficult to love fellow-believers?

> To live above with the saints we love
> will all be bliss and glory.
> To live below with the saints we know
> is quite a different story.

It may be that we are divided over big and significant issues in our church, and we find it hard to love and serve people who are so clearly wrong! Or it may be that it is the smallest and most trivial aspects of others that make it hard for us to love and serve them. We may not do them any harm, but that is not enough. We are called to lay down our lives for others. And I guess, if that is what God wants, then we are actually harming people by not treating them as God wants us to do.

For me, I don't mind loving people and serving them when I am ready to do it, when I chose to do it, when I have the spare energy and time to do it, and when it is in my diary. I am a happy servant when I choose the time, place, and action. That is why I find Esther such a powerful personal challenge. She did not choose the time, place, or action—they chose her. Or rather, God placed her there and gave her that opportunity as a precious gift. She recognized the hidden hand of God in her life, prayed to God, and acted to serve Him by loving His people.

In a way, I suppose that the big gesture is easier than the daily discipline. But our likeness to Christ is more likely to be required in daily discipline than in big gestures. And daily discipline trains us for big gestures, when and if they come our way.

I think that one of the lost arts of our age is that of embracing suffering. We are trained to avoid it at all costs, unless we are training to be elite athletes! We need to learn the art of embracing suffering, because it is sure to come our way. We need to learn the art of embracing suffering, otherwise it will have us on the run, and be our master. We need to be victors over suffering, not victims of suffering. We need to express our full human dignity, our full glorious humanity, by choosing to suffer, as Esther did, as Jesus did, as we are called to do.

Listen to these wise words about suffering. The Lord Jesus said, "If anyone would come after me, let him deny himself and take up his cross daily and follow me" (Luke 9:23); and, "The cup that I drink you will drink" (Mark 10:39).

Nellie Saunders, missionary martyr in China, said, "It is only in this life that we shall have the privilege of being partakers in Christ's sufferings, and the priceless honor of glorifying him in suffering." Dietrich Bonhoeffer, German theologian and opponent of Hitler, wrote, "When Jesus Christ calls people, he calls them to come and die" (adapted). Paul Billheimer said, "Don't waste your sorrows." John Piper wrote, "Don't waste your cancer."

Our light afflictions

We read in Job, "The LORD gave, and the LORD has taken away; blessed be the name of the LORD" (1:21). We read in Hebrews that "The Lord disciplines the one he loves" (12:6). We read in Paul, "For this light momentary affliction is preparing for us an eternal weight of glory" (2 Cor. 4:17), and it "has been granted to you that for the sake of Christ you should not only believe in him but also suffer for his sake" (Phil. 1:29).

We think that suffering is the worst thing that can happen to us, but God works good through our suffering, as He did through the sufferings of Christ. Suffering for Christ is part of the normal Christian life. It is exceptional not to suffer for Christ. Because we want all our happiness now, we cannot bear to be unhappy. But pain now means gain later. "No cross, no crown." We follow our world in wanting everything now. We are like children; we cannot wait. The gospel is a free gift that we cannot pay for, but the gospel may cost us everything to receive. Living by faith is risking all for Christ. Great sacrifices are part of the normal Christian life. Like little children who have to learn that parents love them even when they say *no*, we have to learn that God loves when the answer to our prayer is *no*. If God is doing good through our sufferings, we should not fight His good gifts. God works through suffering, God blesses us in our suffering, and God blesses others through our suffering. Praise God!

God loves us as we are, but loves us too much to leave us as we are, and He loves us too much not to include us in His costly work in His world. Don't be a victim, avoiding suffering whatever the cost. Drink the cup, embrace your cross, offer your sacrifice, follow Christ.

Personally speaking, I don't mind suffering and laying down my life for others when I choose to do so, when I choose the occasion, the time and place, and what I have to do. What frightens me is when I am called to do so by circumstances, when I feel unprepared and unwilling, when I feel out of control of the situation, when I am not sure it will be worthwhile.

I should remember Esther, "If I perish, I perish." Better to serve God even if I fail, than to fail to serve God. Better to serve God, better to follow the Lord Jesus, whatever the cost.

Remember that Jesus Christ told us what earthly kings such as Ahasuerus were like. He said to His disciples, "You know that those who are considered rulers of the Gentiles lord it over them, and their great ones exercise authority over them" (Mark 10:42). Then He told them, "But it shall not be so among you. But whoever would be great among you must be your servant, and whoever would be first among you must be slave of all. For even the Son of Man came not to be served but to serve, and to give his life as a ransom for many" (Mark 10:43-45).

The "not be so among you" is so powerful, isn't it? Our default setting is to want to be served, like King Ahasuerus, or like James and John, and like many of Christ's disciples. But "not be so among you" cuts across our assumptions and our preferences. Serving others is not only the call of Christ, but also the means He used to save us, as He gave His life as a ransom for many on the cross, His crucial act of service.

"If I perish, I perish": the words of Esther, and the example of Christ. Except of course that while Esther did not know if her offering of her life would be productive, Christ laid down His life as an effective sacrifice to take away our sin. And He not only laid down His life in His death, but took up His life again in His resurrection, and is alive forever more. His death was powerful, effective, glorious and wonderful, with eternal consequences for His people, and our praise for that death will never end.

But that death was also an example for us to follow. "For to this you have been called, because Christ also suffered for you, leaving you an example, so that you might follow in his steps. He … continued entrusting himself to him who judges justly. He himself bore our sins in his body on the tree, that we might die to sin and live to righteousness. By his wounds you have been healed" (1 Pet. 2:21-24).

And who knows when the call will come, who knows when God will provide the opportunity, who knows when it will be "such a time as this." At the right time, Christ died for the ungodly (Rom. 5:6). At "such a time" the opportunity came for Esther to risk her life to save God's people: "If I perish, I perish." Who knows when your time will come?

Well I know when your time will come. The time for you to lay down your life for your brothers and sisters in Christ, to sacrifice yourself for others will come today, and tomorrow, and the next day, and the day after that, and every day, for the rest of your life. Ask God to help you remember Esther's words, "If I perish, I perish." Praise God for every opportunity God will give you to follow the example of His glorious and only Son, the Lord Jesus Christ.

All our times are in God's hands, and every day is a day to follow Christ by laying down our lives for others. "If I perish, I perish," said Esther. But for us ... "If I perish, I perish. But if I perish, I suffer with Christ and will be glorified with him."

Forgive the dated language, but here is a wonderful poem by Amy Carmichael that has haunted me since I was first converted to Christ.

No Scar?

"For to you it has been granted on behalf of Christ, not only to believe in Him, but also to suffer for His sake" (Philippians 1:29 NKJV).

Hast thou no scar?
No hidden scar on foot, or side, or hand?
I hear thee sung as mighty in the land;
I hear them hail thy bright, ascendant star.
Hast thou no scar?

Hast thou no wound?
Yet I was wounded by the archers; spent,
Leaned Me against a tree to die; and rent
By ravening beasts that compassed Me, I swooned.
Hast thou no wound?

No wound? No scar?
Yet, as the Master shall the servant be,
And pierced are the feet that follow Me.
But thine are whole; can he have followed far
Who hast no wound or scar?[1]

Remember Esther! Follow Christ!

---

1. http://www.crossroad.to/Victory/poems/amy_carmichael/no-scar.htm (accessed Nov. 27, 2012).

3 Mind the Details and Mine the Details

RHETT DODSON

When I entered full-time pastoral ministry, I soon realized that I needed not only to work diligently on my sermons but to work methodically as well. I had done a good bit of preaching while in seminary and had always tried to be careful in my preparation. Getting from text to message for one sermon, however, often looked quite different from another. While it is true that the process will vary slightly from sermon to sermon depending upon the length of the passage, the genre, and one's own familiarity with the text; without a disciplined, step-by-step process, one can easily flounder about in search of "a few blessed thoughts."

In those early days of ministry, I began to search for a method that would focus on verse-by-verse exegesis and would also serve me well as a means for keeping a systematic and detailed record of my work. What you find described in this chapter is the method that has developed over the years, and continues to develop.[1] It is a method that has enabled me to accomplish both of my preliminary goals and hopefully to feed the flock God has given me to shepherd—my primary goal.

---

1. Our methods will change as we grow and develop as preachers, and that's as it should be. As we immerse ourselves in the Word, our progress should be evident to all. See 1 Timothy 4:15.

As I have studied books on homiletics, listened to numerous lectures, and read many articles, I have gleaned bits and pieces from other preachers that have proved helpful. In addition, I have spent a lot of time thinking through just what it is that I need to know and have at hand in order accurately, and faithfully to preach God's Word. All of this has come together into what has become my method. My way is certainly not the only way to go about preparing a sermon, and it may not even be the best way, but it is the way that has worked for me. My prayer is that it, or perhaps at least parts of it, can help to guide others who want to properly handle God's Word of truth and faithfully preach it to a waiting church.

Pray!

The first step in sermon preparation is prayer. The second step is prayer. And the third step is yet more prayer! The preacher's task is to interpret and proclaim the written, living Word of God (cf. Heb. 4:12; 2 Tim. 4:2). Since the Bible is God's inerrant and life-giving truth, we need – indeed we must have – God's help to understand it. From the selection of the preaching passage to the pronouncement of the benediction on Sunday morning, as expositors of God's settled truth, we are dependent upon the ministry of the Holy Spirit to lead us, illumine Scripture, open our minds, give us understanding, and enable us to utter "Thus saith the Lord." Prayer is the key to experience the Spirit's ministry in all of these areas.

The Bible provides no better place than Psalm 119 to supply us with plenty of petitions to bring to the Lord as we begin to work on the sermon.

"Blessed are you, O LORD; teach me your statutes" (v. 12).

"Open my eyes, that I may behold wondrous things out of your law" (v. 18).

"Put false ways far from me and graciously teach me your law" (v. 29).

"Deal with your servant according to your steadfast love, and teach me your statutes" (v. 124).

Our digital world confronts us with myriad distractions. The pastoral life involves many demands that pull at our schedules. When you're able to sit down in your study and begin work on the sermon, the temptation is to dive right into the passage and begin to assimilate information. Yield not to temptation! Begin all of your sermon preparation with earnest prayer that the Holy Spirit will work in you and through you to accurately understand and faithfully proclaim the Bible.

I tell my congregation that I engage in "the exegesis of desperation."[2] The exegesis of desperation is not a new critical methodology. The phrase describes me, a believer with remaining sin and lots of ignorance, desperately wanting to know God's truth for my own spiritual growth and eagerly desiring to stand and teach it to others so that they might meet the Lord in and through His Word.

When all else fails, pray? No! Pray, or all else will fail!

What to preach?

For those who preach, especially those who preach on a regular basis, the first big question is "What do I preach?" No doubt some wag will reply "the Bible!", but that answer hardly settles the matter. The Bible is a rather large book! In his classic *A Treatise on the Preparation and Delivery of Sermons*, John Broadus devoted his first chapter to text selection. He writes, "There are few points as to which preachers differ more widely in talent and skill, than the selection of texts, and few in which diligent and systematic effort will be more richly rewarded."[3]

My practice has been to preach through books of the Bible or extended portions within a book (for example 1 Samuel 1–7 on the life of Samuel). I believe that passage-by-passage expository preaching should be the consistent diet that pastors feed their congregations. Sequential preaching pays honor to the way in which the Bible was originally written. God did not give us random verses or thoughts – He gave us books. To preach

---

2. Douglas Kelly uses the expression "an exegesis of desperation" to describe the work of those who read a gap of millions of years between Genesis 1:1 and 1:2. I obviously use the phrase in quite a different way. See Douglas F. Kelly, *Creation and Change: Genesis 1:1–2:4 in the Light of Changing Scientific Paradigms* (Fearn, Ross-shire: Christian Focus Publications, 1997), 94-95.

3. John A. Broadus, *A Treatise on the Preparation and Delivery of Sermons* (Louisville, KY: The Southern Baptist Theological Seminary, 2012), 24. Southern Seminary has reprinted the first edition of Broadus's work. If you are going to read Broadus, this is the *must-have* edition.

expositional sermons through books of the Bible also helps believers learn how to read the Bible. They more easily become attuned to context, structure, and flow within a passage and begin to look for those things in their own study of Scripture. Sequential expository preaching also helps the preacher. Rather than searching for a verse or a passage to expound, you simply move on to the next verse, paragraph, or chapter in the book.[4]

Though sequential exposition should, I believe, be the consistent diet for a congregation, it does not (and probably should not) be the exclusive diet. I do not feel bound by a liturgical calendar, but I do try to preach special messages at Christmas and Easter. In addition, I will often preach on doctrinal topics in the Sunday evening service (albeit by the exposition of key texts). Overall, however, I am accustomed to and work toward making my way through a given book from chapter 1, verse 1 to the end.

Getting Oriented: The Search for Context

I once attended a men's outing where an Army Ranger taught us a basic course in orienteering. With a map and compass, we were supposed to plot a path to get from our starting coordinates of point A to the destination coordinates of point B. I discovered two things that day: first, the importance of knowing where you are and, second, the reason the Lord never called me to be a soldier! Just as a soldier must know where he is and how to get to his destination, so too must the preacher. For me, orientation is the first step in sermon preparation, and the key word for orientation is *context*.

Some Bible teachers can lose the forest for the trees, or the bark on the trees, or even the veins in the leaves on the trees! But unless you know the forest, you can't make sense of the trees. In his book *The Hermeneutical Spiral*, Grant Osborne writes, "I tell my classes that if anyone is half asleep and does not hear a question that I ask, there is a 50 per cent chance of being correct if he or she answers 'context.'"[5] Context is *that* important. My

---

4. These, of course, are only a few of the reasons for passage-by-passage preaching. Peter Adam lists 15! See Peter Adam, "Arguing for Expository Preaching" http://beginningwithmoses.org/preaching/245/arguing-for-expository-preaching (accessed December 23, 2013).

5. Grant R. Osborne, *The Hermeneutical Spiral: A Comprehensive Introduction to Biblical Interpretation* (Downers Grove, IL: InterVarsity Press, 1991), 21.

first goal, then, is to orient myself to the book I plan to preach and then, as I work through the book week by week, to orient myself to the individual passage for that week's message.

In order to familiarize myself with a Bible book as a whole, I have to plan ahead and begin to read and study the book long before the sermon series actually begins. This is not always easy to do given the often hectic pace of pastoral life, but the effort is well rewarded. You will become a much better expositor if you begin with the big picture in mind. I read and reread the book looking for its major structure and theme. Since I want to discover the author's main point, as I read I constantly ask myself, "Why did Moses (or Jeremiah or Luke, etc.) write this?" If I don't know how the book I am preaching is put together and what the author's big idea is, I may have to make major corrections and changes in the middle of the series. This could be quite disconcerting for the congregation (not to mention the preacher!).

With the big picture of the book in mind I then, on a weekly basis, have to concern myself with the context of the passage I'm going to teach on the coming Lord's Day. Discovering this context, however, involves much more than reading a few verses before and a few verses after the ones I plan to study. I need to know where the particular passage fits within the book (this is where my prior work pays off), where the book fits within the canon of Scripture, and where the passage fits within the flow of redemptive history. So at the outset of my weekly preparation I am asking serious textual and biblical-theological questions.

It can take a great deal of time and effort to understand the context of a passage, but the investment is well worth it in the end. If you preach passage by passage through books of the Bible, your understanding of the book as a whole and where the parts fit to make up the whole will only deepen and expand. Sequential exposition will, in the end, make you a better preacher because it will strengthen your knowledge of the Word.

Structure and Content

After I have spent time getting a handle on where the passage fits in Scripture, I begin to read and reread it numerous times. I don't have a goal to read it a certain number of times. I read until I am comfortable that I know the content of the verses.

As I read, I begin to look for the structure of the passage. I want to know, "How did the author put this text together?" Clues to a text's structure will often depend upon the genre of the passage. For narrative literature, I look for scene or character changes. In poetry, parallelism is key. In epistolary literature, I look for transitional words or a clear shift in topic. These are not the only clues to be aware of, but they are a good place to start. The more familiar you become with the book you plan to preach, the more easily you will begin to see the ways the author puts together his thoughts.

At this stage in the process, I often find it helpful to develop a propositional display. A propositional display analyzes the clauses and phrases of a passage and arranges them in their logical order. This can easily be done by copying the text from Bible software and pasting it into a word-processing program. Then, by means of indentation and subordination, you can arrange the propositions of the passage to demonstrate the kernel statements of each sentence (subject, verb, object) and how they relate to the remaining subordinate statements (adjectives, adverbs, participles, infinitives, etc.). A propositional display enables you to see the main points the author makes (the kernel statements) as well as the ways in which he fleshes out those points through further description, amplification, explanation, etc.[6] Another way to accomplish the same goal is to use the method known as *Bible Arcing*. Dan Fuller developed this process to demonstrate the relationship between propositions[7] and Fuller's well-known student John Piper popularized it.[8]

It is important for you to understand the structure or movements in the passage so that you can follow the flow of thought. If you do not know the logic of the passage, you cannot

---

6. For those interested in learning more about propositional displays, see John Beekman and John Callow, *Translating the Word of God* (Grand Rapids: Zondervan, 1974), 267-342.

7. Daniel P. Fuller, *Helps for Hermeneutics* (unpublished class syllabus, Fuller Theological Seminary, 1993).

8. John Piper, *Biblical Exegesis: Discovering the Original Meaning of Scriptural Texts* (Minneapolis: Bethlehem Baptist Church, 1999). A website, app, and instructional videos are now available to assist the exegete in this process. Go to www.biblearc.com.

adequately express its message. The more clearly you understand the text, the more clearly you will be able to explain it to others. The structure will then, in turn, provide you with a basis for an expository sermon outline.

The Main Point

As I read the passage and analyze its structure, I ask myself, "What is this passage talking about? What is its subject?" I'm in search of the main point, the theme, or the big idea. A number of clues can help me to answer my question. I look for a key verse, a pivotal point in the text, repeated words or phrases, or concepts that seem to receive the most emphasis.

Once I have determined the subject, I then begin to ask, "What is Paul (or John, or Moses, or Isaiah) saying about this subject?" If the theme of the passage is obedience, am I being told *how* to obey, *what* to obey, *why* obey, etc.? If I know the subject of a passage and what the author is telling me about the subject, then I have arrived at the main point.[9] Once I have the big idea, I essentially have my sermon proposition. This main point is going to drive the sermon. Everything, from the opening words of the introduction to the final words of the conclusion, will be designed to drill *this one truth* down into the minds and hearts of my hearers.

The temptation is to short-circuit the process. For example, if you determine that the subject of your passage is repentance, you may begin to turn your sermon into a discourse on everything you know about repentance instead of what that particular passage says about repentance. I have to keep asking, "What is *this* passage saying about *this* subject?" Otherwise I will stray from the author's (and ultimately the Holy Spirit's) intent. If I preach something about the subject that is true but not what

---

9. Those familiar with homiletic literature will know that this approach to the big idea is not original with me. See Haddon W. Robinson, *Biblical Preaching: The Development and Delivery of Expository Messages* (Grand Rapids: Baker, 1980), 31-48. Robinson's two main questions of a passage are (1) "What is the author talking about?" (the subject), and (2) "What is he saying about what he is talking about?" (the complement). *ibid.*, 41. Ramesh Richard refers to the concept of the big idea as "the central proposition of the text" and labels its two parts *theme* and *thrust*. *Preparing Expository Sermons: A Seven-Step Method for Biblical Preaching* (Grand Rapids: Baker, 2001), 65-71.

that particular text says about the subject, then I have not faithfully handled God's Word, and I have robbed the message of its power.

Capturing the Preliminary Data

So far I have discussed the first three areas that I focus on when I begin to prepare a sermon. I look at the *context*, the *structure*, and the *main point*. These three steps alone can generate a lot of information, and it is important to capture this data so that I can retrieve it throughout the sermon preparation process, review and expand it should I preach or teach the passage again, or use it for a writing project. For this purpose I have created an exegesis template for Microsoft Word. This template has developed over the years, and I'll tell you more about it later. For now, the preliminary data I've collected usually takes up the first three or four pages of a Word document, and I organize the data under bold, italic headings: Context, Content/Structure, The Big Idea, etc..

Throughout this process I endeavor to *mind the details*. I want to be a careful reader of the text. After collecting and organizing the preliminary data, I am ready to delve deeper into the text to *mine the details*. I should point out, however, that moving from the preliminary, big picture questions to the more microscopic inspection of the passage doesn't mean that I'm finished with my big questions. All of my exegetical work, from the preliminary determinations regarding the verses I'm studying to the detailed grammatical work and research in commentaries, should result in a cross-fertilization process. For example, knowing the context, structure, and big idea of the passage equips me to dig deeper into the verses, while digging deeper enables me to refine the work I've done up to this point. More detailed work also enables me to answer another series of questions I always ask about a passage: What is the *tone* of this verse, paragraph, or pericope? What was the author's *purpose* in writing it? How will I combine the tone and purpose when I preach this passage to my congregation? I also gather this information on the first few pages of my exegesis notes, and it too is organized under bold, italic headings.

Digging Deeper

Any miner will tell you that his job entails a lot of hard work. But for those willing to dig and sift, there are diamonds and gold to be found! I want to be a faithful miner!

A number of years ago I listened to a series of lectures by D. A. Carson on "The Pastor and Scholarship".[10] In those lectures, Carson shared that in his exegetical work he devoted a single sheet of paper to each verse he studied. He wrote the verse reference in the top left and right corners of the page and kept all of his notes for that particular verse on that page. Using this method he could easily insert pages into his notes as his work on a particular verse grew. Carson's approach appealed to me as a good way to keep my notes organized. I adopted and adapted that approach, and it has proved valuable ever since. As I begin the more detailed verse-by-verse exegesis of my passage, I simply insert as many page breaks in my Word document as I need, keep them numbered in sequential order, and can easily navigate to the particular place that I choose.

Beginning with the verse reference in the top corners of the page, I copy and paste the text just below the reference. I use Bible Works for this and work with the original Hebrew and Greek, though this method can easily be used for those who work primarily with the English Bible. Below the verse I insert a parsing and location table. This, again, is based on working with the original text. Here I am able to list any vocabulary I'm unfamiliar with; parse the verbs, participles, and infinitives; list grammatical uses; and have a chart to help me with reading and translating the text. My goal is to gather as much detailed grammatical and syntactical information as possible. I want to know how the various parts of the sentences work together.

Once I have a good handle on the grammar and flow of the verse, I begin to write my own commentary. I do this by asking another series of questions: What do these words mean? Why did the author write them? Do these words or similar expressions occur elsewhere

---

10. Carson presented these lectures at Biblical Theological Seminary in Hatfield, PA. I have a set of four cassette tapes of these lectures, but they have no date. I have been unable to find them online.

in the Bible? Here I make use of as many cross references as I can find so that I allow Scripture to interpret Scripture. How do these words connect to what proceeds and what follows? How can I express these ideas in my own words to teach others?

I also begin to ask questions about application: What are the implications of this verse? How does this verse impact my life? Would people in my congregation struggle to believe this verse or to live it out at home or work? If I were to live out this verse in my life, what would that look like? How can I teach people to implement its truth? Again, all of these questions feed the cross-fertilization process.

This exegetical process takes me through each verse in the passage I'm studying. When I've finished with one verse I insert a page break, type in the reference for the next verse, paste the text from Bible Works, insert a parsing/location chart, and work through the next verse.[11] All during this time I am asking question after question of the text. How is this participle related to that verb? Why did the author choose that word? For me this is all a part of mining the details. There's gold in the text! Dig diligently for it and you will be amply rewarded!

When I've finished this process and have essentially written my own explanation and exposition of the passage, I go back through it again, refine any parts that need refining (and many parts often need it!), check to see if I have missed any grammatical or interpretational details, and then I stop. There always comes a point in any project where you just have to stop. I let my mind rest and focus on other things so that when I come back to the passage I have a fresher perspective.

I wish I could say that these exegetical steps always work out according to schedule and that by Monday, Tuesday, or Wednesday I have a certain amount of work accomplished. Alas, the best-laid schemes o' mice an' ministers gang aft agley (with apologies to Robbie Burns)! What I would say is that it is important to begin the work as early in the week as possible.

---

11. For longer, usually narrative, texts the reference at the top of the page will encompass several verses, typically a paragraph or scene. I will then use as many or as few pages as necessary to exegete and comment on that paragraph.

I don't take Monday as my day off. I'm too nervous about next Sunday! I get started early in the week so that I have plenty of time to meditate and pray over what I will preach.

Communing with the Commentators

After a break that allows me time to refresh my mind, I come back to the study to start working through the commentaries I plan to read. I only turn to the commentaries, however, *after* I have done my own work. If you do not do your own study of the text first, you will be tempted to adopt too quickly and uncritically the ideas of others. Study the passage. Arrive at your own interpretations and conclusions. Then be humble and willing to change those interpretations and conclusions if an author mounts a stronger, more Scriptural argument.

My friend Doug O'Donnell loves to read commentaries. This comes out clearly in his chapter "Spirit-filled *Sitzfleisch*." I, on the other hand, have a love/hate relationship with them. I love commentaries because I love books about the Bible. Commentators, at least those who write substantive works, have obviously spent a great deal of time and effort to study and explain Scripture. When I read commentaries, and I have in mind here those written by individuals who respect the Bible as God's Word, I am able to glean from the best minds in the Church from throughout the ages.

But I also find that commentaries frustrate me (that's the *hate* part of the relationship). Older commentaries often answer questions that readers no longer ask. Newer ones often include such a mass of information that they become difficult to wade through in search of the pertinent points. I realize that commentators have to be thorough, but very often a lot of material makes its way into a commentary that does not necessarily make the text clearer. My personal goal is to conduct such a thorough study of the passage that the commentaries lend very little by way of information or raw data. For me, the commentary becomes a debate partner as I weigh the various arguments for disputed interpretations.

I suggest that when you begin to preach through a book, find the single best commentary that you can on that book. Read reviews, ask friends, e-mail your seminary professor, but find the best resource that you can find. Then, use it as a training tool. For example, when I preached through Philippians, I studied the text as thoroughly as I could. I then turned to Peter O'Brien's commentary and carefully read it.[12] As I worked my way through O'Brien's exegesis, I saw gaps in my own work, and I also saw how O'Brien filled in those gaps. At the end of that preparation time, I knew *where* I needed to improve my exegetical skills. I also had a better idea of *how* to improve them, *what* questions to ask, and *where* to look for the relevant information. Don't read a commentary just to glean facts or interpretations for a particular passage. Find an excellent commentary on the passage you are studying and use it as a training or refresher course in exegesis. Ask not merely what the commentary says but try to discover the kinds of questions the author asked of the text and the way he arrived at his answers.

How many commentaries should you read in the preparation of a message? Only as many as you need to read. Don't feel obligated to read every commentary you can lay your hands on, nor should you necessarily read everything in the commentary. After you have a good grasp of the passage and the issues and problems involved in its interpretation, carefully read your best one or two commentaries on the text and skim the others.

As I read through the commentaries, I will take notes in the margins or mark off a certain phrase, paragraph, or cross reference. After I've finished with a commentary, I will then type the notes and quotations that I have gleaned into my exegetical document and insert footnotes to keep track of the source. This enables me to combine my own notes and explanations with the best material that I discover in other places.

Where is Jesus?

Though I've placed the question "Where is Jesus?" near the end of this chapter, it is by no means the last step in the process. As with all of my exegetical work, it is a part of the cross-fertilization that occurs from the very beginning. But I have listed it near the end of the process because before I write my sermon or draw up

---

12. Peter T. O'Brien, *The Epistle to the Philippians*. The New International Greek Testament Commentary (Grand Rapids: Eerdmans, 1991).

my preaching notes, I want to be sure that I have accurately and thoroughly answered the question.

At times we can become so caught up in mining the details that we can forget what we're looking for! As we dig into Scripture, we will discover many beautiful gems that we will polish and admire and show to our congregation. Our people need to see those gems! But don't forget the diamond! Don't forget Christ! All of the other beautiful gems in the Bible provide the setting for the center stone. Let that center stone shine, and let all of its facets glisten to show the beauty of the Savior.[13]

Writing the sermon

After the preliminary work of exegesis, commentary writing, and commentary reading is complete, it is time to write the sermon. But with many explanations and even applications already written out in the exegesis notes, a sizeable portion of the work is already done.

In order, however, to insure that the sermon flows well, I typically begin the formal writing process with an extended outline. Throughout my preparation time I attempt to tease out various ways to structure the message. Once I have arrived at the way I think best explains the passage, I will write each main point on a separate sheet of paper. From there I will write down the subpoints and leave plenty of room to fill in information such as explanations, applications, and illustrations. Once I have this outline in place, I then begin to write the sermon.

Though I have written full sermon manuscripts for a number of years, I am not convinced that this is always the best way to proceed. The Lutheran pietist Johann Albrecht Bengel advised

---

13. The scope of this chapter does not allow me to delve into the ways we should see and preach Christ as He is revealed throughout redemptive history. To help you develop your skills in this area, I suggest the following resources: Michael P. V. Barrett, *Beginning At Moses: A Guide to Finding Christ in the Old Testament* (Greenville, SC: Ambassador–Emerald International, 1999), Edmund P. Clowney, *The Unfolding Mystery: Discovering Christ in the Old Testament* (Colorado Springs: NavPress, 1988), Graeme Goldsworthy, *Preaching the Whole Bible as Christian Scripture* (Grand Rapids: Eerdmans, 2000), and Dennis E. Johnson, *Him We Proclaim: Preaching Christ from All the Scriptures* (Phillipsburg, NJ: P&R Publishing, 2007).

"Much thinking, little writing."[14] He may well be right. What I do know is that each man must discover what works best for him. No two preachers are alike, and no two should try to be alike. Each should discover how his mind works and whether few notes or full notes lead to the best delivery. Then he must do his best to speak for his Lord as he proclaims to men and women the whole counsel of God.

Once the sermon is written, I prayerfully review and edit the manuscript. At this stage I want to be sure that the message is clear and that I remove any unnecessary weight. It can be difficult to delete a paragraph that I worked hard to write, but if it doesn't add to the sermon and the single point that I am trying to make, then it detracts from the message and has to go. Deciding what to leave out of a message is often as important as deciding what to put in it.

The final step before preaching is to familiarize myself with the sermon so that it becomes embedded in my heart through prayer and personal application. I have first to preach the sermon to myself in the study before I can preach it in the pulpit. If it doesn't move and change me, it is unlikely to have an impact on others.

Each Lord's Day morning, just before our worship service, the elders of the church gather in my office to pray. We ask the Lord to come and bless the preaching of His Word, and then we proceed to the service with the conviction that God's Word will not return to Him empty (Isa. 55:11). Though the grass withers and the flower fades, His Word will stand forever (Isa. 40:8).

---

14. Bengel, quoted in J. W. Alexander, *Thoughts on Preaching* (1864; repr., Edinburgh: Banner of Truth, 1988), 156.

4 Gain + Loss = Gain
The Mathematics of the Gospel
(Philippians 3:4-9)

RHETT DODSON

In 2010, Oscar Mayer, the hot dog people, announced a campaign called *The Good Mood Mission*. To accomplish this mission, the company offered to help people keep track of their good deeds. If you joined *The Good Mood Mission*, you could record your acts of kindness online and receive rewards along the way.

I think this kind of promotion makes sense to us. If someone puts forth the effort to do a kind deed, that should be acknowledged. No good deed should go unrewarded. And, at a certain level, that's true. We do want to take note of the good things people do for us. We want to be thankful. And sometimes that thanks leads to a reward. So I have no beef with Oscar Mayer.

We make a serious mistake, however, when we believe that all of life should work like *The Good Mood Mission*, especially when we think that way about our relationship with God. Our hearts naturally gravitate to this error. We have it ingrained in our thinking. We believe that God is a kind of cosmic Oscar Mayer, keeping track on His heavenly hard drive of all the good things we have done, and that He has a plan to reward us in the end. All that He has to do is count up our gains and losses, and if the gains outweigh the losses, we're in good shape to receive our reward. This is the message our hearts tell us. This is the religion with which we're born. But it is far from what God tells us. It may be popular religion, but it is not the religion of Christ.

In the early verses of Philippians 3, Paul warns the believers in Philippi that there are people who claim to speak for God, but they do not preach a message of grace. "Look out for the dogs, look out for the evildoers, look out for those who mutilate the flesh" (v. 2). Paul's tone is strong, even harsh, because those to whom he refers were perverting the gospel. These false teachers were the Judaizers. They did talk about Christ, but theirs was not a gospel of Christ *alone*. They preached a message of Christ *plus*—Christ plus Moses, Christ plus ceremony, Christ plus the law. In fact, their emphasis on the necessity of circumcision for salvation led Paul to describe them as "mutilators of the flesh."

Paul had lived a conscientious, meticulous life of pious Jewish observance, as we shall see in this passage, in an attempt to win favor with God. But he discovered that all of the righteousness, all of the good works he was adding up for his reward, could not bring him salvation and peace. They could not make him right with God. Paul discovered that he didn't need something more to add to his religion—he needed something completely different. He did not need a righteousness that he could achieve but an "alien" righteousness, a righteousness outside of himself that comes from God. He needed a perfect righteousness that's received by faith alone.

Paul learned this lesson one day on the road to Damascus when he met the risen Lord Jesus. He learned the lesson of the good news of Christ and the free gift of justification in Him. We learn the basics of this lesson when we first believe the gospel, but we need to learn it over and over again. The gospel teaches us to lose what we have worked to gain in order to gain what we cannot lose.

Paul clearly makes this point as he demonstrates from his own life the losses and gains of knowing Christ. As we work our way through this passage and look at the apostle's personal testimony, I want you to see the two main things Paul emphasizes. They are first, *the gain that is loss,* and second, *the loss that is gain.*

The Gain that is Loss
Paul has been at pains to make clear to his readers the distinctions between Judaizers and true believers. While, in

the end, Judaizers are unclean doers of evil whose adherence to ceremony proves to be a distortion of God's intention (see v. 2), those who follow Christ are the true circumcision. They worship by the Holy Spirit, glory in Christ, and do not rely upon their own efforts. That is, they "put no confidence in the flesh" (v. 3).

This final description regarding "confidence in the flesh" prompts Paul to begin an autobiographical reminiscence. Believers do not put confidence in the flesh, *but* if anyone could brag about and trust in his superiority, Paul was the man. "Take a look at my résumé," says Paul. "If anyone thinks he has reason for confidence in the flesh, I have more" (v. 4). That's a bold, almost brash, statement to make, but the Philippians needed to hear it. The Judaizers who were troubling the church made much of their status and achievements, and they were trying to get the Philippians to conform to the standards of God's ceremonial law as well. But Paul argues from his own experience that conformity to that law is not the way of true salvation. If these teachers want the Philippians to conform to the law, then says Paul, "Let's see where this conformity will get you." The apostle then proceeds to describe his own pre-conversion gain. He lists seven things that form a picture of a complete Jew who could outshine any Judaizer. How does he describe his gain? He sums it up in terms of *status* and *achievements*.

As to his *status*, Paul was a Jew of the Jews! He was "circumcised on the eighth day" (v. 5). He received the sign of the covenant exactly as God had prescribed (see Gen. 17:12). Circumcision was to take place on the eighth day. This date is significant because it symbolizes newness or renewal. Many of the ceremonial cleansings took effect on the eighth day (cf. Lev. 9:1; 12:3; 14:10, 23; 15:14, 29; Num. 6:10; cf. Lev. 23:36; Num. 29:35). By Jewish reckoning, the eighth day was the first day of a new week, a new cycle of time and hence a picture of newness, a new start. The eighth day of the Jewish calendar corresponds to the first day of the week or Sunday, the Lord's Day, the day of new (resurrection) life. The eighth day of a child's life may not be the same as the day after the Sabbath. Statistically most children would reach eight days old on other days of the week. The eight-day cycle, however, carries the weight of the symbolism and makes the timing significant.

A male convert to Judaism would be circumcised despite his age. But Paul received circumcision, not as a proselyte, but as one born into the nation whose parents were careful to observe the law.

Paul had not only received the initiatory rite of Judaism, he was "of the people of Israel" (v. 5). He was racially a Jew. He was not a convert from among the Gentiles. Under the old covenant, it was good to convert to Judaism. But for Paul, the blood of Abraham flowed in his veins.[1]

Next, Paul narrows down his Jewish identity by pinpointing his tribal lineage. He was "of the tribe of Benjamin" (v. 5). A proselyte to Judaism became a member of Israel in general and not of a particular tribe. Paul readily classed himself as a Benjamite. This tribe played a prominent role in Israel and was the source of Israel's first king, Saul, after whom Paul (Saul of Tarsus) was likely named. This is not the only time he refers to his tribe. In Romans 11:1 he writes, "I ask, then, has God rejected his people? By no means! For I myself am an Israelite, a descendant of Abraham, a member of the tribe of Benjamin."

Moses had blessed the tribe of Benjamin as the beloved of the Lord.[2] "Of Benjamin he said, 'The beloved of the LORD dwells in safety. The High God surrounds him all day long, and dwells between his shoulders'" (Deut. 33:12). Why was it so significant to be a Benjamite? Peter T. O'Brien points out that, "Benjamin, the son of Jacob's favourite wife Rachel, was the only son born in the land of promise (Gen. 35:16-18). The tribe of Benjamin gave Israel its first king (1 Sam. 9:1-2) and remained loyal to the house of David after the disruption of the monarchy (1 Kings 12:21). Together with the tribe of Judah it formed the core of the new fellowship of people (cf. Ezra 4:1)."[3] *Belonging to this tribe was an notable point of pride.*

---

1. "Having been born into the chosen race of Israelite parents and subsequently circumcised, Paul inherited all the privileges of the covenant community, privileges he enumerates in relation to Israel, even after his conversion, at Romans 9:4-5." Peter T. O'Brien, *The Epistle to the Philippians.* The New International Greek Testament Commentary (Grand Rapids: Eerdmans, 1991), 370.

2. Gordon D. Fee, *Paul's Letter to the Philippians.* The New International Commentary on the New Testament (Grand Rapids: Eerdmans, 1995), 307.

3. O'Brien, *Philippians*, 370.

As Paul continues to enumerate his qualifications on his spiritual résumé, the fourth item he mentions is "a Hebrew of Hebrews" (v. 5). He was a Hebrew son born to Hebrew parents. He spoke the Hebrew language. But there's more to this expression. The grammatical construction is a Hebraic way to express the superlative. We see this happen in other places in the Bible. For example, the Most Holy Place in the tabernacle is literally "the holy of holies" (Exod. 26:33). The Song of Songs (Song 1:1) is Solomon's greatest song. And Jesus is the King of kings and Lord of lords (Rev. 17:14), the greatest king and the greatest Lord! So Paul writes, "Of the Hebrews, I am a Hebrew." In one sense he says, "I am the greatest Jew!" You would have had to search long and hard to find a more dedicated, loyal, and observant man among God's old covenant people.

What Paul lays out here is an impressive pedigree, a status not to be ignored. Next, near the end of verse 5, Paul shifts the discussion to focus on his achievements. And he enumerates three.

First, as to the law, he was a Pharisee. The Pharisees were a strict religious sect in Israel. They adhered closely to the law, tithing even small amounts of spices (Matt. 23:23). Unlike their contemporaries the Sadducees, the Pharisees believed in the spiritual world of angels and in the resurrection (see Acts 23:6-8). Paul was a scrupulous observer of all that God commanded. He lived "according to the strictest party" of Judaism (Acts 26:5) and advanced beyond many of his contemporaries because of his zeal for Jewish traditions (Gal. 1:13-14).

When it came to keeping the law, Paul quickly identified himself as a strict and conscientious adherent. But, second, when it came to zeal, to a consuming pursuit and passion in life, Paul was "a persecutor of the church" (v. 6). The story of Paul's early career as a Pharisee was one of oppressing the followers of Christ. When we first encounter Paul (or Saul as he was then) in Scripture, we find him standing by, quietly but approvingly observing the martyrdom of Stephen (Acts 7:58–8:1a). In the wake of Stephen's death, a great persecution arose against the church in Jerusalem. "Saul was ravaging the church, and entering house after house, he dragged off men and women and committed them to prison" (Acts 8:3).

Later, when the apostle gave his testimony to the Jews, he recounted these former deeds: "I am a Jew, born in Tarsus in Cilicia, but brought up in this city, educated at the feet of Gamaliel according to the strict manner of the law of our fathers, being zealous for God as all of you are this day. I persecuted this Way to the death, binding and delivering to prison both men and women, as the high priest and the whole council of elders can bear me witness. From them I received letters to the brothers, and I journeyed towards Damascus to take those also who were there and bring them in bonds to Jerusalem to be punished" (Acts 22:3-5). Prior to his conversion, Paul saw this kind of barbaric behavior as a point of honor. He thought he was serving God.

The third achievement Paul refers to was his unimpeachable pursuit of merit: "as to righteousness under the law, blameless" (v. 6). According to the law, that is with regard to its interpretation, Paul was a Pharisee rather than a Sadducee. But when it came to the righteous deeds of the law, he was blameless. No one could find fault with how Paul observed the dictates of God's commands. Paul followed the Pharisaic interpretations and applications of the law, and he did so flawlessly.[4]

Paul bore the mark of the covenant. He lived in the covenant community. He spoke the language. He was religiously zealous and conformed to the accepted code of conduct. But where did all of this leave him? Religious, but lost. As far as Paul and his contemporaries could see, his life was one gain after another. Rung after rung he had climbed the ladder of Jewish religious success and eventually found himself at the top, but then he suddenly realized that the ladder was leaning against the wrong

---

4. Commenting on Paul's final assertion O'Brien writes, "Paul's statement not only describes the exertion with which he scrupulously observed the law's requirements' it goes even further, indicating that in his observance of the OT law, as interpreted along Pharisaic lines, he had become blameless.... Clearly this is not pessimistic self-portrait or recollection of one tortured by an unattainable ideal, a conclusion that has often been drawn from Romans 7. Here is a man well satisfied, reminiscent of the rich young ruler in the Gospel story (Luke 18:21) who claims to have kept all the commandments from his youth" (O'Brien, *Philippians*, 379).

wall![5] That explains why Paul writes as he does in this passage. His argument is this: "If anyone had good reason to boast in his religious accomplishments in Judaism, I'm the man." But, as he will go on to contend (vv. 7ff.), "Christ is of such greater worth than all that I can attain, that I turned from my self-righteous pursuits."

Now, if Paul abandoned his confidence in his strict religious performance, so should everyone! If Paul couldn't trust in his good works, then neither can we. Works righteousness, however, is the natural religion of every heart. Because we are born in sin and alienated from God, our sinful instinct is to try to earn our way into God's favor. Our hard hearts are naturally resistant to grace.

This has been the testimony of some of God's greatest servants throughout the history of the church. They began a life of self-righteousness only later to see the beauty of Christ's righteousness. Martin Luther followed the dictates of his monastic order to the nth degree. He spent hours in the confessional. He beat his body. He fasted and prayed, but he could find no peace with God until he realized that none of his works could buy him one bit of favor with the Father. The Father had already demonstrated His love and grace in the gift of His Son. When Luther began to understand the gospel and justification by faith alone, he abandoned his religious efforts to make himself right with God. Luther said,

> My situation was that, although an impeccable monk, I stood before God as a sinner troubled in conscience, and I had no confidence that my merit would assuage him .... Night and day I pondered until I saw the connection between the justice of God and the statement that "the just shall live by his faith." Then I grasped that the justice of God is that righteousness by which through grace and sheer mercy God justifies us through faith. Thereupon I felt myself to be reborn and to have gone through open doors into paradise.[6]

---

5. Stephen Covey uses this imagery to describe the lack of fulfillment so many feel when they have given their lives to career success and neglected more important matters, like family. Stephen R. Covey, *The Seven Habits of Highly Effective People* (New York: Simon and Schuster, 1989), 98. How much more tragic is it when one tries zealously to earn favor with God and fails to see the goodness of grace.

6. Roland H. Bainton, *Here I Stand: A Life of Martin Luther* (Nashville: Abingdon, 1978), 49.

The same was true of John Wesley. Raised in a pastor's home, Wesley himself pursued the ministry. He was self-disciplined. He joined Oxford's Holy Club with his brother Charles and George Whitefield. He pursued a holy life under his own power and became a miserable, doubt-filled man. One evening on Aldersgate Street in London, he heard someone read Luther's preface to his commentary on Romans. The Lord used those words to open Wesley's heart to the truth of justification, and he felt his heart strangely warmed.

Are you making the initial mistake that Paul, Luther, Wesley, and countless others have made? Do you believe you can work your way to God? Do you think you can satisfy His wrath against your sin by your religious observance and good deeds? How religious will you have to be? How many good works will you have to do?

Young people easily fall into the same trap as Paul. Often they have been baptized as covenant children; they spend a lot of time in the midst of God's people; they speak the language. Perhaps you've experienced these kinds of privileges, and you know the right answers to give about sin and salvation. But is salvation a living reality in your heart and life? Are you trusting in your privileges or are you trusting in the Savior who gave them to you?

Paul added up all the positive things, the things that any good Jew would be proud of, the things that gave him a high ranking and status among his people, and then threw them all away! It was the gain that was loss. He threw it all away because he realized that there is a loss that is gain.

The Loss that is Gain

Verse 7 is a summary of Paul's message: "But whatever gain I had, I counted as loss for the sake of Christ." The phrase "whatever gain" refers back to the list of seven statements of status and achievement in verses 5 and 6. These were the things Paul considered profitable in life. But whatever advantage he previously thought he had he was willing to give up or count "as loss for the sake of Christ."

Paul refers to this loss three different times in this passage, once in verse 7 and twice in verse 8. The only other time the word *loss* occurs in the New Testament is in Acts 27 where Luke uses it (reporting Paul's speech) to describe the loss of cargo (predicted, v. 10; actual, v. 21) from the storm at sea when the apostle was being transported to Rome. In that context, it was a commercial loss, the loss of something valuable and worthwhile. The implication, therefore, is that this loss involves suffering of some kind.[7] What did Paul lose? All of his status and achievement, all of his good deeds and religion.

How did Paul lose these things? They were still true of him. He was still Jewish; he had persecuted the church; he had followed the dictates of the Pharisees. He couldn't change his past. What had changed was his outlook.

Note the way Paul describes his loss. He says, "I counted as loss ..." (v. 7); "I count everything as loss ..." (v. 8). His heart and mind were changed so that he did not look at or think about things the way he once did. Whereas he once saw his law-keeping and persecuting zeal as something God would look upon with favor, he now realizes that he was heaping up one sin after the other. His religious zeal was working an exceeding weight of eternal damnation. Only the grace of God can account for this transformation of his thoughts. Only his encounter with the risen Christ on the road to Damascus could bring about such a radical change in the smug, self-righteous heart of this Pharisee.

Paul then intensifies his description. Near the end of verse 8 he writes, I "count them as rubbish." Rubbish is the kind of refuse you throw out into the street. It's the rotting scraps that aren't fit for anyone but dogs to eat. No doubt Paul is playing on that very image. The Jews, especially those enamored with their own self-righteousness, considered the Gentiles to be dogs. Gentiles were unclean and to be avoided. Now, however, the tables have been turned. The Gentiles are no longer the dogs, the Judaizers are (see Phil. 3:2). And here are the scraps they can eat! Listen once more at Paul's confession: "All that I worked for, all my attainments are merely street garbage!" That's the loss. Everything Paul once held dear. And the gain?

---

7. "To suffer the loss of something which one has previously possessed, with the implication that the loss involves considerable hardship or suffering." Johannes E. Louw and Eugene A. Nida, *Greek-English Lexicon of the New Testament Based on Semantic Domains*, 2nd edition (New York: United Bible Socities, 1989), electronic version, entry 57.69.

In verses 7 and 8, Paul uses two different expressions to describe the gain he looked for. The first expression begins with the words "for the sake of" or "because of". Trace that phrase through these verses with me. Verse 7, "I counted as loss *for the sake of Christ.*" Verse 8, "I count everything as loss *because of the surpassing worth of knowing Christ Jesus my Lord.*" Again in verse 8, "*For his sake* I have suffered the loss of all things...." If you placed Paul's achievements in one pan of a balance-scale and placed the value of knowing Christ in the opposite pan, knowing Christ far outweighs anything he could ever hope to achieve.

The second expression begins with these words at the end of verse 8: "in order that I may gain Christ and be found in him." Paul's reason for considering everything else to be rubbish is so that he can gain Christ. He cannot hold on to his self-righteousness and to Christ at the same time. To *gain* does not mean to earn in the sense of *deserve*. To *gain Christ* is Paul's description of the wonderful advantage of having Christ, of being in Christ. To gain Christ is to be saved, rescued from sin's penalty, and to be united to God's Son.[8]

When does Paul want this to happen? The words *gain* and *be found* look forward to the day of judgment. Paul wants to gain Christ and be found in Him on that day. But not just on that day! Here's another great example of the New Testament's tension between the *already* and the *not yet*. Believers are already in Christ. We have gained Christ. We are found in Him. But we look forward to that day when we will stand before the Lord. We want to gain Him and be found in Him on that day as well.

How does Paul want to be found? Perfectly righteous! But not with his own righteousness. He had already tried that route (vv. 4-6). Can you blame Paul for rejecting self-righteousness? Would you want to stand before a perfectly pure and holy God and offer Him your good deeds and religious observances as your hope for entering heaven? I hope not, because all of our righteousness is like rubbish, street garbage. The prophet Isaiah used another image of uncleanness when he wrote, "We have all

---

8. On the relationship between union with Christ and justification, see Robert Letham, *Union with Christ: In Scripture, History, and Theology* (Phillipsburg, NJ: P and R Publishing, 2011), 73-83.

become like one who is unclean, and all our righteous deeds are like a polluted garment. We all fade like a leaf, and our iniquities, like the wind, take us away" (Isa. 64:6).

If Paul has rejected all of his previous attempts to become righteous through his own efforts, how could he then be found righteous? With another's righteousness! Paul wants a righteousness that comes from God! Luther called this an *alien righteousness*. It belongs to another. It comes from outside us. It's the pure and spotless righteousness of the Lord Jesus Christ! When Christ came, He offered to the Father perfect obedience. He remained sinless and pure (1 Pet. 1:18-19; 2:22) and thereby provided a righteousness for us that we could not obtain (2 Cor. 5:21).

How do we receive this righteousness from God? It comes by faith. Paul describes this in verse 9 as a righteousness "which comes through faith in Christ, the righteousness from God that depends on faith." You can't work for this righteousness, but if you trust Christ to give it to you, He will! This is what preachers and theologians mean when they refer to the doctrine of justification by faith. When you trust in Christ for forgiveness and everlasting life, He not only delivers you from the penalty of sin, He also imputes or credits His righteousness to you so that you have a perfect standing before God (see Rom. 5:1).

If you're not a Christian, don't depend upon what you can accomplish to make you right with God. Turn from your sin and your good works to believe on Christ. Christ is the one who has pleased the Father. His perfect life, perfect death, and perfect resurrection combine to form the only way of salvation. He simply asks you to receive it, to trust Him for it.

If you call upon the Lord for salvation today, He will forgive all your sins, He will forgive you for trusting in your goodness and religion, and He will take His righteousness and credit it to your account (Rom. 10:13). When you turn to the Lord Jesus, you aren't losing anything that's worthwhile or valuable, you're gaining everlasting life. Unbeliever, justification is by faith alone.

Believer, justification is by faith alone. As a Christian, you've already started down the path with Christ. He is your Savior and Lord. God sees you clothed in Christ's righteousness. But the temptation you face is to go back to your old religion of works. Even the heart of the believer wants to gain favor with God. We fear that, if we sin, He won't love us; but He still does. If we do sin, we try to counteract it by Bible reading, prayer, church attendance, being nice to someone, or some other good thing that we can do to get us back into God's favor or make us feel better about ourselves. But the fact of the matter is, we have all of God's favor in Jesus. We have His grace that is free, we have His forgiveness that is complete, and we have His righteousness that is spotless.

What kind of religion do you have? Sit down and do the math. Are you trying to work your way to God or are you resting in the work of Christ? Are you working hard to gain favor with God, or have you lost all your self-righteousness for the favor that Christ has already gained? There is a gain that is loss and a loss that is gain. Where do you stand in the equation of gospel mathematics?

5 Tell Me the Old, Old Story

Preparing to Preach Old Testament Narratives

IAIN DUGUID

The Holy Spirit has chosen to fill the Bible with stories, and so the preacher wanting to preach the whole counsel of God will need to work out how to preach stories sooner rather than later. As the Scriptures tell us, the stories of the Old Testament are written down for our instruction (1 Cor. 10:1-11), and are profitable for teaching, for reproof, for correction, and for training in righteousness (2 Tim. 3:16). Yet at the same time, the central focus of the whole Old Testament is the sufferings of Christ and the glories that will follow (Luke 24:44-47). Thus my goal in preaching Old Testament narratives is to show people the glory of the gospel in the sufferings and resurrection of Christ, in a way that instructs and trains them in righteousness, while at the same time constantly returning their eyes to Christ, the founder and perfecter of our faith (Heb. 12:2).

I have an unusual calling: I am a bi-vocational church planter in a church with multiple part-time staff. We presently have two half-time pastors, including myself, a part-time intern who oversees our music ministry, and a part-time staff member who prepares our order of service. I work full-time for a Christian college and I currently preach around 40 per cent of the Sundays, which means that my schedule for preparation doesn't necessarily look like that of the more normal full-time solo pastor, who preaches 90 per cent of the Sundays, perhaps twice each Sunday, and may have a midweek Bible Study as well. Yet I will try to focus on what is universal in the preparation process.

Select the Text

The process of selecting a text is usually fairly straightforward for me, since we follow the practice of preaching consecutively through Biblical books. The advantages of this approach are many, especially when it comes to narratives. It enables the members of our church to grasp the connection between each story and its wider context in the Biblical book, without having to build all of those connections from scratch in each sermon. For example, the story of David and Goliath does not occur in a vacuum in 1 Samuel 17. It connects back to the previous chapter in which the Lord chose David to be Israel's future king over his taller brothers because God looks on the heart, not on outward appearance (1 Sam. 16:7). It also connects back to Israel's desire for a king who would go out in front of them and fight their battles for them in 1 Samuel 8:20. Situations like this were supposedly why Israel needed a king in the first place. Preaching a whole book helps the congregation (and preacher) to get the bigger picture and therefore see more clearly the themes that are important to the author of the text.

Occasionally, we will do a more selective overview series, but usually we cover every single narrative in a Biblical book. This forces me to wrestle with hard texts that I would otherwise skip. For example, in my series on the book of Numbers, I was faced with preaching on Numbers 33, which is a travel itinerary listing the various places Israel camped on their journey through the wilderness. If I had been preparing a twelve-week series on Numbers, I would certainly have skipped it. Yet as I prepared to preach it, I realized that the list of place names and events that Moses was instructed to write down (by the Lord!) actually had a profound purpose in shaping Israel's thinking about the wilderness experience, a purpose that resonates with our own wilderness journeys through this world.[1] In God's providence,

---

1. See "Pilgrim People" in Iain Duguid, *Numbers*. Preach the Word (Wheaton, IL: Crossway, 2006), 345-54. The audio version is available at http://thegospelcoalition.org/resources/a/ Pilgrim-People.

the most unlikely text became the basis for one of the most helpful and memorable sermons in the entire series. Indeed, even when that is not the case, I would argue that these "hard passages" are often the texts that our people need the most help to understand, and we shirk our calling as preachers if we dodge them.

On the other hand, we also need to feed our people a balanced diet from God's Word. While I preached through the book of Numbers for eighteen months, my co-pastor was preaching from the New Testament in roughly equal amounts. At other times, we have chosen to preach through shorter sections of a long book and then shift to a series from a different book and different genre before returning to the next section (for example, preaching the Abraham stories from Genesis, then preaching a section from Ephesians before returning to Isaac and Jacob).

Even when preaching continuously through books, though, I still need to decide what constitutes the narrative unit. In many cases, the Biblical chapter divisions match up with literary divisions, but this is not always the case. What I am looking for is a narrative unit that contains a beginning, a middle, and an end. A complete narrative unit typically starts with an exposition that sets the scene for the story, followed by a series of episodes with increasing narrative tension in which the events play themselves out, and then a final resolution. Taking a shorter section as your preaching unit can easily lead to missing the main point of the story and preaching about something that is incidental rather than central to its purpose.

In the Old Testament, that typically leads to long preaching texts. For example, the story of David and Goliath is 58 verses long. In many of our churches people are not used to having such long readings from Scripture, yet since this is indeed the Word of God should we not be seeking to encourage people to develop an appetite for more of it? I therefore never apologize for a long Scripture reading, though I do take account of it in setting the boundaries of how long I can preach. I don't want to exhaust the patience of young or weak sheep. I also always read my own Scripture passage at the beginning of the sermon because I believe that that is, in a profound sense, the beginning of teaching the story. Since I have been living with this story for a week, often I can read it in a way that highlights important aspects and themes.

Understand the Text

Having decided the parameters of my text, I now need to grasp the structure, flow and details of the passage. To do this, I generally begin by reading the passage in the Hebrew. This is not easy for most preachers given the length of the passage and the fact that many pastors do not have a strong background in the original languages. Yet I would encourage you to do the best you can with what you have, using all of the helps that are available to you. Many computer programs will help you look up vocabulary in a lexicon and parse difficult verbs simply by pointing a mouse, and it is not "cheating" if you need to do this.

If you don't read Hebrew, read the narrative several times slowly in several different English translations, including a more word for word translation like the NASB and a more dynamically equivalent translation like the NIV or the NLT. My goal at this stage is to start to soak in the story and develop a close familiarity with it. In fact, every morning before I start work on my sermon, I usually read the whole story again. There is no substitute for knowing the text well.

While I am reading, I am looking for unusual or repeated words, or for phrases that may suggest things that are being emphasized by the narrator. For example, why is Sarah's maidservant Hagar so often called "Hagar the Egyptian"?[2] Words that are repeated frequently in the original will not always be repeated in an English translation, however. In the book of Jonah, for example, the Hebrew word *ra'* in different contexts is variously translated as *evil, harm, displeasing, angry*. Reading from a translation may not pick up all of these connections, though some will still be there.

I also look for any programmatic sounding statements that may give a clue to the purpose of the narrative. For example, Joseph's statement to his brothers, "As for you, you meant evil

---

2. For my answer, see "Hagar the Egyptian. A Note on the Allure of Egypt in the Abraham Cycle", *WTJ* 56 (1994): 419-21. This article stemmed from an observation made while preparing to preach.

against me, but God meant it for good" (Gen. 50:20), clearly describes an important point being made in the narrative, as does Jonah's declaration "Salvation is of the Lord" (Jonah 2:9, KJV). In addition, I'll make notes about anything that seems out of place or irrelevant. Nothing in the Bible is irrelevant, of course, but sometimes there are seemingly odd details. I can't always figure out why they are there, but if I can explain why the narrator has chosen to include these details, I am probably getting close to understanding his goals.

Next, I try to break the narrative down into individual scenes. Scenes are typically defined by location, time, or the characters taking part. When one of these elements changes, so also does the scene. Often the paragraph breaks in the English Bible will give basic clues to scene changes. Again, looking at several English translations will help me see where there is general agreement that there is a break and where there may be a division of opinion about which verses are most closely connected together. Having identified the scenes, I will often try to summarize the function of each scene individually to build up a composite picture of the flow of the narrative plot. Again, this forces me to wrestle with the details of the text, not just the big picture.

Sometimes a narrative has a chiastic structure which invites the reader to look for the event or events that provide the turning point. The book of Esther has a strongly marked chiastic structure which highlights the key turning point in the fortunes of the Jews—not Esther's decision to appear before the king in chapter 4 but rather King Ahasuerus' sleepless night in 6:1. On that seemingly chance happening (and the subsequent series of "coincidences" that follow) hangs the fate of the entire people, whatever Esther does or does not decide to do.

At other times, there are scenes that are narratively unnecessary for telling the story. For example, in Judges 11, the story would flow smoothly from verse 29 into verse 32 if verses 30 and 31 (where Jephthah makes his vow) were omitted. In that way, the narrator is showing us how unnecessary (as well as how wrong) Jephthah's vow was to winning the battle.

I also list out all the characters that are involved in the narrative, since stories generally work by inviting us to compare the characters and plot of the story with ourselves and the plot of our lives. With whom in the story do we naturally identify? Are there other characters in the story who are actually more like us? These identifications will tend to suggest potential avenues of application for the story. For example, if we identify with David in the story about his encounter with Goliath, the natural application will be about the need for us to have faith as we encounter the giants in our lives. Yet in reality, most of us are probably much more like Saul, hiding in our tents and shirking our calling to fight. Or perhaps we are like Eliab, David's older brother: we are not willing to fight ourselves but instead speak discouraging words to those who do have faith. Putting ourselves into the place of a variety of characters (including characters like the people of Israel as a whole) will suggest a variety of different ways in which the text may have been written down for our instruction (1 Cor. 10:11).

There may also be characters in the story that indicate ways of preaching this text to non-Christians who may be present. Where are the people in this story who look like my non-Christian neighbor or friend? If I am thoughtless about their presence in the congregation, I may preach David and Goliath in a way that presents the secular world like Goliath, an enemy to be slain! In some ways, of course, that would not be a false presentation of the text. Yet if I remember that I am preaching to some unbelievers, I might point out that this is not the only way in which Israel is called to interact with their unbelieving neighbors. There are also the models of outsiders like Rahab and Ruth, who repent and are incorporated into the covenant community by faith.

If we only find the connections between the characters and ourselves, however, our application will tend to be moralistic, treating the passage as if it were only law: "Don't be like Saul or Eliab. Dare to be a David." I am, therefore, always also looking for the line that goes from this passage to Christ. I want to show people how the plot of the story connects with the wider plot of the Biblical book, of the Old Testament, and with the grand narrative of Scripture that always finds its focus in the sufferings of Christ and the glories that will follow (Luke 24:44-47). In other words, how does this passage draw us to see more richly the gospel of Jesus?

At this stage, it is sometimes helpful to ask what message the original hearers of the story would have heard. How would it have addressed them in their immediate circumstances and pointed them forward to their need of the Messiah? In the case of David and Goliath, the immediate issue was Israel's need for a king—and not just any king, but a king after God's own heart. Saul's role in the story is to fail and show Israel their need of David. But as the horizon widens to the whole of 1 and 2 Samuel, we see that even David, the king after God's own heart, was far from perfect. He committed adultery with Bathsheba and had her husband killed (2 Sam. 11). He did not manage his own family well, nor did he oversee his subordinates wisely. Second Samuel ends with his sinful census. And who will take his place after his death? Is he really the king that Israel needs?

Widening the horizon further to include the book of Judges and the books of 1 and 2 Kings, we see that these themes have a longer trajectory. Samson's calling was to "begin to save Israel from the hand of the Philistines" (Judg. 13:5), of whom Goliath is the classic example (he is called "The Philistine" in 1 Samuel 17:8). Yet Samson failed, instead doing what was right in his own eyes (notice the prevalence of sight as the source of Samson's problems). A key issue in the book of Judges is the absence of a king (17:6; 19:1; 21:25). Yet having a king does not prevent Israel from descending into chaos and apostasy once again. Indeed, the kings themselves often lead the people astray, and it is their sins that provide the catalyst for the exile, as the Book of Kings repeatedly makes clear. The first readers of the Book of Kings would have known that great though David was, he was not the answer to their problems.

Ultimately, the answer to Israel's need and ours comes in a new David, Jesus Christ, who comes to the battle line as humble and as unrecognized as David and conquers our true enemies (sin, Satan, and death) not by his skill with a sling, nor even by his willingness to risk his life by faith in the name of the Lord, but by actually laying down his life in our place. In Jesus Christ, the Good Shepherd takes the place of His sheep. We have all often fallen short like Saul and Eliab, instead of stepping out in faith to serve God as David did. Even when we have tried to do what is right, Eliab's words of critique may (in our case) actually be close to the mark: we are seeking the glory for ourselves rather than for the name of the Lord. Yet David's role in the story is to anticipate his greater son. Jesus doesn't just re-do what David did on a larger scale. He is not simply a clearer and better model. He has won the victory for us, in our place, as our covenant head. In the active obedience of Christ, God provides specific righteousness to cover our personal lack of faith and confidence in the Lord's power and might. Through His suffering and death, He atones for our specific failures in this area, as well as for the times when we have succeeded with deeply sinful motivations.

Use Good Resources

At this point, I'm ready to turn to the commentaries. In some cases, I may already know in a fair amount of detail what the text is about, with some clear ideas about application and how the passage points to Christ. At other times, I'm still completely in the dark at this point. I've also discovered that different preachers use widely ranging numbers of resources. I know some pastors who use a dozen or more commentaries each week in studying every passage. I don't personally find that profitable, since after the first three or four the amount of benefit gained typically drops off sharply. For any sermon series, I usually try to find four different commentaries that will become my main resources, though if there are particular questions that a passage raises, I may search through a few more for specific answers.

Of those four commentaries, I try to make one a literary analysis of the narrative. Even if not written by a Christian, a good literary analysis (such as the works of Jan Fokkelman) will bring out the themes and structure of a story and its connections with other stories in ways that can be enormously illuminating. Unfortunately, such academic works can be very expensive, so if you have a local college or seminary library or access to interlibrary loans it will be helpful. In some cases, books. google.com or the "search inside" feature at Amazon.com can provide enough access to decide whether it is worth paying for the book. I will often choose to read a commentary by a Jewish scholar as well, especially for the Pentateuch. Their insight into rabbinic discussion of texts can be very helpful, for example, in discovering why particular laws are inserted in connection with particular narratives. Traditional academic commentaries like the New International Commentary on the Old Testament are often useful to answer specific background questions. I don't generally find much profit in devotional commentaries, as they are usually not grounded sufficiently in a good understanding of the text. However, works by pastor-scholars like Ralph Davis (Focus on the Bible) and Philip Ryken (Reformed Expository Commentary) are very helpful.

Start writing

I can research a passage forever. It's much easier than the hard work of writing, so I have to discipline myself to sit in front of my computer and get to work. Sometimes I sit down and the sermon seems to write itself. At other times, I spend a lot of time staring at a blank screen. Occasionally, I even remember that I ought to pray! God often uses the process of writing to humble me and remind me that producing a sermon is not a matter under my control. He has never yet left me with nothing to say on Sunday, though there have been a few Saturdays when I have tossed out everything (apart from the research) and started from scratch.

In general, when I hit a block, I try to keep on writing something, even if I know that it isn't any good. Often the next day when I come back to it and ask the question, "Why isn't this any good?" the answer points me in the direction of what "good" looks like. In any event, I try to start writing early in the week, since I firmly believe that the art of writing is rewriting. If I start writing on Tuesday, I have several days in which to come back fresh, look over what I have already and try to develop it further. Given my teaching load, Fridays often end up as my main writing day. However, by that point I have been working with the text all week, so there have been plenty of opportunities in the course of life to think about connections between the passage and my life.

Traditional homiletics books tend to stress a deductive approach to sermon structure, in which the unity of the sermon comes from a structure that is to some degree imposed on the text. Often, the preacher starts out with a thesis statement and gives his points at the outset. This approach generally works well for Pauline epistles, where there is a clear flow to Paul's arguments, and many of my favorite preachers follow the same approach when it comes to narratives. It makes for a clear, simple outline and at its best can really unpack the points that the Biblical storyteller is making.

At other times, however, an approach that restructures the complexity of the narrative into three simple, connected points moves the sermon too far away from the text itself, flattening out the fine detail of the story. Particularly with narratives, therefore, I often prefer to adopt a more inductive approach where I walk the congregation through the story, examining all of its details like the facets of a jewel. Application may be scattered throughout the sermon or gathered together at the end, once we have a really rich appreciation of the narrative. Something is lost in the unity of the sermon, perhaps, but I think that something is gained in appreciating the nuances of the text. I think that this inductive approach also trains my congregation over the course of time how to read a Biblical story and how application (including gospel-centered application) flows from the story in a way that a more deductive approach sometimes may not make so clear. Like life, stories are complex and can have many applications.

I always begin my sermon by writing the introduction. I know that many homileticians advocate writing the introduction at the end, when you actually know where the sermon is going, but my linear-thinking mind can't cope with that. I have to start at the beginning, even if I am aware that I may have to come back at the end and make sure that the introduction still matches where the sermon ended up going.

I always write a full manuscript of my sermon. Writing a full manuscript forces me to think through not only what I want to say but how exactly I am going to say it. It allows me to polish each phrase and sentence so that it has exactly the right wording, and to work on precise and effective transitions. It also means that if I ever come back to preach the sermon again, I have a complete understanding of what I said. I know some preachers who will never preach the same sermon twice. I don't understand that concern: if it was worth preaching once, it is worth preaching again, while if it wasn't worth preaching in the first place, it is time to repent and try to do better. I try to write in oral style, in the way I will deliver it, not in written style as if for a book. I don't worry too much about details when I am first writing, though, because I know I will be going back through it again (and again). Initially, what I am seeking to get down is a coherent flow of thought. My goal is to have a complete and polished manuscript by the end of Friday, in a form that I can then show my wife (see below).

I don't take a full manuscript with me into the pulpit. I think that if I did, I would find it too easy to be tied to my manuscript and lose eye contact with people. On the other hand, given my bi-vocational schedule, I don't have time to memorize the entire sermon and deliver it without notes. I can see the significant advantage of preaching without notes for those who preach to large congregations of skeptics, or where there are always many visitors. Preaching without notes gives great directness and is very engaging. Yet in my context, where most of the people know me and are already to some degree engaged with the sermon, I find that it works well enough for me to have an abbreviated version of the manuscript with which I am very familiar. This reduced manuscript consists of half sentences and single words that act as memory triggers. Illustrations, for the most part, can be identified by a single word, while important phrases and transitions are retained in more precise form. The result is something that probably no one apart from me could decipher but it enables me to know exactly where I am and where I am going.

Practice delivery

Once I have my reduced manuscript, I work from it a couple of times until I am completely familiar with it (normally on Saturday and early Sunday morning). When I started out as a preacher, I would actually do this out loud so that I could figure out appropriate inflections. Now I am able to do it entirely in my head, which helps me not to disturb sleeping family members. At this stage, I am often still adding illustrations and application points as they occur to me.

Typically, this is also the point where I get input from my wife. I am blessed to have a wife who has enormous wisdom and theological acumen, combined with great people skills and sensitivity. As a result, I ask her to read the manuscript of my sermon each week, usually on Friday. This is an exercise in humility as the sermon is rarely finished at that point. My pride would always like to wait until it is in better shape before giving it to her; however, I have learned that it is far more helpful to have her input, positive or critical. She helps me in a variety of ways. Sometimes she will flag a sentence or thought that would be unnecessarily offensive to people in a particular situation. Often, she will suggest a possible line of application. She will frequently ask "How have you failed in this area? Can you give an example?", encouraging me to be open about the specifics of my own sin and failure. Sometimes she will suggest appropriate lines of connection to Christ. Not every ministry wife has the time or gifts to help in this way, but it is a tremendous asset to my preaching. If your wife is not able to do this, you may be able to find another pastor, an elder, or a gifted layman who can fill this role for you.

Deliver the Sermon
Not much needs to be said here.

Debrief
In my early ministry, I pastored a church plant in an area of low-cost, government subsidized housing in England. Our most fruitful ministry was with 7-11 year old street kids. As a result, about half of our small congregation was made up of 7-11 year olds who attended our service, ate lunch with us, and then hung around for our afternoon children's program. It was a fabulous apprenticeship in learning how to preach profound truth simply. To keep the kids engaged, I produced a children's sheet each week to go along with the sermon, with questions for them to respond to and spaces for them to draw their own picture. After church, I would often go around and see what the kids had drawn. It was a great (and often humbling) way to find out what they thought my sermon had been about.

In the same way, the time after church provides an opportunity for us to find out what people are hearing in our sermons. It is also often a time when we are physically and emotionally drained, so it is not the time for detailed critical analysis of the sermon's strengths and weaknesses. However, if someone says "That was a great sermon", it can be a good idea to ask what they found helpful. Track down some kids and teenagers and ask them what they learned. As you build up an inventory of answers over time, you will get a sense of what it is that people are hearing clearly and also, perhaps, what they are missing.

This can usefully be combined with more formal or informal feedback mechanisms. It can be difficult to hear people point out our weaknesses and flaws. We would rather that they only told us our strengths. Yet I need to remember that if this is what my friends are thinking about my preaching, there are probably other people in the congregation who are thinking it less charitably! There may be bad habits that can be corrected or other areas to work on that will help the gospel to shine more clearly in my preaching. Why wouldn't I want to do everything in my power to pursue that goal?

Suggested resources for further reading:

Dale Ralph Davis, *The Word Became Fresh: How to Preach from Old Testament Narrative Texts* (Fearn, Ross-shire: Christian Focus Publications, 2006).

Jan Fokkelman, *Reading Biblical Narrative* (Louisville: Westminster John Knox, 2000).

6

Like Father, Like Sons[1]

(2 Samuel 13)

Iain Duguid

Family resemblance is a remarkable thing. Sometimes, when I am greeting people before church, I see a pair of adults walk in and even though I have never met them before, I know immediately which of the students at the college they go with. There is some similarity of look or mannerism that tips me off to the relationship. Often that similarity is a good thing: a charming and endearing physical resemblance. Yet not everything that we pass on to our children is equally attractive. We also pass on family patterns of sin and dysfunction. There are particular besetting sins with which our children will struggle that they learned from us. We didn't set out to teach them those sins, of course. Yet as they watched us interact with God, with our neighbors and with our circumstances, their little hearts were busy taking notes and filing away strategies, for good or for ill. That's what we see in this chapter of Scripture: the father's sins bearing bitter fruit in the lives of his offspring. It is not coincidental that the two protagonists in this chapter, Amnon and Absalom, are each introduced with the descriptor "son of David" in the very

---

1. This is a sermon I preached in our church as part of a series on the life of David. I chose it because it is both a "hard text" that we might be tempted to avoid and because it demonstrates well the kind of inductive approach to a narrative that I described earlier.

first verse. David's sons have, unfortunately, been watching and learning a great deal from their father's behavior in the whole affair with Bathsheba and Uriah in 2 Samuel 11 and 12.

That could make this chapter of Scripture a very depressing study. There is indeed much to weep over here. Real people's lives were ruined in the making of this brutal and tragic story. Yet from another perspective, that is precisely the power of this chapter, because we too live in a world where brutal and tragic things happen, and not just to other people. Nor do tragic and painful events just happen *to* God's people. Sometimes they are perpetrated *by* God's people, as those in positions of authority abuse their power over others. How do these things fit with God's purposes in this world, and especially the promise of a son of David that God gave back in 2 Samuel 7? Will human sin prove too strong for God's promise in the end? Will Israel's story— and our own stories—end in tears, shipwrecked by the evil of human folly and frailty? Or can God redeem the stories of failing parents, broken children and abused women? Specifically, can God redeem your story and mine and make them a showcase of His powerful grace?

Sin is certainly powerful. The family dysfunction that was on open display in 2 Samuel 11 is repeated in amplified form in 2 Samuel 13. We see it first of all in Amnon, David's oldest son and heir-apparent. Amnon is in love with his beautiful half-sister, Tamar. At least, that is what the text says, although I think that the narrator is being profoundly ironic in calling it that. A more telling description of Amnon's "love" for Tamar is that "it seemed impossible for him to do anything to her" (v. 2 NIV), which pretty much sums up Amnon's intentions. He wasn't interested in a relationship with her; he saw her, she was beautiful, and he wanted to have her. Does that sound familiar? It is David and Bathsheba all over again. David wasn't attracted by Bathsheba's wonderful personality: he saw her bathing, she was beautiful, and so he figured out how to do something to her. Of course, Tamar wasn't married like Bathsheba had been. She was still a *betulah*, an unmarried woman under the authority of her father. Yet she was equally forbidden to Amnon under the law of Moses because she was his half-sister. Amnon had the same sinful desires as his father for a woman who was off limits, but since he wasn't the king, he lacked the power that David had to make his sinful desires come true.

Enter Amnon's wise friend, Jonadab. Again, the text is more than a little ironic in calling him *wise*, though our English versions soften the irony by translating the word as *shrewd*. Jonadab knows exactly how Amnon can get what he wants; he explains to him how to get Tamar alone by pretending to be sick and asking for Tamar to come and feed him. Jonadab's "wisdom" also maintains plausible deniability, however, so that if he were to be challenged later he could say "Amnon did what...? I'm shocked, deeply shocked. I had no idea. I thought that he just wanted to get to know her better in a more private setting..." Jonadab is the consummate skilled politician, as we shall see later in the chapter.

The plan played out exactly as Amnon (and Jonadab) expected. Amnon deceived the king into having Tamar come and cook for him. In a revealing touch, what Amnon said he wanted her to bake were literally *heart-shaped* cakes (v. 6). He then pretended to be so weak that he needed her to feed him like a baby, and sent everyone else out of the room. Once Amnon got Tamar alone, he overpowered her, ignoring her desperate pleas for him to ask the king for her hand in marriage, anything other than this abomination. Immediately after he was done with her, however, his "love" turned into hatred of the object that he had soiled. And he had his servant toss her out like so much garbage, bolting the door behind her (v. 18). Tamar was left to walk away in deep mourning, her prospects of any kind of life completely ruined. What a devastating betrayal of trust and care, the exact opposite of love!

Worse still, the text tells us that David heard all of these things and was very angry, yet he did absolutely nothing about it (v. 21). This was no act of childish foolishness by Amnon but a considered and premeditated act. Tamar was right when she said that this was an abomination—something so awful that it ought hardly to be contemplated happening in Israel. Yet it had happened with the crown prince as the perpetrator, and David did absolutely nothing. There was no punishment for Amnon, which meant that there could be no justice and not even the slightest vindication for Tamar. Everyone acted as if the whole thing had never happened. The same court machinery that covered up David's affair with Bathsheba swung into action to cover up Amnon's rape of his half-sister in a conspiracy of toxic silence, leaving Tamar to a lifelong lonely fate in the house of her brother, Absalom.

Meanwhile, Absalom plotted his own revenge. As next in line for the throne behind Amnon, Absalom had more than one reason to wish him out of the way. Yet Absalom was in no hurry to carry out his plan; he waited two years until the moment was right. As the old mafia saying goes, "Revenge is a dish best served cold." To avoid suspicion, Absalom invited the king and all of his sons to come and join in the feasting that would accompany the sheep-shearing at his country estate, probably knowing that David would decline (v. 23). Yet he persisted in his request until David agreed to send all of his sons along to the feast. As was the case with Amnon's request, David was once again completely deceived by one of his sons. At the key moment, Absalom instructed his servants to strike Amnon down (v. 28). Absalom wasn't right to take justice into his own hands and appoint himself as Amnon's judge, jury, and executioner, but the outcome was what the law demanded. There can be few tears for Amnon.

In the chaotic aftermath, as all of the king's other sons fled the scene fearing for their own lives, a messenger came to David telling him that all of his sons had been killed by Absalom. What must David have thought in response to such devastating news? Perhaps he thought that the Lord's judgment on his own sin was complete, taking away not only the child born out of his affair with Bathsheba but all of his children at one stroke. Yet right on cue, Jonadab was at hand to reassure David that actually only Amnon was dead, not all of David's sons, because that had been Absalom's plan from the beginning (v. 32). This revelation makes you wonder about Jonadab, who was introduced in verse 3 as Amnon's friend. What kind of friend knows about a plot against your life and doesn't tell you? What kind of government official knows about a plan to kill one of the king's sons and doesn't tell the king? Well, one like Jonadab, whose "wisdom" is all about protecting and advancing his own position. All is not well in the Davidic administration. Justice, righteousness, and truth seem in short supply on all sides. Meanwhile, Absalom fled to his grandfather's court in Geshur, safely out of David's reach.

The chapter ends with David mourning for his son, day after day, as happened in chapter 12. But which son? Not Amnon. We read that David was comforted that Amnon was dead. I think David recognized in Amnon's death the Lord's judgment on Amnon, and the Lord's continuing judgment on himself. He mourned over the loss of Absalom, who was forced into exile for doing what the king himself should have done in a judicial context. David's failure to act against Amnon caused Absalom's exile, and set in place the rift between them that would lead into the next tragic episode in David's story.

Yet this story has deeper echoes that take us all the way back to the book of Genesis. The narrator specifically mentions Tamar's clothing, describing it as a long robe with sleeves (v. 18). This is exactly the same description as the special coat that Jacob had made for Joseph, setting him up for equally unbrotherly conduct; these are the only two places in the Bible where such a piece of clothing is mentioned. Even more significant are the links back to Genesis 34 and the rape of Dinah. In that episode, a Canaanite prince of the land, Shechem, saw Jacob's daughter Dinah and violated her. Jacob did nothing in response, and her brothers were outraged, calling what had happened an outrageous thing, something that must not happen in Israel (34:7), exactly as Tamar described her abuse by Amnon. Dinah's brothers engaged in their own vigilante-style revenge, killing not just Shechem but all of his fellow-citizens as well. Yet the differences between the two stories are equally compelling. It is after Shechem violated Dinah that he is said to have loved her, not before, and he at least wanted to provide for her welfare after the event by marrying her. Shechem comes across in a far better light in Genesis than Amnon does here.

It is a truly shocking critique of the state of affairs that has been reached in Israel when the pagans who occupied the Promised Land before them actually behaved better than the

Israelites do. Likewise, in the dark days of the judges, everyone did as was right in their own eyes because there was no king. Yet now that Israel had a God-appointed king, people were still doing exactly what was right in their own eyes, and were being led in that direction first by David himself and now by David's son. Time after time, the storyline from Joshua through to 2 Kings relentlessly exposes the sins of each generation of God's people until it climaxes in the sin that will finally end up in their exile in Babylon.

This surely is the first point of application: the dysfunction of the people of God. Israel was a broken community, congenitally unable to keep God's commandments. The people who responded so confidently at Mount Sinai to the demands of the law with "All that the Lord has spoken we will do" (Exod. 19:8) did not in practice behave even with the kind of common decency that might be expected from pagans. Instead, in the midst of a people called to be holy and uniquely set apart to God, a horrific act of abuse took place that the authorities sought to cover up because of its connection to the royal family.

The same dysfunction is evident in the contemporary church. We too are a broken community, a community of sinners not just in theory but in practice. The tragic fact about Christians is that we don't just believe in the doctrine of total depravity, we live it out. Many people can tell you awful stories of abuse within the family and within the church, and of pastors and elders who just want to cover it up and live in denial. The story of Amnon and Tamar, and of David's refusal to act, is not so very far from our own experience. It is terrible that we have to admit that we don't even live up to the standards of the pagans in these matters, but sadly it is often true. Why is it that Christians are not better and more moral people than pagans? Why does God tolerate such sinfulness in His own people?

Yet we have to bring it even closer to home than that. It is too easy for us to condemn Amnon, David, and Absalom as big sinners without recognizing just how like them we ourselves are in our own hearts, even if we never copy their outward crimes. Amnon's sin against Tamar flowed out of a heart that viewed her as an object that he wanted to do something to, yet it took

Jonadab's counsel to enable him to see how to turn his thoughts into actions. Without Jonadab, Amnon might never have acted, but he would still have had exactly the same thoughts. So too there are many sinful thoughts in our hearts that thankfully never get acted upon, either because we lack the opportunity or the ability to carry them through. We are no better than Amnon; we just lack his position and power. Likewise, many of us who are in positions of leadership are quick to condemn the cover-ups of others, yet which of us really knows what we might do in a similar situation? We may hope and pray that we would do the right thing, but it is easy to be an armchair quarterback or a backseat driver. Some of us know what it is to have Absalom's boiling rage for justice that wants to hurt someone who wronged us, or who hurt a family member that we love. Thankfully, the Lord has protected us from having the power or opportunity to murder the other person, but we know that we are capable of it, especially if the other person seems to be getting away with his crime. Why is it that we are not better people? Why does the Lord tolerate such sinfulness in us?

One response to these questions is to try to clear God of blame by questioning his control of these things. Some will therefore insist that God really, really wants us to be better people but He just can't manage it because of our free will. Yet that doesn't fit with the Bible's portrayal of God's sovereignty over all things. God could have prevented these events simply by removing Jonadab from the picture, or by having him give different counsel to Amnon. God's sovereignty is precisely the point of the link that the narrator makes between Tamar and Joseph's clothing. The stories of Tamar and Joseph both tell of profound and devastating events that humans meant for evil and that God would work for good. We are eager and happy to confess that the Lord is sovereign over all things when a series of providential "coincidences" puts us in exactly the right place at the right time to get the perfect job, or when against all odds the cancer goes into remission. We find it much harder to confess God's sovereignty, however, when what should have been a minor surgery is fatal because of a doctor's mistake, or when your sister is sexually abused, or when your own son is the one who rapes someone. Is God still in control if you yourself commit a sin that you hardly thought possible, or you discover that the church that you love has been covering up something truly dreadful for years and years? What is a sovereign, all-powerful God up to in the midst of these devastating tragedies that rip families and churches apart and reveal the absolute worst in us?

Perhaps that is exactly what God is up to: He is revealing the absolute worst that there is in us and in His church, even after He has redeemed us, to make it plain that there is no hope at all to be found in us. John Newton said that no one ever came to a conviction about total depravity simply by being informed of the doctrine. We come to believe it about ourselves and about others by being shown it. We are naturally inclined toward the belief that we ourselves are inherently good, even practically perfect, and so are our families and our churches. The truth is that we're not close to perfect, and neither are they. You are a mess, your family is a mess, and so is your church. Much of the time we live in denial about that basic reality. Sometimes, though, God opens the door for the ugly truth to be clearly seen. By God's grace, not every person, family, and church lives out that dysfunction in quite as devastating a way. Total depravity doesn't mean that we all commit every sin that we could. God's restraining grace prevents you from doing many evil things that you would do if left to yourself, and gives many of us the incredible blessing of more-or-less functional personal lives, families, and churches. But God's grace doesn't immediately transform the fundamental reality of our deeply ingrained sinfulness.

At the same time, however, God is also gracious even when He removes the restraints on our sinful acts. What we mean for evil, God still means for good as He exposes the truth about us as individuals and as a people. Israel was not God's chosen people because they were more holy than the Canaanites. So too we who are Christians are not saved and loved by God because we are more holy and righteous than our non-Christian neighbors. Sometimes, God chooses to reveal that fact to us in dramatic ways by turning us over to our sin.

So how would you counsel the various participants in this story? Suppose you had the opportunity in the middle of the chapter to speak to each of them, what would you say?

To Tamar? Oh Tamar, I am so sorry for what you have been through. That must have been an absolutely terrible experience for you to endure. My heart breaks for you. You have been betrayed and sinned against by so many people who ought to have loved and protected you. Your father and your brother have both hurt you in ways that you can't simply get over, and that will leave deep scars on your life. You may be tempted to blame yourself for what happened to you and think that you somehow deserved this or brought it on yourself. You didn't. What happened to you was not your fault. You'll also be tempted to respond to what has happened to you in sinful ways, reacting against God and other people with anger, self-protection, and bitterness. Yet God is sovereign even over this event. God did not abandon or betray you: instead He will use your pain and suffering to grow you in deep ways that you can barely even imagine right now. He cares for you far more than anyone else ever could, and He knows far better than anyone else what it is to be deeply betrayed and sinned against by people you should be able to trust.

Tamar, how I wish you could have known the rest of the Biblical story! I wish I could tell you how your salvation will rest in the hands of a different and better son of David than Amnon, or even Absalom. Absalom is deeply angry right now and wants to make Amnon pay, yet his brand of justice will not redeem anyone. You need a son of David who is willing to take into himself all of the hurt and pain that you are feeling right now, as well as all of the guilt and shame—not just your guilt and shame but the guilt and shame of all of his people. Tamar, this coming son of David is going to take all of the pain and curse that sin has brought into the world into Himself on the cross and pay for it all, so that you can be accepted and loved by God as His child. In this suffering Messiah who is yet to come, you can stand before God not merely unstained by what has happened to you but unstained by all of the wrong things you yourself have thought and said and done. There is hope for you to find peace and rest in your loving Heavenly Father's arms through the death of that son of David in your place.

To Amnon? Amnon, you don't look a bit sorry or repentant for what you did. That is very sad but not surprising. I know that

I am capable of doing what you did too, if God were to leave me to myself. Only God can soften your hard heart, as He did for your father David, when his heart was similarly hard. Amnon, I wish you too could know the rest of the Biblical story! You have sinned terribly, but even if you were the worst sinner in the world, what Jesus Christ, the true son of David, will do is enough to cover you too. When Jesus took His Father's wrath on the cross, He took all of it for His people: He paid the penalty for murder, rape, blasphemy, lust, anger, pride, malice, gossip, coveting and so on. Jesus paid for all of that, and He covers us instead with His perfect purity and righteousness: He clothes us with His true, pure and self-sacrificial love for others in place of our filthy, self-centered using of others to serve our own lusts.

Yet if you remain hard-hearted and closed to the gospel, Amnon, you will have to bear the wrath of God yourself. You may think that you have got away with your sin because your father is the king, and he refuses to do anything, but no one ever really gets away with anything in God's universe. God is just, and He is not mocked. Repent while there is still time and throw yourself on the mercy and grace of God which are your only hope!

To Absalom? Absalom, I can see that you are angry and bitter right now and I understand why you are feeling that way. It is absolutely awful that Amnon did this to your sister and still more awful that David refuses to provide justice. But beware of allowing a root of bitterness and anger to spring up in your heart that may lead you to do something you shouldn't. God is able to judge Amnon for his sin, with or without the king's help, or yours for that matter. Don't compound Amnon's sin and David's sin with a sinful response on your part. Submit your unruly heart to God's wisdom and His sovereign right to be the just judge of all the earth. God is not mocked. Amnon will not get away with this. But you need to guard your own heart and confess your anger to God, asking Him to take it away. Human wisdom does not accomplish God's justice and our search for vengeance simply compounds the problem.

Of course, we can't go back in time and counsel Tamar, Amnon, and Absalom. But we can counsel the Tamars and Amnons and Absaloms who are here this morning, which probably covers all of us in some way or another. This passage addresses each one of us and exposes our hearts through the ways in which we respond to the events it describes. Allow God to speak the gospel to you in the face of the particular challenge that you face this morning, whether you are broken-hearted and shamed by someone else's sin against you, hard hearted and comfortable in your own sin, or angry and eager for vengeance against your brother. Perhaps you are angry with God because He ordains such things to happen, or bitter about your own sins that you seem powerless to overcome.

The only hope for all of us is in another son of David—but a Son of David who would not share this particular family pattern of sexual sin and violence. Jesus Christ is the true Son of David, the seed of the promise given in 2 Samuel 7, whose kingdom will endure forever. It wouldn't be good news to hear that Amnon or Absalom would rule forever, or even Solomon (see 1 Kings 11). Yet in Jesus, we see a different Son of David. Jesus was literally descended from David and Bathsheba, yet He was the heir apparent not only to the throne of Israel but to the throne of the universe as well; He is not simply the son of David but also the Son of God. Far from abusing His position of power and glory for His own pleasure and treating people like objects, as Amnon did, He humbled Himself and was Himself treated like dirt for us. His own brothers and sisters thought He was crazy. His disciples abandoned Him and fled at the time of His arrest; one of them, Judas Iscariot, betrayed Him with a kiss. The Jewish people, who should have joyfully bowed to Him as their king, rejected Him, choosing to have a convicted terrorist released to them instead of Jesus.

Jesus' body was given over to the Roman soldiers to abuse physically, not merely once but over many shameful hours. They first scourged His back brutally. Then they took advantage of His weakness, blindfolding Him and hitting Him, saying "Prophesy! Who hit you?" They dressed Him up in a mocking robe of purple and a crown of thorns, saying, "Hail, king of the Jews!" After all that, they nailed His bleeding body to a cross and killed Him. Jesus can therefore empathize perfectly with Tamar, and with you and me when we are sinned against. He knows what it is to be profoundly sinned against and abused, to be treated as so much trash.

Yet instead of responding to that sin with anger and violent outrage, as Absalom did, Jesus loved His enemies and forgave His persecutors, even as He was being nailed to the cross. On that dreadful day, Jesus's Father also held His peace in the face of this abomination—not because He was like David and didn't care about justice but precisely because He *did* care about justice. He knew that at the cross His justice and mercy could meet in a way that would fully and finally cleanse His people from their sins once and for all. At the cross, justice would see sin atoned for and be satisfied, while mercy would be poured out upon broken sinners and see them reconciled to God. Only those who remain hard hearted and refuse to repent are left outside, determined to cling to their sin and face its consequences on their own. The cross means that we will not be stuck forever with our brokenness. We shall all be transformed and become new creations, cleansed of all of our filth.

Do you see how this gospel speaks to you this morning, whether you are the abuser or the abused, the sinner or the sinned against? In Jesus, there is cleansing from your deepest shame, mercy that covers your blackest sin, and hope of a justice that transcends anything this world can offer. As the Father, the Son, and the Spirit work together, they are creating a new and holy people for themselves—a people who may continue to struggle throughout their lives in many ways with their own sin and the sin of others around them, but who can look forward with joy to the inheritance that is theirs in Christ. On that last day, all of our sin will be finally washed away and we shall be pure as He is pure, washed clean forever, as we bear the true likeness of our heavenly Father, made His perfect sons and daughters forever. On that day the true glory of God's grace will be seen in all of its shining magnificence as it welcomes in former abusers and prostitutes, former drug addicts and adulterers, former coveters and greedy people like you and me who in ourselves could never be part of the kingdom of God, and it cleanses away our sense of guilt and shame once for all, replaced forever by the perfect holiness of Christ.

7 Sermon Preparation On the Run

AJITH FERNANDO

I am writing as a non-pastor who has been actively involved in the same church, which my wife and I helped "restart," for thirty-three years. I preached there regularly during the early years, but most of my preaching has been as a visiting preacher in churches, camps, conferences, and mostly in gatherings of Youth for Christ. Despite that irregularity, I have generally preached about five or more times a week. So preparation of sermons is as challenging to me as it is to a pastor of a local church.

One of my great aims as national leader of Youth for Christ for thirty-five years was to develop a model of ministry where everything came out of biblical theology. Biblical preaching and teaching therefore have been key aspects of my life and ministry. Now, after stepping down from overall leadership and taking on the role of Teaching Director, I am preaching and teaching even more than before (20-35 times a month). Because of the itinerant nature of my ministry I frequently repeat my messages, but I am always working on new ones.

Two Inaccessible Models
Most preachers who love to preach look longingly at two models of sermon preparation that are impossible for them to follow. The first model is that of the Senior Pastor of a large multi-staff church in North America who is expected to concentrate on

preaching and so is able to spend thirty or more hours a week in preparation. Other staff will handle most of the other duties relating to pastoral ministry.

I fear that this may not be a very biblical model. Good preaching comes out of a lifestyle of ministering personally to people. Acts and the Epistles show that Paul gave a lot of his time for personal ministry. That is messy and calls for us to do many different things for people with which we may be uncomfortable. I think one of the glories of the call to be a preacher is our call to be a generalist. This can be very frustrating, but it gives us close contact with people, and that provides a background for the kind of theologizing that produces great preaching. When the frustration of working with difficult people combines with careful study and reflection, the result is penetrative insight.

In his early years of ministry, Augustine had a little community in a place called Tagaste where he taught the Bible and was able to give himself to a contemplative life. He feared becoming a pastor because he knew that this would deprive him of the time for reflection he desired and had in the monastery that he led. Since he was a good preacher, he was often invited to preach at various churches. But he would not accept appointments at churches where there was no pastor. He feared they might ask him to come there as pastor!

On one occasion Augustine was invited to Hippo to counsel someone. He was not afraid to go to Hippo because there was a pastor, Bishop Valerius, there. He went to church to hear the bishop preach, and the bishop, on seeing him, told the people that there was an urgent need for a second ordained man there. "At once the congregation laid hands on Augustine and brought him to the front amid general acclamation. There was no escape .... He was ordained on the spot." He began to weep. Some thought that he was weeping because he had not been made bishop (elder) right away. "But the real reason was that he knew ordination meant the end of his dream of a tranquil Christian life, withdrawn from the pressures and strife of the world."[1]

---

1. David Bentley-Taylor, *Augustine: Wayward Genius* (London: Hodder and Stoughton, 1980), 58.

Augustine served in Hippo until his death almost forty years later. But what an influence this one man had! He has been called, "The greatest Christian theologian since the apostle Paul."[2] Some of his books took a long time to write because of the pressures of ministry. One, called *The Trinity,* took seventeen years to finish. He had to drop this project each time a challenge came his way that needed to be addressed.[3] The solitude Augustine desired he got only during the last ten days of his life when, confined to his bed, he asked not to be disturbed.[4] Some of the most influential theologians in history, like Martin Luther, John Calvin, and John Wesley, were generalists who preached and wrote out of active grassroots ministry.

The second model of sermon preparation that is impossible for most preachers today is that of "the country parson" of a few generations ago. He lived in a peaceful, idyllic setting and was able to devote the whole morning on weekdays for study and preparation.

When I was a student at Fuller Theological Seminary in the mid-1970s, John Stott visited the seminary. At a question and answer session a student asked him how a pastor should devote time for study. He said that the old model of the pastor giving the whole morning to preparation is almost impossible to follow today. Instead he said that we should squeeze in whatever time is available for preparation. Few statements about preaching have helped me as much as this one. It is a huge challenge to keep up with the preparation we need to do in this rushed world. But it is amazing how much time preachers could find if they discipline themselves to use the little moments of free time they get for studying.

Sources for Preaching

Keeping ourselves enriched in order to have a wealth of insight to use in our preaching is a great challenge. I rely on five indispensable sources.

---

2.   Tony Lane, *The Lion Concise Book of Christian Thought* (Herts: Lion Publishing, 1984), 40.

3.   Bentley-Taylor, *Augustine,* 189.

4.   Bentley-Taylor, *Augustine,* 238.

Reading and Listening for Personal Renewal

We need to be exposed to means that feed our heart and mind. The most important thing here, of course, is exposure to the Bible. To that I would like to add the need to be exposed to the thinking of other Christians. There is a great danger that, in today's digitalized world, preachers get exposed to limitless bytes of information that fill (not feed) the mind but do not feed the soul. A pastor who left the ministry as a result of burnout left behind his library at his office in the church. When his successor came and looked at his library, he noticed that many of the books he had acquired early in his ministry were on the Bible and theology, but most of his more recently acquired books were on practical topics relating to techniques of ministry and leadership.[5] He had probably neglected the work of feeding his mind and soul.

Theological and devotional books based on exegesis feed us with security-building realities. These realities give us strength to go through the rigors of an active ministry. We confront so many uncertainties and receive so many blows in ministry that without this strength we can become very insecure people. This is what gave the psalmists the courage to persevere against all odds. As the psalmist wrote, "If your law had not been my delight, I would have perished in my affliction" (Ps. 119:92). Deep down we are braced by the reality that "the world is passing away along with its desires, but whoever does the will of God abides forever" (1 John 2:17). With so much uncertainty around, we cling to the belief that truth will finally triumph. As Peter said, "The grass withers, and the flower falls, but the word of the Lord remains forever" (1 Pet. 1:24-25 NIV). As we are bombarded daily with messages that seem to deny this, it is easy to imbibe the insecurity of the world. This is why we need to be fed by a regular dose of the truths of God. These abiding truths give us the security to persevere amidst so many obstacles and setbacks in ministry.

I am convinced that burnout takes place more as a result of insecurity than hard work. Paul uses the verb *kopiaō*, which

---

5.   This was related by Bishop Robert Solomon of Singapore in a seminar he conducted in Sri Lanka many years ago.

carries the idea of toiling or working to the point of exhaustion, thirteen times,[6] and the corresponding noun *kopos* eight times,[7] in connection with Christian ministry. This suggests that hard work and tiredness are inevitable in ministry. But if our hard work and passion for success come from trying to overcome our insecurities, we will never be content in ministry, and we will keep pushing ourselves until we get burned out. Therefore feeding our minds with truths which affirm our security should be a priority in ministry. So is time spent alone with God in prayer. But that is beyond the scope of this chapter.

When I was a student at Asbury Theological Seminary, Bishop Stephen Neill, who served with distinction in India, Kenya and England, visited us for two days. He had one of the most brilliant minds I have ever encountered. During a question and answer time he recommended something to the students which I have found very helpful. He recommended that when we launch into ministry we regularly read theological books slowly, a little at a time when we can find the time, even if it takes several months to complete them. Over the years I have tried to do this with not only theological books but also expository books, exegetically derived devotional books, and biographies of people whose ministries have stood the test of time. Among my favorite authors are Joe Bayly, F. F. Bruce, Don Carson, Robert Coleman, David Gooding, E. Stanley Jones, Dennis Kinlaw, C. S. Lewis, Leon Morris, Robert Murray McCheyne, J. A. Motyer, Lesslie Newbigin, John Piper, A. T. Robertson, Tom Schreiner, John Stott, Chris Wright, and Philip Yancey.

Another lesson that has been helpful to me has been something I learned from John Piper who said, "Books don't change people; paragraphs do. Sometimes even sentences."[8] What I learned from this is that sometimes one does not have to read a whole book to be blessed by an author. When you are reading a large book slowly, it may take a long time to complete

---

6. Acts 20:35; Rom. 16:6, 12; 1 Cor. 4:12; 15:10; 16:16; Gal. 4:11; Phil. 2:16; Col. 1:29; 1 Thess. 5:12; 1 Tim. 4:10; 5:17; 2 Tim. 2:6.

7. 1 Cor. 15:58; 2 Cor. 6:5; 11:23, 27; 1 Thess. 1:3; 2:9; 3:5; 2 Thess. 3:8.

8. John Piper, *A Godward Life* (Sisters, OR: Multnomah Publishers, 1997), 13.

the whole book. Sometimes we may leave a book after reading a substantial portion of it, as we have imbibed enough of the author's burden for the time being.

Of course, we will skim books and magazines in order to get a sense of some of the issues being discussed today. I also read book reviews, and they give me a glimpse of the issues being talked about. I have found that the e-journal *Themelios* (which is found on the Gospel Coalition website) and *The International Bulletin of Missionary Research* have a good variety of helpful reviews. Today, of course, many preachers will find nourishment through listening to talks through podcasts, DVDs, etc.

Observation

We preachers need to know what is happening in the world in which we live. This knowledge leads us to good avenues for the application of truth and also tells us the issues we should address from the pulpit. For this television, newspapers, the internet and magazines can be very helpful. Preachers should consider keeping up with the news (religious and other) as an important aspect of their calling. I work with the poor, and most of them travel by bus. So I usually do several short trips by bus a year and one or two longer trips. The discomfort is more than compensated by the potent preaching material that is gained through observing what is happening.

I also have decided to do my exercise walk in my neighborhood rather than the nice walking areas available close to my home. This is also so that that I can stop and chat to neighbors and get a little involved in their lives. We preachers have to search diligently for opportunities to interact with non-Christians because it is easy to become so involved in the affairs of the church that we end up limiting our contacts to Christians. John Wesley was walking with one of his preachers when they encountered two women quarreling. The preacher suggested that they walk on, but Wesley checked him saying, "Stay, Sammy, stay, and learn to preach!"[9]

I must give a warning along with this call to find out what is happening in the world. Some terrible things are taking place.

---

9. From W. T. Purkiser, *The New Testament Image of the Ministry* (Grand Rapids: Baker, 1974), 64.

There are sordid stories that are circulating as news, which should be categorized as gossip or pornography, which can arouse unsanctified feelings within us and leave us impure. This is why I think it is good for every preacher (indeed, for every Christian) who spends a lot of time on the internet to install some accountability software which both blocks unhelpful sites and sends a weekly report of internet use to an accountability partner. I use the program Covenant Eyes and have found it very helpful.

Personal Ministry

Using a metaphor popularized by John Stott, we could say that the preacher's job is to build a bridge between the biblical world and the world of our hearers. Knowing both the world we live in and the Scriptures is important. But we must take the knowledge we have and present it in a way that is relevant and challenging to people. All preachers must develop skills in the art of integration. Few things help a keen student of the world and the Word to integrate as effectively as personal ministry. To be sure personal work is often frustrating and filled with disappointments. When we make ourselves open to helping people we find that their needs often crop up at the most inconvenient times. Yet personal ministry is a key to penetrative preaching.

Personal ministry forces us to theologize. We are forced to ask how we can effectively apply what we know of the Word and the world to the lives of the people we are ministering to. This often brings us to the point of desperation. We ask questions like, "How can I help this person?" "What went wrong in this situation?" "How was it that I was able to help John while I couldn't help Jerry?" All this helps us to develop skills so that we can penetratingly apply the Word to people's lives.

In the first few years of ministry after completing my seminary studies, most of the illustrations I used were explanatory. They explained what a biblical truth meant. Now I find that most of my illustrations are applicational. Their purpose is to help people to apply biblical truth in their daily lives. I believe this shift is directly related to experiences in personal ministry. When you work with people, you become desperate to help them. So one of the great aims of preaching becomes helping people to think and live like Christians.

I have had to live with a measure of prominence because of my call to be a writer and to speak internationally. But I have come to recognize that the prominence of public ministry is a burden to be endured rather than an honor to seek. Our badge of honor is personal work. Public ministry must never detract from personal ministry. Personal ministry is the context out of which good public ministry emerges.

Research

I suppose I should say something about specific research relating to the content we are going to present in a sermon. The internet of course presents us with a marvelous array of material, which can be very helpful. But we have to be cautious about this because sometimes what you find on the internet is not reliable. I have found dictionaries to be very helpful. I do a lot of my study when I am travelling. So, thanks to the kindness of some friends, I have been able to install on my laptop several dictionaries on a variety of topics which I can refer to when preparing a message. I have Dictionaries/Encyclopedias of the Bible, of Biblical theology, of theology, of church history, of biography, of pastoral theology and ethics, and of counseling. These are augmented by books on topics that would figure in my preaching and teaching; but most of those are hard copies rather than digital copies. Of course, I must mention Bible commentaries which help enrich our study. For me inductive study of the text comes first and only after that do I refer to a commentary.

Usually I use the BibleWorks software for my basic study of the Bible and Logos Bible Software for research and broader study. The Logos program is so large that I have had to keep changing my computer to keep up with it because it can get very slow on an older machine. Thank God for friends who help with such purchases!

Often, when preparing a message, I call friends whom I consider experts to check whether a point I am making is correct. I will call a doctor if I am making a medical point or a lawyer if I want some clarification on a legal matter. When preparing a message for young people, I often ask my children or other staff of Youth for Christ for guidance in helping me make my talk relevant. We must look at application as an exacting task that requires the same kind of rigor that we would give to doing accurate exegesis of the text from which we are going to speak. If I have a serious exegetical question that I cannot answer from the books I have, I am blessed with two friends who are top Bible scholars whom I can write to or call. Sometimes when I visit the U.S.A., I take a list of things I want to ask them. I am amazed at the versatility of their scholarship and thank God that He gives the church this kind of genius.

Bible Study

The core of a good preacher's preparation should be time spent studying the Bible. I am grateful to have had the privilege of studying under Dr. Robert Traina at Asbury Theological Seminary and Dr. Daniel Fuller at Fuller Theological Seminary. They introduced me to inductive Bible study, and I use what I learned from them almost every day. The well-known steps of observation, interpretation, and looking for legitimate applications continue to serve as a sure way to get myself and others into vibrant Bible study.

Such study is, however, a time-consuming task, and it requires people to think hard about what they are reading. In today's digital world, people are not accustomed to spending so much time thinking. Many people would not regard spending large amounts of time on careful observation and thinking about a short passage as a meaningful and fulfilling activity. Ours is a surfing culture that is used to skimming through material and accumulating facts that have been presented in easily digestible bytes. Our generation seems to be more skilled at producing technicians than thinkers and theologians. People say that expository preaching is out of fashion today because it seems culturally distant to people. I feel that the primary reason for the loss of popularity of biblical exposition today is that preachers find it difficult to devote so much time to the tasks of serious study of the Word and thoroughgoing application of the text.

In promoting biblical preaching today, we do face some serious cultural challenges. There is an aversion, in this postmodern generation, to fashioning one's life by submitting to objective truth (truth that is outside of us). This makes exhortation from the Scriptures a culturally unacceptable practice to many.

Related to this is the subjective reader-oriented hermeneutic which places a greater focus on the way a text affects the reader with a resulting decrease in attention given to the intention of the author.

About twenty-five years ago, when I was discussing the possibility of some of my work being published in the west, I spoke with several publishers. They told me that people are not interested in reading Bible expositions. Even Bible expositions that sell should be camouflaged as something else so that the fact that it is an exposition does not figure in the decision to read the book. I remember someone in the publishing world telling me that my publisher made a mistake in having a sub-title *Applying the Book of Daniel Today* to my book *Spiritual Living in a Secular World.* This person felt that the main title was attractive, but the sub-title would betray the fact that the book was a Bible exposition and would thus deter some prospective readers. I determined at that time that I would labor to make Bible exposition exciting and relevant.

I am grateful for a lively correspondence in those early days with Jack Kuhatschek, then at Zondervan. He urged me to be conscientious in presenting the results of solid study in ways that are attractive and relevant. It was a joy and privilege to be able to write the volume on *Acts* in Jack's brainchild, *The NIV Application Commentary.*[10]

My dream is to preach in such a way that people will be attracted to the Scriptures; that they will be amazed at how relevant the Bible is to their daily life; and that they will find themselves developing an inclination to live under the objective truths in the Bible. So preachers today need to be not only expositors of the Bible but also evangelists for the Bible and for objective truth. They have the task of convincing people that the truth of the Word is worth taking seriously. And one way to do that is to present the truth of Scripture in such a powerfully relevant way that it will trigger life change in the hearers. The exposition must demonstrate what living under the Word means as it applies the Word to everyday life. In this way, we can raise

---

10. Ajith Fernando, *Acts: The NIV Application Commentary* (Grand Rapids: Zondervan, 1998).

up a generation of Christians who learn to respect and eagerly sit under the objective truth of the Word.

A Daunting Task

Yet we are asking a lot from preachers when we say they must study the Word and the world and theology and also do personal ministry. Many find this to be too demanding and they compromise somewhere. Sometimes preaching is very relevant but not exegetically sound. Other times it is based on good biblical study, but it is boring and not relevant to the lives of the audience. Those who choose to follow the path I am advocating may experience tiredness. I have been in vocational Christian ministry for thirty-seven years, and I think I have been exhausted for thirty-seven years! I have been preaching since I was about eighteen years old, that is, for about forty-six years. Though exhausted, I must say that I am more enthusiastic and thrilled about preaching than I was forty-six years ago.

I believe my exhaustion is because I have tried to live a balanced life (though I cannot say I have "arrived" at the best balance yet). I see the balanced life not as doing everything in moderation but as being obedient in every area of life. So we give time for study, for reading, for observing what is happening in the world, for preparation, for prayer, for fun times with the family, for other family responsibilities, for exercise, for weekly Sabbath rest, for personal ministry, for neighbors…. Just reading that list could leave you exhausted! However within this stretched and balanced life are sources of renewal. There is a balance between output and input, between fun and work. For example, when we study the Word we are fed, and when we pray and play with family we are refreshed. So we are tired, but we are also refreshed. And if we are happy about our work and relatively healthy—what more do we want?

Quite often I am so busy with other things or I get stuck in my preparation because of an exegetical or other problem, that I am forced to work almost the whole night on a message for the morning. I go and preach and then come home to catch up on lost sleep. I do not detest this discomfort. Preaching is such a great privilege and such a thrilling call that I am happy to pay whatever price needs to be paid to prepare for it. I concur with the sentiments of Robert Murray McCheyne who said, "I will tell you why we faint not. Because it is so sweet to preach. I would say with Henry, 'I would beg six days, to be allowed to preach the seventh.'"[11] I am so grateful for the homiletics course I took under Dr. Donald Demaray in my first term at Asbury Seminary in 1972. The biggest impression it left on me was that preaching was a grand and glorious task. That impression has not left me all these years.

Preparation and Writing Sermon Notes

Let me tell you something about the specific process that goes into my preparation. One day in Dr. Demaray's homiletics class we had a local Methodist pastor Dr. David Seamands come and tell us how he prepared his sermons. Dr. Seamands had been in the same church for almost two decades at that time and had preached two different sermons of about fifty minutes each in the morning and evening on most Sundays. He was a brilliant preacher, and I was always inspired and stimulated by his preaching. He told us that he would go on a retreat and decide what he would preach on for three months. Then he would have a large envelope for each sermon and, if he read something in a paper or magazine which he thought would help him in a particular sermon, he would cut it out and put it in the appropriate envelope.

I use a similar method, though I put my material on a clip board or in a notebook. I try to decide what I am going to preach on as early as possible, and then I let the sermon grow. If I am giving an expository message (which is what I do most of the time), I will print out the passage. I usually use sheets of paper with plenty of space for writing notes. I place the Scripture passage on the left side of the page in an area about three inches wide. This leaves a very large margin on the right and also large margins on the top and bottom. A sermon requires several such sheets. If I am speaking from one or two verses I will use a page for a phrase, which will be typed out at the top. The rest of the page is for notes. The text will be only on one side of the paper

---

11. Robert Murray McCheyne, *A Basket of Fragments* (1848; repr. Fearn, Ross-shire: Christian Focus Publications, 1979), 8.

so that the other side is also available for writing notes. These pages will be clipped to a clipboard. Usually I am preparing more than one message at a given time, so I have a clipboard for each sermon. Some sermons are prepared using smaller notebooks but with a similar idea of having a page or two for a point.

Usually I will read the passage devotionally during my quiet time for about two days. After that my preparation will be outside the quiet time. I will study the passage inductively, taking notes as I go along. Once I have an idea of what my main points are, I keep adding notes to each point. My diary has several blank detachable pages, and if I do not have my notes with me, I will write down ideas in the diary as soon as they come to my mind. Later I will paste or write these into the main notes I am collecting for the sermon. If I do not have my diary, I will look for a paper in my wallet and write it down. If I did not write it down immediately, I would probably forget it.

Sometimes something I hear in a sermon triggers an idea for a sermon I am working on, and I write it down at once. An incident on the road, something I see on TV, something I read, or a conversation may trigger ideas. Those are also written down as soon as possible. Sometimes when I am driving my vehicle, a thought comes and I park somewhere as soon as possible and write it down before proceeding on my journey. Applications spring from day-to-day experiences. What we learn through our personal ministry is a potent source for applications, but we must be careful not to embarrass the person through whom we learned the truth.

Since it is difficult for me to study at home, except at night, I have a few hideaways where I can study undisturbed. I got this idea from John Stott who had a cottage in Wales. My sister and mother live next door, and sometimes I go there. Our Youth for Christ drug rehabilitation center, which is about ninety minutes from my home, is my favorite home away-from-home where I can study undisturbed. During my travels abroad I have friends who open their homes to me for a few days of uninterrupted writing. Without trying to play host, they just leave me alone to study. Sometimes if I have a little free time, like fifteen minutes or half an hour between appointments, I will park my vehicle somewhere and study in the vehicle during that time.

So the sermon grows with time. I am usually modifying the sermon until the time I preach it because ideas keep coming. Something that happens or that is said or sung during the service/meeting triggers an idea, and that is incorporated into the message. This may mean that I will decide to drop something in the original sermon in order to stick to the time allotted to me. Since I modify all the time, I write on only one side of the page so that I can put additions on the opposite side. I also take scissors and tape with me wherever I go, so that if I need to do a major revision it can be pasted over the discarded material.

I usually handwrite my sermon notes because I am more comfortable reading my own writing than I am reading typescript. Sometimes when I am speaking in a conference, I need to present the manuscript ahead of time. So I do that, and then I transfer the material into a handwritten form! This may sound strange to younger people from the digital generation. But this is what is easier for me. I want to see rather than read the notes. This way I can look at the audience most of the time. I color-code my messages using highlighters—again so that I can see without having to read. My main points are colored blue. Subpoints are in green. Scripture is in orange and illustrations and applications are in pink.

I must add that my preparation is slowly getting more and more digitalized and that I am progressively using my computer more during my preparation. Those who are more computer-savvy than I would see that all the processes described above can be done using an iPad or computer. The main thing is to find ways to access the material in our notes, while we are preaching, with minimal distraction so that we concentrate on the huge challenge of communicating effectively to our audience.

I tell our Youth for Christ workers that if they go to speak in a service without adequate preparation, they should be put in prison. One of the most terrible things that could happen on earth is for God to be dishonored. A poorly presented message dishonors God. And if we are responsible for that we should be considered criminals. A vision of the glory of God and our call to uphold it drive us to prepare well before we speak.

Yet sometimes we have to preach without any preparation. On Pentecost Sunday this year at our church, I led the worship up to the sermon. The preacher had not come, and we kept expecting him to turn up at any moment. The offertory hymn was just before the sermon, and he had not yet come. I realized that I would have to preach. I pleaded with God for a message and took the first two chapters of Acts and delivered a sermon making it up as I went along. I think the message went well!

I was able to do this because it was an exception to the rule. A preacher is always thinking about the things of God. Out of the thinking (or theologizing) we have been doing, once in a while, we can come up with things worth sharing without much preparation. But we cannot do this often, for our resources would soon be exhausted. The norm for preachers is hard praying and conscientious preparation before preaching.

8 Moving from Judgment to Blessing

(2 Chronicles 7:11-22)

AJITH FERNANDO

Second Chronicles 7 records God's conversation with King Solomon after some momentous events in the life of the nation of Israel. David had wanted to build a temple for the Lord, but God had told him that this plan would be executed by his son Solomon. After the record of Solomon's inauguration in 2 Chronicles 1, chapters 2–4 describe the construction of this temple, and chapters 5–7 describe its dedication. Chapter 6 includes Solomon's famous prayer of dedication.

Chapter 7 describes what happened after the people had done their part in the dedication. God first responds with the fire falling from heaven and His glory coming to the temple (7:1-3). Then the temple is dedicated (7:4-7). The people celebrate a feast for seven days (7:8-9) and go back happily to their homes (7:10). Verse 11 sounds a note of having completed a great assignment: "Thus Solomon finished the house of the LORD and the king's house. All that Solomon had planned to do in the house of the LORD and in his own house he successfully accomplished." After this, in verse 12, God speaks to Solomon reconfirming his acceptance of what has recently taken place. "Then the LORD appeared to Solomon in the night and said to him: 'I have heard your prayer and have chosen this place for myself as a house of sacrifice.'"

The conversation that follows focuses on the need for ongoing obedience by the people and by Solomon. It is good to have acts of dedication and joyous celebrations over God's blessings. But these mountain-top experiences must lead to a life of obedience.

Do These Promises Apply Today?

First, God tells how He will punish the land if the people disobey and how He will heal the land if they repent (2 Chron. 7:13-14). These promises were made to the nation of Israel, and we must ask how much of them we can apply to our nations, churches, and personal lives today. First, we must note that the many land-related promises in the Old Testament were specifically given to Israel, God's chosen nation. So those who are to respond to God in this passage are described as "my people who are called by my name" (7:14). This passage is based on God's covenant with the people Israel. Other nations have not entered into such a covenant. Therefore this passage would not directly apply to them.

However, today Christians are "called by [God's] name", and this passage should have relevance for Christians. The principles of what God requires of His people remain the same in the Old Testament and in the New. The land-related promises and other promises with tangible blessings and curses relating to Israel may not necessarily work exactly as they are predicted in the Old Testament. God does, however, sometimes intervene and punish sin in an overtly physical way even today. This happened when Ananias and Sapphira lied about how much they gave as a gift to the church. Both died instantly (Acts 5:1-11). In the church in Corinth, many were "weak and ill, and some … died" because there was abuse of the Lord's Supper in that church (1 Cor. 11:30). During the period Scripture was being written God seems to have shown the church what His standards were in unmistakable ways. So we know what God thinks about sin and disobedience. He does not always punish with direct physical punishments. But we know that He is displeased by the disobedience and that, as the New Testament says, "It is a fearful thing to fall into the hands of the living God" (Heb. 10:31).

We know that, living in this world where people suffer, we too may have to suffer physical problems. Paul says that the whole creation has been subjected to futility or frustration (Rom. 8:20). So, even though we live righteous lives, we may get sick, be victims of natural disasters, or suffer economic reversals like other people in this world. But sometimes these problems may be an indication of God's disapproval of our behavior.

What we can say for sure is that we forfeit God's blessings when we sin and that we receive God's blessings when we obey. This applies to individuals and to the church. We can also say that because God is the Creator of the world, the nations of the world will be blessed if they follow God's commands. These blessings and curses may take physical forms, like good health and sickness. Blessings may also take the form of other evidences of God's intervention like His sovereign working for our good and His giving us deep joy and peace which make life worth living.

Judgment for Sin

Verse 13 describes God's physical punishment on Israel if they sin. "When I shut up the heavens so that there is no rain, or command the locust to devour the land, or send pestilence among my people...." The theme that God punishes sin is very common both in the Old and New Testaments. Most Christians, however, tend to ignore these passages. A few months ago I completed reading the book of Isaiah for my devotions. I was struck by the fact that the main theme of the first part of Isaiah (chapters 1–39) is judgment. Once in a while there are positive statements of blessings that are almost like sections in parenthesis. But many Christians completely ignore the judgment aspects of this book and focus on the more emotionally inspiring passages.

Something like this happens when people come to me for advice about a decision they have to make, such as deciding on a spouse or on whether to leave a church and go to another. Sometimes I may give one positive point and ten negative points about what they want to do. And they will latch on to the one positive point and forget the negative points. For example, I may say that the church this person wants to join is a good church, and then give several reasons why this person should not leave his home church. After the conversation he may go about saying, "Ajith said that this is a good church." But he would not mention that I advised him against leaving his home church.

In the Bible the prospect of God's judgment is presented as a strong incentive to obedience. And that is an important truth to always have in our minds.

When we face a reversal of fortune, such as a disaster or a sickness, it does not necessarily mean that it is a chastisement from God. But it would be good for us to ask whether God is telling us something through this. Is there something wrong that we have done or are doing which needs to be corrected? In most cases, this will not be so. Yet it is a good question to ask when something goes wrong.

Called by God's Name

Verse 14 describes the way back to God. It starts by identifying God's people: "If my people who are called by my name." This refers, of course, to the Jewish nation. But now believers in Christ are also called by God's name. So this can refer to us too. This statement tells us two things. God describes the Jews as "my people." That declares ownership. We belong to God; or as the Bible says, "And I will be their God, and they shall be my people" (Jer. 31:33). That is our identity. We are God's people.

Then God says "... who are called by name". In the Bible, a name is often used to signify the character of the person identified. So, when we pray in the name of Jesus, we are saying that the confidence we have in praying is because of who Jesus is. When we are called by God's name, it means that we display His character. This is a way the world will know about God. People look at how those who belong to Him behave and say, "O, so that's what God is like!" They will judge Christianity by the behavior of those who call themselves Christians.

John Selwyn was a missionary to the South Pacific Islands who ran a boys' home and school. There was a very disobedient boy in this home, and no matter what Selwyn tried to do, he did not seem to be willing to change his behavior. One day Selwyn had reproved him for a wrong he had done. In a fit of rage, the boy slapped Selwyn in the face. Selwyn decided that it would be best not to respond with punishment. He quietly turned and left. The boy got worse and worse until he had to be sent back to his island. A few decades later this boy, now an elderly man, called for a pastor saying that he wanted to become a Christian. The pastor explained the gospel, and he accepted it and was baptized as a Christian. The pastor then asked him whether he wanted to take on a new name, now that he was a Christian. "Yes," he said, "call me John Selwyn, because I found out what Christ was like the day that I slapped him." Our behavior shows people what our God is like.

Humbling Ourselves

What happens if we sin and do not behave as people who belong to God? God shows what we should do when we sin. First, God says, sinners must "humble themselves" (7:14). Walter Kaiser, in *Revive us Again*, comments that the theme of self-humbling is very common in the Old Testament.[1] There are more than twelve Hebrew words for it and over eighty references to it. The word used here *kana'* has the idea of subdue. The picture is one of bending the knee or the neck. This verse is describing an attitude of humble acceptance of our faults. It is like saying, "I am wrong;" "I have no excuse to make;" "I have nothing to stand on."

None of us are perfect. James reminds us that "we all stumble in many ways" (James 3:2). If so, humbly accepting our faults should be a frequent thing in our lives. That is why the Old Testament refers to it eighty times.

Yet many do not have the strength to accept that they have done wrong. It requires strength—the strength that grace brings. When we sin, we lose our joy, and joy is one of our greatest treasures in life. The happiest thing about us is that God loves us and rejoices over us. We are thrilled to know that God looks at us in this way. Indeed we pay a huge price to take up our cross and follow Christ. But we have joy. Without that joy our cross would be an unbearable burden.

When we do wrong, we lose our joy. At first we may not be eager to humble ourselves. But soon we become homesick for God; we begin to yearn for the smile of His approval. And we become wise, wanting to be rich with joy again. So we humble ourselves.

1.　Walter C. Kaiser, Jr., *Revive Us Again* (Fearn, Ross-shire: Christian Focus Publications, 2001), 131ff (ch. 9 of book).

Those who don't accept they're wrong and humble themselves are weak people. I have heard both husbands and wives say that they have never heard their spouses apologize to them. These spouses are not angels who do no wrong. They do wrong, but they don't have the strength to accept that they have done wrong. As a result they will not have joy in their lives and invariably their homes will not be happy places.

In an Asian culture, people see admitting to sin as a great shame. This attitude is gaining ground in the west also. People consider it wrong to accept that they have done wrong because of the shame that action brings. How does the Bible answer this problem? I want to suggest two ways.

First, the Bible teaches that the greatest shame for wrongdoers will be at the judgment. In the Bible, judgment is often associated with shame. Jesus talks of the secrets we have whispered in private rooms being proclaimed on the housetops (Luke 12:3). He describes the successful farmer, who retired with a lot of wealth, as a fool because he was not ready for death. We must remind people that not accepting wrong is a foolish thing because they are headed for huge shame at the judgment.

Second, when we deny sinning we become fake Christians. First John 1 has a lot to say about such. Verse 8 says, "If we say we have no sin, we deceive ourselves, and the truth is not in us." According to John we need to "walk in the light" if we are to have "fellowship with one another" (1 Jn. 1:7). The context shows that walking in the light means being honest and open about wrongdoing.

We have situations today where everyone knows that a father or a pastor or a leader has done wrong. No one talks about it openly, and the individual keeps up appearances and goes on as if nothing has happened. But what that person has is fake fellowship. People will privately mention how the leader has done wrong. That leader may command authority and respect by virtue of his position. But spiritual authority and spiritual respect are lost. People will accept him as the boss. But they won't say he is a good person. There may be hugging and public expressions of fellowship, but it is only an act. It is fake fellowship.

So if we don't humble ourselves when we do wrong, we will be fools and our fellowship will be fake. These are also categories that are related to shame. Earlier the shame was in being caught. Now in the Christian community the shame is from the opposite direction. It is the shame of not having the strength to admit our sin.

Praying and Seeking God's Face

Verse 14 goes on to give the next step to take after humbling ourselves; we must "pray and seek [God's] face" (2 Chron. 7:14). Prayer is characterized by seeking God's face. In the Bible, people seek God's face when they seek a word from God, or some seal of His approval. Things have gone wrong; the person who prays feels forsaken by God. Now he comes to God yearning for the smile of His approval. We want to have the assurance that Paul refers to in Romans 8:31, "If God is for us, who can be against us?"

The greatest blessing in life is the joy of knowing that God delights in us. When that joy is gone, we want it back. A child displeases her father and earns his rebuke. She is very sad about it. So she draws a card apologizing to her father. When she comes to his room, he is busy working at his desk. She waits even though he seems to be ignoring her. She won't give up until she has won his attention. And when he sees the card, he hugs her and tells her, "Now let's forget about the wrong you did. That is forgotten."

Unlike that father, God is never too busy for us. But still we have a strong sense of urgency in our prayers. Our sins have brought a barrier between us and God. We want that barrier removed as soon as possible. So our prayer has a sense of urgency. The New Testament uses the idea of earnestness to describe such prayer. The Greek word translated *earnest* has the idea of being stretched out. Our whole being is stretched in urgent pleading with God. This word is used in the description of the prayer of Jesus at the garden. "And being in an agony he prayed more earnestly; and his sweat became like great drops of blood falling down to the ground" (Luke 22:44). It is used for the church's prayer when Peter was in prison, probably awaiting execution (Acts 12:5). God answered that prayer miraculously by sending an angel who rescued Peter.

This is the kind of prayer prayed by those who return to God after sin. Their relationship with God has become a matter of life and death. They know that they cannot go on living in sin. They desperately want to change and receive God's pardon. Jesus told a parable of two people who went to pray. One was a Pharisee who thanked God that he was not like other sinners. The other was a tax collector, despised by his own people for his disobedient lifestyle. He "beat his breast." The breast or the heart was considered the seat of sin. So he is expressing grief over his sin. And then he says, "God, be merciful to me, a sinner!" Jesus said that it was this sinner who went home justified rather than the Pharisee (Luke 18:9-14).

History has shown that this is the kind of prayer that often precedes revival. When people are aware of their own shortcomings and urgently seek God, they can become instruments of His mighty work.

Turning from Wicked Ways

It is not enough to be sorry about our sins. We must also give up the sinful behavior that ruined our lives. So the next thing God says is that the people who have sinned must "turn from their wicked ways" (7:14). Now this is easy to say. But is it possible to practice? Many people do not believe that it is possible to live a holy life. The Bible however often assures us that it is possible for us to be holy. Paul says, "No temptation has overtaken you that is not common to man. God is faithful, and he will not let you be tempted beyond your ability, but with the temptation he will also provide the way of escape, that you may be able to endure it" (1 Cor. 10:13).

The Bible says that God uses many means to help us to live holy lives. Two of these are especially important. The first is *the help of the Holy Spirit*. Romans 8 describes this is some detail. Verse 13 says, "...if by the Spirit you put to death the deeds of the body, you will live." It is the Holy Spirit who helps us to turn from wicked ways. It is we who put to death those deeds; we are not passive but active participants in this process. Our Chronicles passage says that we must turn. But for all of this the help comes from the Holy Spirit.

Leviticus 20:7-8 uses different terminology to tell us how this takes place. "Consecrate yourselves, therefore, and be holy, for I am the LORD your God. Keep my statutes and do them; I am the LORD who sanctifies you." We must consecrate ourselves; that is, we must commit ourselves totally to God. Then we must consciously seek to obey (keep His statutes). But ultimately it is God who sanctifies us. Today we know that we are sanctified through the work of the Holy Spirit in us.

A boy was greatly attracted to a handful of candy that his sister had with her. He asked her for it, but she refused to part with it. After an extended session of asking and refusing, the girl finally relented. She said that she would give her brother all her candy if he would give her all the marbles that were in his pocket. Now this boy was very fond of his marbles, and he did not want to part with them. But he wanted the candy so much that he agreed to the bargain.

The boy could recognize his marbles just by touching them. He reached into his pocket and felt around until he touched his favorite blue marble. He kept that one aside and gave the rest to his sister, even though he promised to give all the marbles. After he got the candy he asked his sister, "Have you given me all your candy?" We are often like that! When we refuse to consecrate our whole life to God, we find it difficult to trust Him to look after us fully. In our insecurity we could, under the force of temptation, succumb to it and end up going back to our wicked ways.

Words such as *consecrate*, *holy*, *sanctifies*, and *statutes* may suggest an otherworldliness that makes holiness something quite distant from us. The holiness described in the Bible, however, is an earthy holiness. Just before describing how the Holy Spirit makes us holy, Paul himself describes his own struggle with sin. He says, "For I have the desire to do what is right, but not the ability to carry it out. For I do not do the good I want, but the evil I do not want is what I keep on doing" (Rom. 7:18b-19).

I have a colleague who was a drug dependant and gang leader before he came to Christ. Now he is a staff worker in our drug rehabilitation program. I was shocked when he told me one day that when he reads the epistles of Paul he feels that Paul must have been a drug addict. I asked him why he said that, and he referred to the passage just quoted from Romans 7. He said that this is exactly what a drug dependent goes through. While I do not believe Paul was ever a drug addict, this shows how close the

Bible is to real human experiences. The holiness it speaks of is a practical lifestyle which is for real people.

This same colleague was assaulted once by some people from the village in which our drug rehab center is located. When I met him shortly after this happened, the first thing he told me was, "Now I know that I am a Christian." He said that in his old life, when something like that happened, his natural reaction was to hit back. The young men in the center had wanted to do that. But he stopped them. He was shocked to find that he did not desire revenge in any way. God can change people from the inside.

The second important means God uses in helping us overcome our wicked ways and live holy lives is *the help of fellow believers*. Second Timothy 2:22 makes a statement similar to the one from 2 Chronicles that we are looking at. Paul says, "So flee youthful passions and pursue righteousness, faith, love, and peace, along with those who call on the Lord from a pure heart." Fleeing evil and pursuing a holy life are not done alone. We do it along with others "who call upon the Lord from a pure heart."

Many people are afraid to come into the vulnerable situation of sharing their struggles with others. Some say they have been hurt by people using the information they shared in the wrong way. They will now, therefore, not trust others enough to share their struggles with them. Indeed, this has happened often. We must not entrust our secrets to unreliable people. We need to raise up a new generation of the kind of sincere Christians Paul tells Timothy about. These will covenant to be honorable and keep in confidence what has been shared with them unless sharing it with someone else will be helpful to the person who shared in the first place.

We are talking here about spiritual accountability. One of the things we can do with our accountability partners is to "confess [our] sins to one another and pray for one another, that [we] may be healed" (James 5:16). This can be a great incentive to holiness and a deterrent to unholy practices. Hebrews 10:24 says that we must "stir up one another to love and good works." The Greek word translated *stir up* is a strong word used for a powerful provocation. When we get lethargic, our Christian friends provoke us to come back to total commitment.

I think spiritual accountability is more needed today than ever before because of the internet and all that happens through mobile phones and computers. Earlier I used to talk about people having one life in church and another life at home and in society. Now I have to talk about another life, which is the private world that people live in with their internet and mobile phones. How dangerous those can be in leading us astray because no one generally sees what is happening. How grateful I am to an accountability partner who gets a report of my internet activity and the questionable sites I may have gone to or tried to go to and was blocked by my filter. I use the Covenant Eyes software for this.

When someone fails continuously in an area, it suggests that there is a weakness that needs healing. Disciplining that person is one of the best ways to bring such healing. Paul mentions the severe discipline of excommunication for two serious errors, one sexual and one theological (1 Cor. 5:5; 1 Tim. 1:20). But in both cases his purpose is that the offender repent and change. Less severe discipline could be helpful for less serious weaknesses too. Hebrews 12 talks about how God disciplines us because He loves us and wants us to be blessed by His disciplining.

When we do wrong and repent, God immediately forgives us, because the punishment for that sin has been borne by Jesus on the cross. When a person is disciplined, it is not a punishment for sin. The sin has revealed a weakness that needs to be healed, and forgiveness alone does not do that. The discipline also acts as a means of healing for the weakness.

Let's see how this works. Here is a good worship leader who has a group of friends to whom he is accountable. He shares with them that he is struggling with controlling his temper when he gets upset with his wife. He often scolds her in insulting language. When this goes on for some time, the friends decide to discipline him by stopping him leading worship for three months. The person who replaces him is very incompetent. He even sings out of tune sometimes. For three months the leader suffers as he sits through low-quality worship leading. Finally, he is able to go back to his former role as worship leader.

Some days after he has been restored to his former position, he comes home and discovers that his wife has done something that really annoys him. The old torrent of unkind words begins to well up in his mind and come as far as the mouth. But before he sends out his barrage of unkind words, he remembers his three months of suffering and he controls himself. He is prevented from doing something which he would later regret and which would be very hurtful to his wife.

This long detour was presented because many today don't believe it is possible for people to give up the wrong deeds that they are accustomed to do. The Bible tells us that it is possible to live a holy life, and it presents aids for doing so. Foremost among these are the help of the Holy Spirit and the help of friends.

God Will Bless If We Remain Obedient

After describing the path of repentance away from the judgment that comes with disobedience, God describes His response to their repentance. He says, "… then I will hear from heaven and will forgive their sin and heal their land" (2 Chron. 7:14). After the healing, there will be free access to God. So God says, "Now my eyes will be open and my ears attentive to the prayer that is made in this place. For now I have chosen and consecrated this house that my name may be there forever. My eyes and my heart will be there for all time" (vv. 15-16). God will always be there to hear and to answer their prayers.

Then God addresses Solomon personally. He tells him that he must continue to be obedient to God and His commands. "And as for you, if you will walk before me as David your father walked, doing according to all that I have commanded you and keeping my statutes and my rules" (7:17). If he continues to be obedient, God says, "… then I will establish your royal throne, as I covenanted with David your father, saying, 'You shall not lack a man to rule Israel'" (7:18).

Sadly, God did not fulfill this promise made to Solomon because he had two big weaknesses. One was that he ruled in an autocratic manner and alienated the people by placing too many burdens on them. The other was that he married too many wives, many of whom worshiped other gods. This corrupted the nation. These wives dragged Solomon away from God's ways. Shrines of other gods were introduced and became a permanent fixture until the people were exiled. After King Solomon died, the kingdom was divided into two, with most of the tribes moving away and forming the kingdom of Israel. Solomon's descendants ruled only their own tribe Judah and the tribe of Benjamin.

Solomon started his rule very well as a humble and eager servant of God. But he did not end well. His weaknesses got the better of him. Will this happen to us too? Sadly many biblical leaders, like Solomon, did not end well. Their weaknesses took them away from righteousness and success. How about us? We also have many weaknesses; we also do wrong. The key is humbly to accept that we have done wrong, to seek God's face in prayer, and to turn from our wicked ways. Is it possible? The Bible says it is! And it tells us that God is the one who will help us truly consecrate ourselves to Him. He does that primarily through the help of the Holy Spirit and the help of sincere Christian friends.

Do you need to return to God? Is there some humbling that needs to be done? Are you asking whether you can make it to the end?

9 Seems Odd to Me

DAVID JACKMAN

There is an old saying that while it may take some hours to prepare a sermon, it takes a life-time to prepare a preacher. Observation and experience over many years certainly tend to confirm its truth. Personally, as I look back over more than forty years of regular preaching, I can see how much my content and style have changed and developed over that period of time—I hope for the better! What I do and the way that I do it today is the product of a complex inter-action of personal, relational, and circumstantial issues which are unique to my own life and personality. God has been growing me as a Christian disciple, as well as deepening my understanding of Scripture and increasing my confidence in its powerful message.

Every sermon will be different because each one is an exposition of a different Biblical text, or passage, which will have its own unique characteristics, in terms of its historical context, its literary genre or style, and its didactic intention. In the same way, every preacher of that text will preach it differently, not only from his fellow preachers, but also from himself as he was twenty, ten, or even five years ago. We are all "works in progress"; each one of us an individual with regard to background, temperament, life-experience, and personality. So, although we can learn a great deal by looking over a more experienced preacher's shoulder during the sermon-preparation process, we can never be anything other than ourselves, as we seek to understand God's truth and express it in preaching. Nor should we want to be!

In a day when it is so easy to download the most popular preachers at the click of a button, what is undoubtedly a great privilege can also become a hazardous danger. It can be very seductive to younger preachers to try to emulate their favorite exemplars, to use their outlines, to repeat their illustrations, even to imitate their tone of voice or gestures. But in the end it is all counter-productive. You cannot be anyone else and to deny this is to reveal a fundamental lack of trust in God's wise providence, which has made you the unique individual you are and given you a specific context in which to preach His Word. We need to have confidence that he has "wired us up" in the particular ways of our own individuality, precisely because, in His sovereign purposes, He has a task and ministry which only we can fulfill. Anything other than being yourself in Christ will not command God's blessing on your work. It will always be second-hand and, sadly, that nearly always means second-rate. God has called you with all your individual strengths and weaknesses to preach this Word of the Lord, to a specific congregation, at this particular moment in time. Don't try to copy anyone else, however "good" they are! As I have often said to my students, "When someone in the future comes to tell you that 'no one preaches like you', don't be flattered; it's just a statement of fact!"

The Driving Seat

With these caveats in place, let me try to explain something of my own methodology, as I lead in to the title of this chapter which lies at the heart of my preparation process. I believe that expository preaching, to which I am committed, involves more than being generally Biblical and orthodox. I remember once attending a conference in which several "outstanding communicators" each preached a "model" sermon. Each one began by reading a Biblical text and affirming their personal dedication to expository preaching. The Bible was then shut and for the next thirty minutes we had a selection of stories and illustrations around a general Biblical principle or idea, often brilliantly presented, in terms of communication skills, warm-hearted, humorous and engaging. But the Bible was not in the driving-seat of the sermon. The preacher was!

So, far from hearing the intended Word of the Lord from that particular text, the preacher's imposition of his (admittedly) talented self between me and God meant that all I heard was the word of the preacher, with all its consequences of limited authority and value, however scintillating the presentation might have seemed. In a contemporary culture like ours, which prizes image over substance and presentation over content, there is an acute danger that the preacher will be squeezed into the world's mold, under the mistaken assumption that he is being "relevant."

My own methodology of conviction for the week-by-week preaching of the Word, in the local congregation, is to work through a book of the Bible, or a section of a longer book, consecutively, passage-by-passage, seeking to expound each successive text in its context. One of the many advantages of this method is that it respects the divine authorship of the Scriptures, not only in expounding the words which make up the context of the revelation, but also in the wider context of the book of which the passage is a part. My assumption is that when God inspired each of the sixty-six books as a literary unit, he knew far better than we how to nurture His people down through the remaining centuries which have followed. So, I want to cut with the grain of the wood as God has provided it. This respects the different historical periods in which the books originated, the literary genres within which the authors wrote in their own times and the preceding revelation on which they built, as well as the individual stylistic choices of vocabulary and structure, which mark them out as distinct from one another. This discipline also guards against imposition from my own limited, culture-bound, contemporary situation, which will always tend to domesticate, if not distort, the plain meaning of the text.

It is this detailed, committed, persistent engagement with the text which produces effective proclamation and for which there is no substitute. A sound-bite culture such as ours is keen to impress upon the preacher that he must be relevant and engaging to his hearers, and that is right, but it often leads the preacher to put the emphasis in the wrong place and so to prioritize his preparation time wrongly. If he engages deeply with the mind of God in the Bible text, his content will be relevant since it will be "the living and abiding word of God" (1 Peter 1:23). But that requires a confidence in the authority and power of the Bible, which many contemporary preachers seem to lack. If our concentration is on the current culture and all our efforts focus on seeking to find appropriate comments on, or answers to, the present pre-occupations of our western secularism then we shall be in the driving seat, but the voice of God may be muzzled at best.

We need to regain an apostolic confidence that the only illumination which can disperse the fog and transcend the confusion of our world today is the light which shines from outside into the mind and heart. Defending the authenticity and consequent authority of the apostolic gospel, Peter affirms not only his own eyewitness account of Christ's majesty, but also his earwitness to the voice from the majestic glory, declaring Jesus to be God's Son, and he also links this to the prophetic writings which it fulfills. Both prophetic prediction and apostolic testimony come together to constitute the Scriptures, to which he tells his readers "you will do well to pay attention, as to a lamp shining in a dark place, until the day dawns and the morning star rises in your hearts" (2 Peter 1:19).

There is no inner light to expel the gloom of sin and despair—not even the bright ideas of the preacher! The light has to come from outside. It is divine in origin. That is why we shall always be in need of it. Expository preachers have as their deepest conviction the work of God. Let us realize once and for all that it is not our job to try to "do something" with the Bible text, as though God's Word needed the helping hand of my ingenuity. How could it ever be anything other than supremely relevant? Expository preaching takes the Bible text seriously by submitting not only to its content for the sermon but also to its intention—application and tone—not the other way round. This means, in turn, that I need to devote my maximum concentration to what the text is actually saying, to read and study it with my antennae up and fully engaged to pick up the signals of the divine messenger. In short, I need to expect the unexpected.

Looking for the Odd Things

"Seems odd to me" is a strapline, coined first by my friend and colleague Dick Lucas, and now used widely in our work in the Proclamation Trust, which sums up what we are looking for as we come to any text to be preached. It is a way of reading the text, observantly and thoughtfully, which generates a fresh engagement with its meaning, however well known we may imagine it to be. As I read and reread the passage, usually in more than one version, I often jot down on a piece of paper, both the things that I find difficult about the text and the surprises I encounter. "Seems odd to me!" is one way of expressing these reactions to the text. There will be puzzles, which are really difficulties of understanding. These may relate to the vocabulary used, or the logical, sequential connections between sentences or ideas. They make me stop and think, and then employ a range of subordinate questions which help to unpack what is beneath the surface meaning. "Why does he say it in this way?" "Why is he saying it in this particular context, at this point in the book, narrative or argument?" "What did it mean to them then, when this text was first heard or read?" But often the most faithful observations occur when I find myself saying "Well, I wouldn't have written that" and at first I find it hard to work out why that is so. "Seems odd to me", but the likelihood that my thinking is right and the Bible is mistaken is as great as the likelihood that a stream could flow uphill!

So then I have to get to work to quarry away at the hidden treasure, which I know is in there and which when I unearth it has the capacity radically to change and develop my perceptions about God and His Word and eventually those of my hearers as well. I am not talking about trying to produce some unexpected meaning from a text, much as a magician produces the proverbial rabbit from a hat. So often people emerge from a sermon saying, "Wasn't it amazing what he got out of it!", when rightly they should be expressing amazement at what the preacher managed to smuggle into it.

We all have our frameworks, and if we do not take preventative measures they will take us over and dominate our preaching. None of us is able to approach any Biblical text as a *carte blanche*. Inevitably, we each wear our own pair of prescription spectacles through which we unconsciously read the Biblical passage according to our training, background, theological convictions, personal life-experience, etc.

Most of us have particular emphases which we have come to treasure and which we can quite effortlessly impose on any given passage. Some preachers can be relied on always to move towards their favorite themes in any sermon—the Lord's second coming, experiences and gifts of the Spirit, election and predestination—and so on. These emphases may be theological, cultural, or pastoral, and they may be entirely right and beneficial in themselves. But what is read into the text usually ends up controlling the sermon. Even though what is being said may be Biblically true, if it is not what this text is saying in its context within the book, then the authority for the sermon has subtly shifted from the Bible to the preacher, from the divine revelation to the human channel. The dominant framework then becomes very predictable to the congregation and once the "bees in the pastor's bonnet" are identified, it takes little effort to switch off and screen out the agenda which is being pursued. Such preaching loses authority, even as its content becomes increasingly repetitive and predictable.

Clearly, if we are to do better than this, we shall have to be disciplined and diligent about our preparation. Too many sermons fall at this first fence. Because the preacher has allowed insufficient time for his preparation, he cuts corners with the result that his hearers are disappointed and the God who gave His Word is dishonored. Preaching is a calling from God, a stewardship for which we must give an account. When Paul opened for the Colossians a window on his own heart and apostolic ministry, he left them in no doubt about the cost of his fruitful service. In Colossians 1:25, he describes the nature of this stewardship as "to make the word of God fully known". He goes on to identify this as the rich and glorious mystery, the open secret which God has now chosen to reveal, which is "Christ in you, the hope of glory" (v. 27). He continues, "Him we proclaim" (v. 28) because Christ is Himself the Word of God in its fullness. Paul is motivated, however, not only by faithfulness to the Lord's commission, but by heart-felt love and concern for his hearers, "warning everyone and teaching everyone with all wisdom, that we may present everyone mature in Christ" (v. 28). The final verse of the paragraph underlines that this does happen casually, or on the back-stroke, as it were. "For this I toil, struggling with all his energy that he powerfully works in me" (v. 29). The ability and energy of God are limitless and, therefore, more than sufficient for what would otherwise be an impossible task. But the verbs Paul uses to describe his involvement (toil and struggle) come from the spheres of back-aching manual labor and the physical demands of the wrestling arena. Biblical ministry is very hard work and those who are not prepared for that should not be given access to the pulpit.

That balance of all-out human effort, coupled with divine enabling, is stated even more succinctly, and with telling precision, in 2 Timothy 2:7, when Paul challenges pastor Timothy to "Think over what I say FOR the Lord will give you understanding in everything." Divinely-given insight comes through the brain-aching work of our study and reflection. That is why the whole process is bathed in prayer from the very beginning. I know that naturally my eyes are heavy, my understanding is slow, and that the default position of my sinful heart will be to harden itself against God's penetrating, convicting, but life-giving Word. I find that the process of preparation is really a conversation with the Lord, as I ask Him for illumination, understanding, application, faith, and obedience. By God's grace I must seek to relate all that he is saying to my own personal life before I can ever pass it on to others with integrity or effectiveness.

Structuring the Process

Although very few ministers have many "ideal" weeks, yet I do think it is important to have an ideal structure for our preparation time and through prayer, discipline, and hard work to seek on a regular basis to get as near to it in practice as we can. Some preachers were frankly given impossible expectations at college about the time they would need for preparation when out in the ministry. Twenty hours would not be too much, perhaps, but for most busy pastors that is an unreachable target. The danger is that having decided that is so, they then swing to the other end of the spectrum and fit whatever preparation they can manage into the odd corners of their week, which usually seem to occur on Saturdays. There is a middle way. Personally, I find ten hours an achievable target time for preparation, which I divide into four roughly equal periods of two to three hours each. These are ideally located on successive days, to allow maximum marinating to be built into the process. In a settled pastorate, this translates into four mornings in the week at the study desk, with the answer phone switched on and the e-mails switched off. If I am preaching through a book, I will have read and studied the text for the good of my own soul before I begin the weekly series of expositions, so that when each individual passage comes up I am not approaching it cold.

My first study session is occupied with the exegesis of the text, with two major aims. I want to have fixed firmly in my mind, but expressed in my own contemporary language, exactly what this passage says and means. From this, I want, secondly, to write a theme sentence, which will summarize and focus the message which I must preach in order to be faithful to the text. It needs to be a sentence (not a paragraph!), which is not yet set in stone but which is the culmination of all the exegetical work which has occupied me during my first session. Incidentally, the session can of course be broken into two parts, if one can concentrate better that way or if events impose themselves upon the plan. But what is important is not to skimp on the overall time.

Obviously, this session will vary according to the type of literature under consideration. Unpacking a passage of dense theological argument, in a few verses of an epistle, will be a very different task from catching the flow, characterization, turning points and narrator's comments when dealing with an Old Testament story, which may be a chapter or more in length. But whatever the genre of the material, establishing what the passage actually says is always the first responsibility for the preacher, because the text is the message. I try to do as much of this work as I can for myself, with my lexicon and concordance, and delay going to the commentaries too soon. If I go to the commentaries too quickly and they are helpful, they will tend to control my thinking. And if they are not helpful, they will probably only deepen my confusion. But it is that "confusion" which often provides the necessary stepping-stones to real understanding.

My second session sees me using my list of surprises and difficulties as I try to delve deeper, by moving on from questions of meaning to questions of significance. The "what" questions tend to be replaced by those beginning with "why?" My aim here is to explore why this passage is included in the Bible and how it fits into the purposes of the book of which it is a part. This will mean that I have to try to get back to the original situation which generated the text as part of God's infallible Word for His people in all ages, including our own. Why was the original writer committing these words to paper? What did the Holy Spirit intend to achieve for His hearers or readers, as He inspired each word, both then and now? These are context questions, which force you below the surface level, to compare Scripture with Scripture and seek the interpretation in the significance of its message, first to them, and then to us now.

I find it helpful to think of context in terms of three concentric circles. With the text at the center, each circle widens out the implications of what we are reading. The first is the immediate literary context which concerns the surrounding verses and often sheds light on the surprises and challenges of the text, identified in session one. A good example of this might be the famous verse, Romans 8:28: "And we know that for those who love God all things work together for good, for those who are called according to His purpose." "Seems odd to me" leads me to observe that life very often looks the polar opposite of this, even for, sometimes especially for, the Christian. On the one hand we don't want to lose the glorious inclusivity of the text. As Spurgeon said if all things means everything, then nothing is left to work in any other way. But if life seems otherwise, does that mean that I don't really love God (or at least love Him enough), or that I'm not really called by Him, not one of His elect? The text out of context becomes a pretext for all sorts of distorted understanding. The context, in verse 29, defines for us the "good" to which God is working. It is not for a life of undisturbed calm or airlifts out of adverse circumstances. Rather, it is to conform us "to the image of His Son". We may not have a stress-free existence, but God will be using it all for our greatest good, to renew us in His image, to make us more like Jesus. Verse 28 no longer seems a mocking contradiction in the light of verse 29.

Every passage, however, also has an historical context in the whole Bible book of which it is a part, which is why consecutive exposition is so beneficial. Each book contributes its own unique addition to the whole Scriptural revelation. So I need to relate this passage to the theme tune that plays throughout the book, its particular purpose and distinctive message. The story of the wedding at Cana of Galilee, in John 2:1-11, is not in the book to provide a sermon for a marriage service. But it is there to develop John's agenda in the book. As Jesus turns the water into wine, this miracle of creation, John says, was "the first of his signs" by which "he manifested his glory". That is totally germane to his book's purpose (see John 20:31).

The magnificent passage on love, 1 Corinthians 13, doesn't occur in its context to be a purple passage or even a pen portrait of Christ, much less another marriage service sermon. There was no great desire to use it for that purpose when it was first read to the Corinthians, I judge, but rather a good deal of anger and hostility that the epistle should dare to address such a gifted and "impressive" church as it did. Certainly, it is a wonderful statement of the expression and character of *agape*, Christian love. But Paul's point is that though love is "square one in the Christian life" and greater than any and every other spiritual gift, the church at Corinth has scarcely begun. The characteristics of love he outlines in verses 4-7 are all related to the deficiencies and shortcomings of the Corinthian church which the first twelve chapters of the letter have had to expose in chilling and depressing detail. Far from being spiritual poetry for the great occasions, it is actually a stinging rebuke of Corinthian immaturity and failure.

Sometimes a particular phrase within the passage under study can open up a more fruitful and deeper understanding of the whole book context, so that the process potentially works both ways. Take, for example, the phrase, "the heavenly places" in Ephesians 1:3 and trace it through its later appearances in the letter at 1:20; 2:6; 3:10; and 6:12, to see a dimension of the book's teaching which is often given comparatively little attention. Or, I think of how the phrase in Luke 1:2, where the writer describes the apostles as "servants of the word" (NIV), pulled me up short. I wouldn't have written it like that. I would have said "servants of the Lord". It seemed odd to me! But it sent me on a journey through which I came to see that everything in the first half of Luke's gospel proceeds through the Word of God as the executive agent of His authority in this world. The contrast between Zechariah and Mary in chapter 1 is a contrast of reactions to the Word of God spoken by Gabriel. And that is just the beginning.

Everything seems to happen "according to his word" and even after the passion narrative and the crucifixion the gospel ends with the risen Christ saying to His disciples, "These are my words that I spoke to you while I was still with you, that everything written about me in the law of Moses and the prophets and the psalms must be fulfilled" (Luke 24:44). It is so often the work on context which produces the application in our preaching.

The final context is that of the whole Bible, relating this particular passage to the sweep of all the Scriptures of which Jesus is the center and key. This prevents us from preaching the Old Testament like a Jewish rabbi. It demands that we reflect on how our text relates to the unfolding pattern of progressive revelation in terms of Biblical theology, doctrinal balance, and cultural applications. It ensures that the single divine authorship serves as an important practical tool for interpretation, not simply as a theoretical position. All these tools are designed to release the significance of the text for us, its contemporary hearers, and at the end of this session I want to be able to write an aim sentence for my sermon. This will, of course, be derived from the theme, but it expresses what I am praying that the Holy Spirit will be pleased to do in the minds and hearts of my hearers, as I seek to preach the meaning and significance of the text.

In my third preparation session, I am concerned with the structure and strategy of the sermon as I try to think through how the pastoral intention of the text is to be related to our context today, in applications which the writer would have recognized as conforming to his own original purpose. Here I often find myself trying to anticipate the negative reaction some of my hearers may experience to the message of the Word. What is there here that will tempt them to harden their hearts in unbelief or rejection? How I can help them to see the reality of God's truth and the folly of resistance to it, without diluting or compromising the message by one iota? This is where I decide the context of the sermon's argumentation, the main teaching points, which are often better expressed didactically than merely descriptively, and the major applications for today which are the implication of the text. I want to select the most helpful headings or marker posts for the sermon's journey. I shall also want to discover the most suitable illustrations, usually at the points where the text is more difficult or where the applications need to be spelt out with practical examples. If we fail to give sufficient time to this aspect of our preparation, including introduction and conclusion, we often fail to land our sermons in the hearts and minds of the congregation. It does not fly under the radar screens, which are all too often expertly positioned and manned, to intercept all incoming missiles! We cannot be content with "sola exegesis." We dare not miss the heart of the expository value of the passage, because while we may preach quite accurately what it says, we omit to say why it matters.

My final session is spent in producing my written notes for the actual preaching. I like to write quite a full script, so as not to have to rely on my recall memory and so use up mental energy which I could use to communicate with my hearers. I don't usually script my illustrations, but for all the major teaching content of the sermon I will put down on the paper all that I mean to say in exactly the way I want to say it. Far from being restrictive, for me it provides freedom, to concentrate on getting it across and into the hearers' hearts and minds, having spent time in my preparation in trying to get it right.

The secret of good preaching is careful listening. "Let the word of Christ dwell in you richly, teaching and admonishing one another in all wisdom" (Col. 3:16). The more you dwell in the Word and the Word dwells in you, the more you will be a channel of the voice of God to your people as you preach. The more you ask questions, the more you will discover life-changing answers to proclaim, as in His mercy God brings sinners to salvation and saints to maturity.

"For we are the aroma of Christ to God among those who are being saved and among those who are perishing, to one a fragrance from death to death, to the other a fragrance from life to life. Who is sufficient for these things? ... Not that we are sufficient in ourselves to claim anything as coming from us, but our sufficiency is from God, who made us sufficient to be ministers of a new covenant, not of the letter but of the Spirit" (2 Cor. 2:15-16, 3:5-6).

10 Don't Give Up On Believing Prayer
(Luke 18:1-8)

DAVID JACKMAN

We live at an extraordinary time in world history. On the one hand, we benefit from the most amazing developments in science, technology and medicine, which our ancestors would not have imagined possible in their wildest dreams. Communications, travel, the exchange of knowledge and ideas all forge ahead with unprecedented expansion and incredible speed of change. On the other hand, there seems to be developing a landslide away from the values which have made western civilization possible—truth and integrity, loyalty and modesty, steadfastness and decency. The moral and spiritual bankruptcy which we see eroding the foundations of our culture may not yet have really hit home, but the trajectory is clear enough, with our patterns of blame and litigation, distrust and isolation, of which the emptying pews and church buildings up for sale are only one symptom.

Many commentators suggest that there is a major shifting of the cultural tectonic plates on a global scale as the influence, prosperity, and power of the west bleed away in greed and self-indulgence. In Neil Postman's chilling phrase, we are literally "amusing ourselves to death." Nor is this surprising when the pillars of our once "Christian" civilization have been under sustained attack for several decades, from what has been aptly described as "the dictatorship of relativism." Once you decide that there can be no absolutes of right and wrong, truth and error, because there is no God to be the ultimate reference point within His created order, then anything is permitted and everything will be. Everything except the protests of those who persist in believing in Truth. Such intolerance will not be tolerated!

Let's be under no illusion that the decline and disintegration of the spiritual and moral framework of our society are the logical outcome of its determined denial, in its intellectual engine room, of the very existence of truth. The Bible, with its revelation of a loving and liberating God who enters His world in person in order to rescue humanity from the consequences of our ignorance and rebellion, has long been abandoned. The idea that humankind was made in the image of God, or is in any sense a distinct divine creation, let alone having an immortal soul, is routinely rubbished. And so, crack by crack, the pressures of political correctness, the product of secular materialism, crumble the moral foundations on which the laws and customs of a free society were built and depend still.

In the face of such assaults, it would be the easiest thing in the world for individual Christians, not to say whole congregations and even denominations, to cut their losses, throw in the towel and capitulate. Indeed, many have already done so and their numbers are growing by the day. When the storm breaks, it's much easier to go below decks, limit one's profile and attempt to sit it out, hoping to preserve what little faith remains, in an hermetically-sealed ghetto environment. Others will see accommodation as the name of the game, making concessions towards every fresh onslaught, until the relentless chipping away of the old certainties essentially ensures the death of truth through a thousand qualifications. Perhaps the obituaries of the Christian faith so regularly produced by the media are to be believed after all.

Except that our twenty-first century world still echoes to the reality of the apostle Paul's first-century affirmation that "all over the world this gospel is bearing fruit and growing" (Col. 1:6 NIV). As the balance of economic wealth and political world power moves east and south, so does the life-giving ministry of the Spirit, bringing multitudes to faith in Christ in Asia and South America. We do not need to fear for the future of the church. Christ will go on building her as He promised (Matt. 16:18).

But we do need to be concerned for the continuance of our own faith and that of our churches, as the environment becomes more hostile and the circumstantial evidence often seems to be stacked against our very survival.

The Biblical Context

"When the Son of Man comes, will he find faith on the earth?" These are the closing words of the Lord Jesus at the end of His parable (v. 8 NIV). They are both startlingly realistic and deeply challenging, aren't they? The implication is that He might well return to an earth which has lost its faith in Him and His salvation. As such, it is a healthy reminder that the church is only ever one generation from extinction, because everything for the church's future depends upon the present generation. Will we be found holding out the Word of Life and living as salt and light, in our time, here and now? For while it is true that Christ's sheep will never perish and that no-one can snatch them out of His hand (John 10:28), it is also true that God has never promised the continuance of the church in one particular location, or nation, in the next generation. Christ's provocative question is designed to ask us what sort of church He will discover us to be when He returns. Will we prove to be expectant and eager to welcome Him, a people full of faith, anticipating the fulfillment of His promises with confidence and joy? Or will that kind of faith have evaporated, so that the church has become virtually indistinguishable from the culture in which it exists? All that needs to happen for that outcome is for the church firmly to nail its colors to the fence it is sitting on!

"Jesus told his disciples a parable to show them that they should always pray and not give up" (v. 1 NIV). Now we can begin to see just why this parable is needed. The verb translated *give up* is a fairly rare one in the New Testament, but in each of the four locations where it is used, it helps us to be aware of the danger more perceptively. If you look it up in a Greek lexicon, you will find a range of meaning which includes to weaken, to grow weary, to lose heart, to tire, to lack courage. In other words, this is the very opposite of faithful perseverance.

Twice in 2 Corinthians 4, where Paul is writing about his own apostolic ministry, proclaiming the good news of Christ, he affirms "we do not lose heart" (vv. 1, 16) because of the realities which the gospel expound concerning the mercy of God and the certainty of His eternal kingdom. In Galatians 6:9 he exhorts his readers, "And let us not grow weary of doing good, for in due season we will reap if we do not give up (lose heart)." Waiting to see the results, which seem to be taking a very long time to appear, could be really disheartening in Christian ministry. But it is God who makes the seed grow and who produces and determines the harvest time, so don't give up. Or, he tells the Thessalonians, "As for you brothers. Do not grow weary in doing good" (2 Thess. 3:13). In each case, and Luke 18:1 is no exception, faith is seen as an expression of perseverance or persistence, which keeps serving and trusting, even though the circumstances seem not to be very conducive and the results minimal. The Bible has many warnings about those who started well, but pulled out of the race, or who left the track, or who failed to finish, so we would be very foolish if we thought this parable was anything less than urgent in its demand for our attention.

The Immediate Context

In verse 1, there seems to be some ambivalence about the expression of the meaning. Give up on what? At first sight, it seems that Jesus is telling us not to give up praying and that is certainly true. But there is perhaps a deeper significance here. Perhaps the "giving up" is in the wider context of our whole Christian faith and experience. Jesus may be saying that the only way to keep going in the Christian life is by the exercise of faith, through prayer, since that is the only antidote to the down-drag of our sinful nature, pulling us away from Christ to compromise with the world, the flesh, and the devil.

These implications become sharper and even more compelling when the parable is read in the context of its own position in the Gospel of Luke. It is, of course, unique to this Gospel. The story of the persistent widow comes as the climax of a section which began at 17:20. The Pharisees are questioning Jesus about His kingly claims and so about the coming, or appearance, of His kingdom. Bible writers often bracket their sections together by using vocabulary or ideas at the start which are echoed or replicated at the end and which provide a summary of the big idea between the "bookends." This is the device by which Luke is shaping this part of his narrative. In 17:20 the focus is on the coming of the kingdom and in 18:8 on the coming of the king. This is probably why Jesus refers to Himself as the Son of Man, the figure from Daniel 7:13-14, to whom were given authority, glory, sovereign power, and an everlasting dominion, as all peoples and nations worship Him. This is the king whose return is described in Luke 17:22-37. Thus the parable acts as the culmination of Jesus' teaching about how His people are to live in the expectation of His return, however delayed it may sometimes appear to be.

There are several negatives, which Christians have frequently ignored over the past two thousand years, to their cost. So, Jesus warns us against becoming obsessed with looking for observable signs (v. 20). We are not to waste our energies nostalgically longing for the return of the days of His earthly ministry, or even trying to repeat them (v. 22). Nor are we to be diverted by all sorts of spurious claims that He has already arrived and is actively doing these things again (v. 23). The corrective Jesus gives lies in the understanding that His kingdom is already here as He exercises His kingly rule in the lives of His followers (v. 21), as they wait for the fullness of the kingdom at His return, by living in holiness and expectation. They keep on praying and do not give up!

In context then, Jesus is looking for His people to stand firm in their faith, confident that God will certainly keep His promises and building their everyday priorities on that assurance. The emphasis in 17:27 is on the suddenness of Christ's return, through the comparisons with the days of Noah and of Lot. No one then really expected the judgment to fall. And isn't that exactly our temptation too? Nobody, outside the Bible-believing community, seriously believes that God will "judge the world in righteousness by a man whom he has appointed" (Acts 17:31). No one thinks that the return of Christ is anything other than an outdated, primitive myth. The point of Jesus' parable, however, is that the church may also easily drift in that direction, because of the pressure of the tides with which she is battling. "Will he find faith on the earth?" Everyone has confidence in modern technology, scientific intervention, further research to be able to solve the multiplicity of problems facing Planet Earth. We will find a way through… which is "just as it was in the days of Noah" (Luke 17:26). But that is not the product of faith.

Christians persevere by always bringing all the apparent contradictions and uncertainties of the present to God in prayer, because praying and giving up are mutually exclusive. Put it this way—the one sure way to give up on your faith is to give up on prayer, simply because prayer is the articulation and exercise of our personal trust and confidence in the Lord Jesus as our king, the Son of God. Prayer is the last resort of the self-reliant but the first recourse of the true believer. And I can tell which I am by the part prayer does, or does not, play in my own life. If we are not going to give up living today in the light of His coming, ready to meet our Savior face to face, then we cannot give up on believing prayer.

As with many of the parables Jesus told, this story has an unexpected twist, which is the means by which its essential message is impressed on our minds and hearts. It is designed to surprise us into challenging our accepted way of thinking, so we will try to preserve as much of that as possible in unpacking the message.

There Is Something Which Seems So Obvious

"He [Jesus] said, 'In a certain city there was a judge who neither feared God nor respected man. And there was a widow in that city who kept coming to him and saying, 'Give me justice against my adversary'" (vv. 2-3). There is little doubt that you could see this story being played out in many communities across Israel, when Jesus first spoke it, just as you can across our world today. The two central characters are polar opposites. The judge has all the power; the woman has none. According to Old Testament teaching, a widow in Israel should be able to expect the judge to use his considerable authority to secure justice for her. But this judge is less than promising! The description that he neither feared God nor respected men means that he was totally corrupt. No superior authority, divine or human, crossed his mind or bothered him, even for a moment. He constantly broke both of the great commandments—love for God and love for neighbor. So, it would do no good to appeal to his better nature, because he seems to have had none. The situation for the widow is as grim as it could be.

By contrast, she is total vulnerability. She has an adversary. Jesus Himself spoke elsewhere of those who devoured widows' houses and clearly this woman was facing a powerful opponent, who either wanted what was rightly hers or refused to give her what was her due. She seems to have had no male relative to plead her cause and she probably had no resources to employ anyone to act on her behalf. She has no means by which she can attract the judge's attention. She is deprivation personified. But she kept coming. You can imagine the reactions she would have experienced from those who knew her. "Why bother? What is the point? He is never going to change his attitude, is he? The sensible thing is to give up and make the best of a bad deal." It all seems so obvious—the classic story of an exploited woman, in a corrupt society, without a single hope. But she kept coming. And at verse 4, the ball starts to spin.

There Is Something That Has Been Overlooked

What is going on in the judge's mind? That is unknown, because it is unseen and so the big danger is to ignore it completely and to act on outward appearances, as though they were the only reality. Christians are often tempted to think and behave like that, when they seem to be up against impossible odds. But Jesus reveals that there is an inner dialogue going on in the judge's consciousness (v. 4b-5). Nothing in his attitude towards God, other people, or particularly the widow actually changes. He is still totally self-concerned, but it is that very priority that changes his behavior. "This widow keeps bothering me" (v. 5). In fact, that translation is rather mild. Some alternative translations which have been suggested are "wearing me out", "beating me down", or "giving me a black eye". Here is the totally unexpected vulnerability, not of the widow, but of the judge. As Joel Green comments, "The language Luke uses is startling, perhaps even humorous, borrowed as it is from the boxing ring, for it invokes images of the almighty, fearless, macho judge cornered and slugged by the least powerful in society."[1]

She will give him a beating by her sheer, dogged persistence, and the game isn't worth it. Whenever he turns up at his office in the morning, there she is in the waiting room day after day;

---

1. Joel B. Green, *The Gospel of Luke* (Grand Rapids: Eerdmans, 1997), 641.

it is all too much. So he will give her what she wants. He doesn't care a jot for her; but he certainly cares for his own comfort and sanity. The powerless widow wins her case by perseverance. The ball has spun; the game has turned. And now the Lord Jesus, who is not only the teller of the story, but the king whose return will light up the sky from one end to the other (17:24), gives us the key to understanding the parable, as He draws the contrast between the unjust judge and the living God.

To move from the story to its interpretation we need to revisit our two main points, but now in reverse order, as we unpack the significance for us today, in our very different context.

There Is Something We Tend to Overlook
What we ignore is the character and consequent activity of our unseen God. Whenever we start to question whether God really knows or cares about us and our circumstances, or to ask whether He will really keep His promises, we are beginning to evacuate the word *God* of all its biblical meaning. The method by which Jesus moves His hearers from the unjust judge to the character of our heavenly Father is that of total contrast. It is the type of argument built on a "how much more" observation. As the polar opposite of the judge, God is loving, caring, deeply concerned and compassionate especially to the vulnerable, the widow, and the orphan, "his elect" (v. 7). As His elect, we are to demonstrate the reality of our confident childlike relationship with Him by crying out to Him, day and night in every situation, and especially when we are oppressed by the world, the flesh, and the devil.

Does God find that tedious or bothersome? That is unthinkable. Will He fob His people off with some self-centered refusal to listen or to act? Of course not. There is no automated reply from the heavenly call center, no out of office response. Will He not be long-suffering with us? Does He not delight to hear His people's persistent prayer, just because that is the evidence of the relationship of trust and covenant commitment, which is the heart of our faith? How then can we begin to think that He will act in any other way than in perfect accordance with His revealed character? But if we forget His nature and start to judge by what we see, we shall give up praying and, sooner or later, we shall give up on our faith. However, when we deliberately apply what we know of God through His Word to the perplexities of life, as we pour out our hearts to Him, then verse 8 becomes highly relevant to us in our personal circumstances.

There Is Something We Should Regard As Obvious

The very concept of God's "elect" underlines the certainty that He is determined to bring every one of His chosen people home to the security of His eternal kingdom, through His overflowing grace. He is not going to abandon us on the way, or to allow our adversaries to overcome us. And once we are aware that persistent prayer is the expression of our continuing, active faith in God, we are not going to look anywhere else for our help or comfort. Jesus gives His own authority and approval to such confident trust, when He says, "I tell you" (v. 8). We do not give up, because we know that God will vindicate and deliver His people and that He will do it *speedily*, or *soon*, at the very first possible moment in the context of His ultimate purposes and our eternal good. He is not holding out on us. His perfect love and wisdom are working everything together for our good (Rom. 8:28) and that *everything* includes even the delays which we find so hard to fathom.

Yet there is still that haunting question of verse 8. "Will he find faith on the earth?" That is perhaps not quite so obvious. *Speedily* or *quickly* is not the same as immediately, which means that Jesus knows that our faith will often be profoundly tested when we experience delays in the answers to our prayers, delays which we are tempted to interpret as lack of love or care, if not of power. The only way to keep trusting is to keep praying, day and night, always relating our little lives and their baffling circumstances to His perfect will and plan. This parable reminds us that appearances can be totally deceptive, which is another reason why we must never give up on believing prayer. Let's keep asking God for the righteousness of His kingdom to prevail.

If we truly know the nature of our loving Father in heaven, we shall keep on praying for God's sustenance of the persecuted church around the world and His intervention on their behalf. We shall keep on praying for God's mercy in the defeated and discouraged churches of the west, for repentance and renewed vision, with fresh faith and zeal. We shall pray the Lord of the harvest to thrust out laborers into His harvest field. We shall pray for many more to come to faith and not only those who start well, but those who finish well too. We shall pray for our own faith to be deepened and our own grasp on these realities to become increasingly strong. "Lord, make my church a praying church and make me a praying Christian." All this is because the Christian life is not based on what we see, but on what God says. In his commentary *According to Luke*, David Gooding puts it this way. "And shall we give up appealing to God and so make him out to be more unfeeling, more unjust than the unjust judge himself? To give up praying would be calamitous; it would imply that God … is so indifferent to justice that we can have no reasonable hope for a coming reign of justice on earth, nor of any heaven above worth going to."[2] As we are pointed to the clear affirmation of Jesus that He will return to bring in His kingdom of everlasting righteousness we are left with this challenge. If meanwhile we have stopped praying, how shall we then satisfactorily explain to Him why we doubted His character? Don't give up on believing prayer!

---

2.   David Gooding, *According to Luke* (Coleraine: The Myrtlefield Trust, 2013), 308.

11 The Treasures are in the Text

SIMON MANCHESTER

I served for three years with a great British preacher, Dick Lucas, a man who has shaped and influenced a generation (or two or three) of young preachers. If I were to put into one word what I learned from him about preaching it would be *listening* — paying attention to the Scriptures until the message of those verses in that book in that canon was really heard and understood so it could be conveyed. Listening is the key to preaching.

The Lord's servant in Isaiah 50:4 puts it like this: "The Sovereign Lord has given me an *instructed* tongue, to know the word that sustains the weary. He wakens me morning by morning, wakens *my ear to listen* like one being taught" (NIV). Or, to put it negatively, the Lord complains of the false prophets in Jeremiah 23:18: "But which of them has stood in the council of the Lord to see or to *hear* his word? Who has *listened* and heard his word?" (NIV)

A friend of mine says that when a passage from Scripture has been truly heard and spoken, especially when it has been explained with integrity, it "preaches itself back at you." The preacher has really heard the point of the passage, and not just what he wanted to say, and conveyed it faithfully. The listeners have heard the point of the passage and know that it has come with integrity — not some bee in the preacher's bonnet but the real Word of God. And when people go back to that text they will remember its meaning.

A simple example of this is the famous chapter, 1 Corinthians 13. How many weddings or sermons have simply lifted this out of context (as if it was a random poem) and then said sweet things about love? Without listening to 1 Corinthians, it is the easiest mistake to make as the preacher is forced — or decides — to elaborate on sentimental things. But the Corinthian letter is a serious blow to selfishness and immaturity, and 1 Corinthians 13 (coming in the middle of the tongues/prophecy discussion) is a devastating attack on the self-loving Corinthians. A thousand sickly sermons on the chapter will be forgotten but no one who hears the true rocket that it is will ever forget it — "Let me tell you impatient and unkind Corinthians what love is like … love is patient, love is kind …." No one will forget this when they hear it properly.

So in coming to a passage of Scripture I want to make absolutely sure, like a messenger boy, that I have listened exactly to what has been said so that I can convey it exactly as intended. What could be more irresponsible than not listening or half-listening so that I end up saying something that is fictional or wrong? The sermon that I have included in this book is an attempt to convey John 17. In "listening" to this chapter, I have tried to grasp what exactly Jesus was praying, especially when it seems to be such a magisterial prayer and yet is so little known (except for famous lines on eternal life or unity). Why have we been told this prayer? Does it fit John's stated aim to help the reader "believe that Jesus is the Christ, the Son of God …" (John 20:31 NIV)? What does Jesus actually pray for Himself, for the apostles, and then for all believers? Is this a unique prayer that only Jesus could pray, or are there aspects we should borrow and echo in our own prayers? What are the message and the point of the prayer?

In coming to the passage I am eager to hear the meaning and application for myself. I don't want to see the word *prayed* and then launch into my own thoughts on prayer. I don't want to turn a descriptive passage into a prescriptive passage—turning indicatives into imperatives—where that would be irresponsible. Before I mention some practicalities in preparation, let me begin with some important convictions.

Convictions: Five Brief But Vital Ones

I hope you will agree with this first conviction that *the Word is the way God works* in creation (Gen. 1), preservation (Heb. 1:3), the church (Deut. 4), and edification (Eph. 4:11). It's His weapon; it's the Spirit's sword (Eph. 6:17). Sunday-by-Sunday preaching may not always be exciting or earth-shattering but it is the way that God makes and transforms new people. Like our dear mothers who cooked for us for years, we may not have had award-winning meals every day but we had (hopefully) life-sustaining meals every day. So we preach God's Word.

Another conviction is that *the pulpit and church tend to rise or fall together*. This doesn't mean that numbers must rise or fall with faithful or unfaithful preaching. We know that numbers are a fickle gauge. But the pulpit is the key to the quality of the church. A pastor who prepares and preaches superficially will create confused people with more pastoral problems that will demand more time away from preparation. The pastor who prepares and preaches responsibly will see clear-headed people who take on the pastoral needs of the flock, leaving more time for his preparation. You must have the conviction of Jesus to stick with the key work and not do everything that people want you to do (Mark 1:35-39), but this does not rule out compassion for the need in front of you (Mark 1:21-45)!

Be sure that *the declaration of the Word is God's plan for all time*. There needs to be someone who says "thus says the Lord" and declares it so that God's Word comes to us with authority and love. The small groups in our churches, or the small groups that substitute for large congregations, are in the business of discussing the Word. That is not the same as declaring it.

Then *huge amounts of pastoral care are done from the pulpit*. Don't fall for those people who divorce the preacher from the pastor, as if one is a truth man and one is a love man or one is a cold man and one is a cuddly man. The real pastor is a preacher and the real preacher is a pastor. A man wrote to me to thank me for "saving his marriage" but I'd never spent half an hour with him and his wife. He was simply hearing the gospel of God's love for him in the Sunday-by-Sunday preaching and translating it into the home. Every faithful sermon is an expression of pastoral care for the people of God.

The last of these five is to *work hard in prayer and preaching so that Christ be glorified*. The Scriptures point to Christ (John 5:39) and so (without rushing too quickly to Christ) every sermon should show how Christ is the fulfillment and goal and hero of God's purposes. It takes sincere prayer to seek Christ's glory when so much of our own sinfulness gets in the road and so much of our blindness sees little way down the road. We need to pray and prepare to get people to go and do business with Jesus and see Him as the key and secret to their life and their joy.

Practicalities

Having been preaching for over thirty years, I find it gets easier and harder all the time. It gets easier in that there is not the same newness to public speaking or the same fear of facing a congregation, but it gets harder in that fresh insights become more demanding and familiar listeners may find the regular preacher pretty predictable! This is where the Bible becomes our joy and treasure-chest because the Scriptures yield new depths and new wonders that we will never get to the end of, like exploring the oceans of the world.

I try to start on Monday (my day off is Thursday), so on Monday morning I read the passage and pray for the Lord's help, then get into "word-by-word" translation. Though we don't want to alarm our listeners by telling them that the original text is sometimes better than the translation in front of them, the fact remains that translating the original will often save us from danger. [At the moment I'm preaching through Galatians and though the NIV tells us that the law was "to lead us to Christ" (3:24) the Greek simply says it was a pedagogue "till Christ" or "up to Christ". This may seem a small point, but it has serious implications for whether the law can "lead" us or simply imprisons us till Christ frees us!] I rarely point out any discrepancies between the original language and the congregational text because I don't want people to doubt the Word in any way and I don't want to set myself up as the High Priest of Scripture. But I might say "the law imprisons us (3:23) and leads us to depend utterly on Christ (3:24) who is the only Person who can free us" etc.

When I've done my translation page, I use a red pen to link up words in the text, add questions that I want answered, and include early thoughts that will need to be addressed and maybe some illustrations or cross references that have occurred to me. For example, in John 17 I will jot down a question like "Why is it right for Jesus to pray for Himself first?" or "Is there any evidence the apostles heard this prayer being prayed?" I have a theory that it's our dissatisfaction with predictable preaching that creates more satisfied listeners. But when we are satisfied with bland preparation our listeners get more dissatisfied. I find it frustrating to listen to preachers who don't grapple with the huge issues that are crying out for an explanation. I once said to Dick Lucas that I would have to ring him every Saturday to make sure that I'd got the point of the passage and he said, "No, brother, I'm just trying to save you from being a water beetle." Water beetles skim over the surface of the water and never break through the film!

One of the greatest dangers in our preparation is simply to regurgitate the accepted wisdom on a passage without proper thought. Let me give you some quick examples of this, one from each gospel.

Matthew 5:13-16. The accepted lesson of this passage is that we must be "salt and light". The problem with this is that Jesus uses three illustrations (salt, light, and a city on a hill) to teach one great lesson — *distinctiveness*. In chapter 6 he uses three again (fasting, prayer, and giving), and in chapter 7 he uses three again (two roads, trees, and foundations). Perhaps if we saw the three illustrations for the one point we would get it right and stop running into social action (salt) and evangelism (light) which is not the point of the passage!

Mark 8:22-26. What do we make of this miracle in two parts, unique to the New Testament? The superficial approach will just state what is there (but we know that!) or blame the man for weak faith (which the passage doesn't do). Surely the context will help us. Before the incident we read that the disciples have eyes but fail to see (8:18) and after it Peter can see who Jesus is (8:29) but not what He has come to do (8:32). Isn't this blind man then a picture of Peter (or anyone) who can see Christ's person but not His mission? What a powerful word to those who preach Christ but not Christ crucified!

Luke 10:25-37. Is anyone more famous in the New Testament than the Good Samaritan? And the easy sermon will simply launch into compassion and the need to cross the road to the needy world etc. But why does Jesus say this to a man who is testing Him (not a good sign) and is also self-justifying (10:25 and 29)? Surely this man is not being told to inherit eternal life by being charitable. When we realize that Jesus is dealing with this man in Luke 10 in a very similar style to the dealings with the Rich Young Ruler in Luke 18, we realize that this is a demolition parable and not a motivation parable. The man is being shown his moral bankruptcy, not his moral duty. If he were to despair and seek a new heart, which would enable him to have something of the amazing love being shown by the Good Samaritan, he might be made new and then be ready for such merciful behavior. Preaching Luke 10 without its context will only be sheer moralism.

John 5:1-30. What's going on when Jesus asks a paralyzed man if he wants to get well (5:6) and then warns him to stop sinning or face something worse (5:14)? Surely the preacher must grapple with what looks like an obvious question and then a bizarre follow up. But the chapter provides the information we need because Jesus is the life-giver (5:21) and the judge (5:22). No wonder He is asking the man if he wants to begin a whole new life and then warns him that without repentance he will meet Jesus the judge and experience something much worse than paralysis.

I mention these four examples not to raise unnecessary questions but simply to show that preachers must work harder at the not-so-neat bits of Scripture. There's a city on a hill, a man healed in two stages, an outsider being given noble things to do, and a paralytic getting strange instructions. So we must think and pray and wrestle till we get the treasure in the text.

Another major danger for preachers is simply preaching our framework. We come to Exodus 20 or Matthew 4 and everything we know about law or temptation is crammed into the sermon. But we have stopped listening and started saying what we already think or know. All of us have a systematic theology, and we need it. But the text is bigger and better. Without a humble view of the text we will squeeze it all into our system, and our system will stay the same (getting more stagnant and predictable every year). What we need is a text that rattles and refreshes our system and shocks and shapes us into people who see more and more of the grandeur of God. Fifteen years into my ministry I was strongly chastened by a brother for a poor grasp of grace in the life of the believer, and he was right. I knew how to speak grace to an outsider but had little for the insider. Without his ministry and God's rattling of my cage, I would have been unable to pastor people for long. My message was too much on responsibility and too little on privilege.

Continuing my preparation process, I will come to commentaries on Tuesday and Wednesday mornings. I have some questions waiting to be answered, and I start reading one after the other, writing down their best thoughts on a notepad. By the time I have finished, I usually have six or seven pages of ideas under the names of the various commentators. I then underline every thought worth keeping and take another page to write these thoughts in sequence. So my one-page outline will have the word *introduction* and how I might recap where we have been so far. Then I will put the verses down the left hand side (e.g. 3:8, 3:9, 3:10) and beside each verse briefly write what I need to say. When I've gone through all the text material I will think about how to structure the sermon. In the case of John 17, it is clearly a three-point prayer (!) as Jesus prays for himself (17:1-5), the apostles (17:6-19), and the disciples (17:20-26). On the right hand side of the page I put down every illustration or application that has come to mind as I've been reading. I put an asterisk beside each one. Then I have everything at a glance on one page. I actually write this page with a red pen so it stands out and doesn't get lost (after all the work). This process has taken me about an hour on Monday to translate and then two hours on Tuesday and two on Wednesday to get through eight to twelve commentaries. What I leave to Saturday morning is my final notes. I tend to write one line phrases that start me off such as "We are preaching through Galatians…" or "Today is a complex passage because…" or "I hope we will see…." Every preacher must work out what suits him best. Some with full notes can preach very freely, and some with few notes can get bogged down in long paragraphs!

On the matter of introducing a sermon, I would say that no rule should apply. There are those who say that you must "begin with a hook" to get people in or "no story is needed" or "just announce your text" or "don't just announce your text". The important principle is to get your listeners to come with you, and there are times when you must work much harder to achieve this. I would even say that a joke has its place if the resistance to a talk is high or there is tension that needs to be broken. Pitting Spurgeon (great humor) against Lloyd-Jones (no humor) shows that we need principles and not rules. My own norm is to explain in a line what we're doing and then simply illustrate the issue. For example, "We are studying Luke on these Sunday mornings and come today to the famous account of the Good Samaritan. You are probably expecting a sermon on being kind and charitable to the needy, but I hope to show you why that is a waste of time—till something else is in place."

On illustrations, I think we should actually *love* our people by including mental pictures or stories that will help them to stay with us and get the point. In setting out a sermon from start to finish we must recognize where things have become long and complex and deliberately move into an illustration that will provide light and a break in the tension. The skill in doing this is not artificial but thoughtful. Watch and see how Dale Ralph Davis keeps injecting stories to make a point (or reinforce a point), and you will see why he is so doctrinal but interesting too. The doctrine is interesting, but he engages those who aren't mature enough to think so!

When I tried to explain how the law works in the purposes of God, I sat for a long while working out a picture that would capture the issue. I settled on a treadmill, sent round as a gift to a doctor's friend, because it doesn't solve heart disease but reveals it. On the other hand, we may know a story from history or personal experience that will anchor the point for all who are grappling with the truth. My point is not necessarily to keep a file of stories but to think hard about what would illumine the teaching you are giving.

Application comes more with prayer, I have found. I talk through the passage in prayer and think through why this is wonderful, what it tells me of God, what it means in my life, what it says to the fearful or careless, what it says to the long-time Christian or the "thinking through Christianity" person, the sad or the silly, the plumber and the professor. Sometimes I look out my window at my neighbors and think what I would say to them if I was asked to explain why my text is so significant. Much application can be driven home during the sermon; try not to save it all for the final five minutes.

In preaching through John 17, you will see (if you read the chapter) that I came to the conclusion that Jesus prays basically two things for Himself (glory in His "hour" and glory in the Father's presence), two things for the apostles (that they may be kept and sanctified) and two things for all believers (that we may be one and finally home).

Part of the challenge was working out why these were so significant for the perfect Pray-er, and what is actually meant in each case for us who read the prayer. For example, should we now be thankful that Jesus was glorified in His death, or should we pray that He would be glorified in proclaiming it? Should the apostles be remembered for their safekeeping and devotion, or should workers be prayed for like this too? Should believers today be praying to arrive in glory one day or be thankful that it is a reality because Jesus died and rose? Hopefully somewhere in the sermon these things were faced and grasped.

My preaching program rotates Old Testament, Gospel, Epistle, and topics, but not necessarily in that order. This keeps me thinking across the Bible. Exposition is easier and more satisfying than topical preaching.

Finally the sermon is over, and I drive home with my sweet wife. She knows how to encourage me often with appreciation for things said and sometimes with the reminder that the work is more supernatural than the sermon felt!

John Stott has a wonderful quote in his book on preaching:

When telling Thy salvation free
Let all absorbing thoughts of Thee

My heart and soul engross.
And when all hearts are bowed and stirred
Beneath the influence of Thy Word
Hide me behind Thy cross.[1]

How kind of God to save and use us.

---

1. John Stott, *I Believe in Preaching* (London: Hodder and Stoughton, 1982), 335.

12 The (Real) Lord's Prayer
(John 17)

SIMON MANCHESTER

We are going to follow the prayer of Jesus Christ in John chapter 17. This is a chapter which helped the great John Knox become a Christian because, when he was dying, he asked his wife to "read where I first cast my anchor", and she read from John 17.

You can work out what people think is important from what they pray about (or don't pray about), so to study the prayer of Jesus means we get to see what was important to the most important person in the universe. That must be significant. And there's nothing more important for a healthy Christian life than good prayer. Everything struggles with bad prayer, and everything is helped by good prayer.

So, do you see what Jesus did after the Last Supper and after such wonderful teaching on the coming Holy Spirit? He looked up to His Father and spoke to Him. God has put an agreement in place that those who belong to Him can speak to Him, and He will hear and act as He sees fit. Most people know that what we usually call the "Lord's Prayer" (in Matthew 6) would not have been prayed by Jesus. He wouldn't ask for sins to be forgiven. But this prayer in John 17 is definitely one that He prayed, and it could be called "the real Lord's prayer."

As Jesus prays, this prayer can be divided into three parts:

- prayer for Himself (17:1-5)
- prayer for the apostles (17:6-19)
- prayer for all believers (17:20-26)

I want us to get this prayer into our heads because, for some reason, what Jesus prayed for has not grabbed the interest (or prayer life) of people as it should. In fact, I think a quick read of this prayer will leave most people confused if not—and this is incredible—unimpressed. But if Jesus was clear about anything, it was what to pray for. And if we get what He was asking for, we can't help but be wiser ourselves.

Jesus' Prayer for Himself (17:1-5)

Here is the Son of God who is about to die and rise again and who knows that His Father in heaven is sovereign, wise, loving and powerful. And that knowledge makes Him pray. It never occurs to Jesus to say, "No need to pray." It never occurs to Jesus to say, "Waste of time to pray." The sovereignty of God doesn't make prayer unnecessary. It just means that God is unbeatably good to pray to!

And now, because the time has come (literally the *hour* has come), Jesus brings His first request to the Father, which is that He, Jesus, would be glorified (v. 1). This "hour" has been coming for a while — you remember at the wedding it had not come (John 2:4), and in talking with His pushy brothers it had not come (John 7:8). But from the arrival of the Greeks in chapter 12 (v. 23) it has come. And it's His hour to die, to rise, and to ascend.

Now you may be shocked to see that Jesus first prays for Himself and for His own glory, but don't miss what immediately follows. If the Father glorifies the Son—and causes people to honor Jesus—then the Father will be glorified (see v. 1) and people will end up with eternal life (see v. 2). There is nothing at all selfish about this request. The way for the Father to be honored and people to be transformed is through the glorification of Jesus (vv. 1-3).

By the way, you can see that eternal life means "knowing God and Jesus Christ" (v. 3), and it begins the moment you turn to Christ. This connection with God and with Jesus then goes on until you see Him face to face. Don't wait to see if eternal life drops into your lap after death. It won't. And don't settle for some vague awareness of Jesus in this life because you must know Him person to person before you die or you don't know Him at all.

Perhaps one way to bring this home to you is to ask whether the death of Christ strikes you as being very wonderful and glorious? Does it seem to you, as you think about that crucifixion, that a great message is screaming out from the cross that says, "God is loving. Look who He has given up for us. God is just. Look who is not escaping. God is wise. Who else could arrange this? God is powerful. Look how the world will be changed and millions (or billions) saved"? The request of Jesus to be glorified was wonderfully wise and wonderfully answered.

But now this request to be glorified also looks past the cross to the throne, and Jesus asks to be glorified in the Father's presence (v. 5). If ever you thought Jesus was saying ordinary things, just look at His prayer here. He is asking to have the glory back again that He had "before the world existed" (v. 5)! If you ever hear me (or anyone) praying that we might end up in heaven, that's a good thing to hear. But, if you hear us ask to be back in heaven, you know we are insane. Jesus, however, calmly asks the Father to restore Him to that glory that He enjoyed—and left behind for us—before the world was made.

So here is His prayer for Himself that the Father would cause the downward path to the cross to be glorious in its impact, and then He asks that the upward path to heaven would be powerfully governed and secured. And I don't think we can escape the absolute priority for our prayers and our lives and our priorities that Jesus has to be glorified. What He prayed for Himself must control our own words and deeds. And if you think this is just pious talk, think about the tsunami of opposition to Jesus. No wonder we need to pray for and seek this glory of Christ. Is this not what Philippians 2:10 is all about? That everyone will kneel before Jesus to God's glory. He prays rightly for this first.

Jesus' Prayer for the Apostles

Then Jesus prays for the apostles. This is the second part of the prayer. The first part for Himself is for glory in the "hour" and glory into heaven. Now, as He prays for the eleven apostles, He again has two main requests— that they be *kept* (vv. 11, 15) and *sanctified* (vv. 17, 19). We can be sure that this prayer is now for the eleven because in verse 11 He basically says, "I'm leaving; they are staying." And in verse 12 He essentially says, "None have been lost except Judas." So, He is focusing on the eleven apostles.

Now, how can Jesus be so narrow and pray for eleven men and specifically say, "I am not praying for the world" (v. 9)? Doesn't He love the world? Well, don't miss His strategy which is to reach the world through faithful apostles and united believers—so that "the world may believe" (v. 21) and "the world [may] believe that you have sent me" (v. 21). He knows what He's doing! You just have to follow the sequence of His prayer.

Notice that these apostles were given to Jesus by the Father (v. 6). Behind the scenes the Father was at work to prompt these people to go to Jesus. A thousand incidents can lead to conversion: hearing Scripture, meeting Christians, getting cancer, finding trouble, but no-one goes to Jesus unless the Father is at work. And when the apostles went to Jesus they therefore "obeyed the word" (v. 6). This doesn't mean they were perfect but that they responded to the gospel word, accepted the truth and got Jesus right (see v. 8)!

I remember reading about a taxi driver speaking to a clergyman in the back seat of his cab, telling the reverend gentleman that he was doing a better job than he was because when the clergyman preaches, people sleep. When the taxi driver drives, however, people pray like crazy. And when God is at work, people wake up and go to Jesus.

So now look at what Jesus asks for these apostles: He says, "protect them" (v. 11) or, literally, "keep them". Then He says, "sanctify them" (v. 17). To keep and to sanctify are two sides of the same coin. He is asking the Father to prevent something and then guarantee something— make sure this doesn't happen and make sure this does happen.

Please notice, He doesn't ask that they will be kept from trouble or suffering. He knows that most of them will be martyred. He is asking that they be kept from the world in which they live (v. 11) and the evil one, that is, the devil (v. 15). He goes straight to the central issue, asking that they will survive the world and the devil, or, if you like, that their souls will be spared and guarded. This is a rebuke to our trivial requests for our children and friends and a stimulus to bigger issues. As Don Carson says in his commentary on this passage, "We spend time today praying about health, projects, decisions, finances, family, even holidays...being materialists at heart we often discern only dimly the spiritual struggle of which He is so aware."[1]

So Jesus asks the Father to "keep them in your name" (v. 11), which means keep them by your faithful character so that they then exhibit some faithful character too. The world is not a playground but a battleground, and he's interceding for their lives. No one knew better than Jesus that the Father had these apostles in His unstoppable hand (John 10:29), but the promises don't cancel our prayers. They fire up our prayers so we pray, "Father, keep your promises"!

Now is this just prayer for their cocooning, to be wrapped up in spiritual cotton wool so they can glide through this life with faith intact? No, the ultimate purpose is in verse 11, "that they may be one, even as we are one." This is not merely that they would get on together and be happy. Instead He prays that they would be united in love and truth and purpose as the Father and the Son are!

Basically, this brilliant request is that the apostles would be so together in the gospel and in sacrificial love and in the task that they've been given, that the world would be impacted for good. And the needs of the world are infinitely greater than the needs of the church when you think about it biblically. Despite the boasting and the laughing and the clapping of the world, it's actually in "sunset." This is as bright as it's ever going to get for the people outside of Christ. And, despite our weakness and unworthiness and doubts, we are in the "sunrise." This is as dark as it's going to get for us! Christ has turned sunset into sunrise completely by grace and by means of His own sacrifice and breakthrough.

No wonder this simple (and brief) but profound (and brilliant) prayer for their safekeeping was so important. And the Father

---

1.   D. A. Carson, *Jesus and His Friends* (Grand Rapids: Baker, 1995), 188.

answered the prayer. Everything in history points to the apostles staying faithful with unity in love and truth and purpose to the end, and we are deeply indebted to their witness and example.

What can we learn from this prayer that God would keep His people? And what can we expect the Father to do as we echo this prayer to Him? Here is my imagination at work as these few words go up to God: "Please keep them." I see in my imagination a thousand darts from the devil being deflected by God. I see a secular campaign to tempt and trap people utterly fail and, in fact, backfire. I see the sin that fills the heart get wonderfully subdued. An inclination to sin arises, but the opportunity is snatched away. Then an opportunity to sin arises, but there is no inclination! Then, more positively, the gospel message of Jesus becomes very real and wonderful all over again, and an appetite for godliness springs up. The value of salvation fills the heart and spills over to prayer and repentance and gratitude and evangelism.

All from the answer to this prayer!

Well now, the flipside to "keep them" is the request to "sanctify them" (vv. 17, 19). Does anyone pray this? Do you ever pray for people that God would sanctify them? Well, the answer is probably *yes* if you mean "make them holy" or "get them growing." But that's not exactly what Jesus is asking, as you'll see in a minute. There are two ways that God sanctifies His people, and if you don't know them both you can get badly confused. One way of sanctification is to be put in a position, as if God were choosing a team. So Paul can say in 1 Corinthians 6:11, "you were sanctified." In other words, God has placed you in a privileged position and a very purposeful position.

The other way of sanctification is to be made to progress in holiness, to be steadily transformed into the likeness of Christ. So Paul can pray in 1 Thessalonians 5:23, "May the God of peace Himself sanctify you completely", that is, "May there be progress." There is positional sanctification and progressive sanctification. One is placement, and one is a process.

Now when Jesus says, "Father, sanctify them" here, He's not likely to be thinking of progressive sanctification ("make them more holy", though that would be a joy to Him) because in verse 19, He says, "for their sake I consecrate [sanctify] myself" which can't mean "I improve myself" but rather "I position myself" (or devote myself) to guarantee their secure position! In other words, He places Himself in the way of the cross so that they will be placed in the way of salvation. And He places Himself in the way of God's will for Him so they will be in the way of God's will for them.

If you put these two requests together, they spell out an incredible combination, something like this:

(a) Father, keep them from a thousand spiritual dangers

(b) Father, sanctify them for one great spiritual purpose (which is their unity, which impacts the world to the glory of God).

We are so powerless to get anyone safe and keen, but God can do it. We can't even get our children free from schoolyard dangers or make them treasure the Lord, but God can do it. We can't get someone to hate sin and love Jesus, but God can do it. Jesus prayed that God would do this through the apostles. What a wonderful combination of prayers! So brief (and apparently unimpressive), but deep and astonishing! "Father, keep them from a thousand spiritual dangers and for one spiritual priority. You are inward strength and outward refuge. Please hear my prayer."

And the instrument the Father uses is "the truth" (v. 17). Jesus is saying, "Please get them into the 'truth'." This sounds so bland and yet everything hangs on clarity and faithfulness in the truth. Unless you're really clear on what you're doing, there is the danger of doing what you think is right, but it has nothing to do with the truth. Two young American writers have recently exposed the confusion so many in the churches have today because of vague language traceable back to the 1970s. Words like *mission* and *serve* have become so elastic that telling someone to focus on God's *mission* and *serve* people will mean evangelism to one and soup kitchens to another. So, when Jesus says, "I am sending you" (John 20:21), what does He mean? Well, a careful reading of John's Gospel will show that Jesus's top priority was to see people get eternal life at the cost of His death. So surely, if we are to be sent to do mission and serve in His name, it will mean helping people get eternal life. That's the eternal priority.

Read the book of Acts and see that *mission* for the early church has no focus on creative care or social planning or community services. Instead the focus is on the Word of God going out and transforming everything. As one of the authors writes, "We want the church to remember that there is something worse than death and something better than human flourishing ... and we will work to relieve suffering ... but especially eternal suffering."[2]

So, when Jesus prays for the truth to be used in sanctifying or positioning the apostles this is no bland request. This is Jesus praying "Make them crystal clear and absolutely united in the truth so that they know what's vital." Here are the apostles chosen out (v. 6), yet left in the world (v. 11). So they are aliens (v. 14), and yet they are missionaries (v. 18). They need the Scriptures!

And Jesus underwrites and guarantees everything because He sanctifies Himself. He positions Himself to die. So the apostles will be kept and sanctified, and all who believe will live eternally. So don't let this prayer for the apostles get lost on you or buried in the tombs of the apostles themselves. Here is a recorded prayer from Jesus, one which is immeasurably wise and significant. "Father, keep us and our loved ones and this church and your servants from a thousand spiritual dangers and for one great spiritual priority."

Jesus' Prayer for All Believers

Finally, we turn to Jesus' prayer for all believers. In this famous section, Jesus prays for all "those who will believe" through the message of the apostles (v. 20). In other words, He casts His mind down the centuries and round the globe to pray for every Christian, including you and me. He is interceding for the millions and millions who will believe.

And His prayer again has two parts: that Christians would be one (vv. 21, 23), and that they would one day be in glory (v. 24). He has two requests for Himself (glory in His hour and glory in God's heaven), two requests for the apostles (that they be kept

---

2. Kevin DeYoung and Greg Gilbert, *What Is the Mission of the Church: Making Sense of Social Justice, Shalom, and the Great Commission* (Wheaton: Crossway, 2011), 27.

and sanctified) and now two requests for the universal church (unity and to be in the glory with Him).

Now this prayer to be *one* is not as wishy-washy as you may think. He is not just praying for a superficial, hand-holding, campfire-singing of *Kumbaya*. This unity is first in the truth (see v. 20). These believers are going to hear and receive and value and agree on the gospel message, which is the scriptural message. Real unity means oneness of mind and heart, as in Philippians 2:2. There is conviction and persuasion on what is true. Remember that Jesus has been organizing this apostolic teaching, as He explains in John 14–16. The Spirit will come and help the apostles remember what Jesus said (14:26) and know what is coming (16:13), so that they can record it for us to read and agree on. Without the oneness of mind in the Scriptures, all external and structured unity is bound to fail. It can only herd people together superficially and temporarily. That's why the so-called "ecumenical movement" to get the churches together can never work while the message of the apostles is trimmed or sidelined. It's not enough to provide tea and cakes along with a desperate avoidance of all essential issues. Truth is crucial.

Incidentally, when Jesus says in John 17:22, "The glory that you have given me I have given to them, that they may be one even as we are one," He probably means, "I've given them the revelation (or display) of what I'm doing", i.e. enough information to agree on.

But then the second key to real Christian unity is relationship. Jesus prayed "that they may all be one, just as you, Father, are in me, and I in you" (v. 21). Obviously the Father-Son relationship is unique and Jesus is not praying that we will be like God. But He has already said in John 15 that there is an organic relationship between Himself and His people (a vine-to-branch relationship), and the Spirit dwells within them. So they are in Christ, and this is a mutual inter-connection and goes way beyond some distant and detached awareness of each other. The idea that a Christian is detached from Christ and only has a book and a building and some coffee and a course to go to is as far removed from real Christianity as saying that a married couple has a house and a fridge as the essence of their relationship. No, real Christianity means profound relationship. We are joined to Christ in an intimate way. We may not feel or even properly grasp this, but He does! For, as far as He is concerned, we belong to Him. He lives in us by His Spirit, and we live in Him as branches in a vine. It is a living relationship.

The third key to unity is that it is progressive. In verse 23 we read, "that they may become perfectly one". This prayer is because Jesus is not satisfied with unity in truth and a relationship that is still dysfunctional. He doesn't want a family that is legally one but practically at war. He wants the truth to be heeded, the Spirit to be transforming us, and for progress in oneness that will let the world know about Jesus (v. 23). One day that unity will be perfect, but even now He longs for it to progress, not just for our joy but for the world to be eternally affected. He cares about the world, and His weapons are Spirit, truth, and a united church to reach the world.

Carson is sharp on the implications when he writes, "Sad to tell, too often Christians do not cherish deeply the things that unite them … they cherish instead the divisive things. Even … defending what we hold to be a point of truth we may endanger the integrity of this witness of loving unity … for this Jesus prays and one day He will see this prayer answered …."[3]

So Jesus prays for Christians to have truthful, relational, and progressive unity.

Finally, Jesus lovingly and generously and wonderfully prays that Christian believers would "be…where I am" to see "the glory" (v. 24). He had prayed for Himself to return to the glory (v. 5), and now He prays that we will arrive there. This is Jesus, about to be crucified, praying for others. Amazing!

And He can ask for this because He pays for this. In John 14:2, He said that He would "go to prepare a place for you", He would go to the cross. And He would pay all the cost that we should pay for our evils and insurrections.

And the *glory* to come is not some Christless pub or golf course—it is to see His glory (v. 24). Unless Jesus is there, there is no heaven nor peace nor perfection! So don't invent a heaven that leaves Him out, or you've invented a mess and a delusion.

---

3. Carson, *Jesus and His Friends*, 196.

That is hell. No, to be with Christ is to be in glory, and to be with all the ransomed saints is a secondary blessing. Don't doubt this now because your sin is great. Believe this now because His grace is greater. It will happen because He paid and because He prayed and because He wills it to happen. The prayer in John 17:24 is not just a request as Jesus often prayed, but here it is, "Father, I will it ... I want it." Astonishing!

So here is this amazing prayer—answered in relation to Jesus already, answered in relation to the apostles already, and being answered in relation to believers who are waiting for the final day: that He be glorified in death and rising, that apostles be kept from dangers and sanctified for faithfulness, that all believers be united here and one day in glory.

When Martyn Lloyd-Jones was dying at the age of eighty-one and people were gathering around to comfort and pray—some thinking that his recovery was crucial for the church as well as the family—he wrote a shaky note to his wife which said, "Do not pray for healing. Do not hold me back from the glory."[4]

Learn from this prayer of Jesus in John 17 what to pray and what to want. It is a priceless gift to us.

---

4. Iain H. Murray, *D. Martyn Lloyd-Jones: The Fight of Faith (1939–1981)* (Edinburgh: Banner of Truth, 1990), 747.

13 The Jeweler's Window

DAVID MEREDITH

Every preacher has that moment when, faced with an open Bible and a blank sheet of paper, he does not yet have the slightest clue of the trajectory his new sermon will take. Of course, it is not a moment for panic, but once again the realization that he is about to lead his people on a journey into the very breath of God, His Word. It's certainly a point which takes one's breath away when we consider the privilege and responsibility of preparing to open up the Word of God to a congregation of God's people.

Planning

The task will be made so much simpler if we know where we are going. A preacher who does not have a plan will waste many hours and fill many trashcans with false starts. While consecutive expository preaching is by no means the only method, it ought to be the central plank of a long-term preaching ministry. In my younger days an older, wiser pastor said to me, somewhat candidly, "Anyone can preach a couple of sermons. The real test is producing new and fresh material, week after week, for decades."

I am not a long-term planner, and I certainly do not stick rigidly to a detailed plan, but I usually know what I will be doing for the next two months. A highly detailed plan does not allow for the obvious fact that other things happen in life, and they do not refer to our plan. I recall when Princess Diana tragically died in an accident during the late hours of a Saturday night, and the next day demanded a more specific pastoral word to my congregation.

It's also good practice to preach series on topical subjects such as "the church" and "meals Jesus had," or even on less controversial subjects such as "worship" or "baptism"! Moreover I want to balance preaching from the Old and New Testaments. I have tried to ensure that in my two Sunday services, morning and evening, both Testaments will be covered.

It's always a bad idea for me to plan alone because I am too close to the situation. So I consult with the church leadership about the specific needs of the congregation. If a congregation has relocated or has suffered from a major corporate trauma, the preaching must feed into the needs of the hour. We don't all have the luxury of other trained preachers on the church staff, but it's always good to share the idea of the sermon content with others, as well as informing them of the broader plan.

Of course, each sermon should be bathed in prayer before, during, and after the writing process. The ministry of prayer is a large part of the calling of the pastor-teacher. But most of us, I suspect, would rather write a couple of sermons than pray about them for two or three hours during the week. I am conscious that there are technical aspects to sermon preparation. We must be sensitive to the hermeneutical demands of the text and the overall theology which is expressed through it. Nevertheless preaching is an act of worship, and we enter our preparation with the shoes off our feet, like Moses, as we meet with the living God. There are some elements of preaching which cannot be prepared for except by prayer. Preaching is a spiritual activity which involves unction and may end in results far greater than the creation of the universe. The conversion of a sinner and the growth of a believer are not things which can be manipulated by technique, so the immediate recognition at the outset that we are in way over our heads will lead to the requisite humility before God and a real sense of dependence on Him. The canon of Scripture is closed, but the supernatural activity of God speaking through it is not.

The Technical Process

My first action in sermon preparation is to print out the passage from the Bible version I use in the pulpit. Personally I favor the 1984 NIV, but I realize that there is now a certain obsolescence with this version. It is probably only a matter of time before we, as a congregation, move to the ESV. But it is not my favorite Bible translation—far too many "ands" for my liking.

The printout will soon turn into a battle zone. I mark key words and note initial thoughts and reflections on the text. The text is always king, but this piece of paper will be the central plank of the whole process. I think we have to be honest about our knowledge and use of the original languages. I have a basic undergraduate level of both Hebrew and Greek. I am thankful that they were both compulsory at my seminary. Yet we have to have a very good and in-depth knowledge of these languages for them to be of any use in bringing original light to a particular text. I am thankful that we are blessed with an embarrassment of versions of the English Bible and outstanding software packages which were beyond the most vivid dreams of a previous generation. I use *Bible Works* for all exegetical work, and I am a total magpie when it comes to the textual insights of the big commentators. For me, the benefit of a basic knowledge of the original languages is that I can follow the arguments of the greats with some understanding. It's rather like my car mechanic telling me about the vagaries of the engine management system. I don't know all that he is talking about, but I have spent enough time with engines to know when he is simply bluffing.

By the way, it is important that your work in the original languages is largely hidden (e.g., never quote a Greek or Hebrew word). It's like a foundation that is never seen on the surface. There are times when the English text does not do justice to the nuances suggested by the original. These instances ought to be noted and engaged with, but with the lightest of touches. There is a very real temptation to present myself as the learned one before an admiring audience.

I love commentaries! My personal library is largely made up of commentaries, and I buy about five or six for each book of the Bible. This practice has meant that I have built up a very useful library, although with the increase of digital media, real libraries are shrinking and virtual libraries are growing. God has given many gifts to the church, not least of which are men and women skilled in rightly dividing the word of truth. It may be difficult to arrange a conversation with Don Carson. I certainly cannot speak with Luther or Calvin, but though they are dead they still speak to me through their writings.

There is no intrinsic value in older commentaries as opposed to more recent works. The older materials have a perspective of a different time and culture, and that enriches us. Prolixity is not intrinsically more noble than brevity, and I usually find that the best of the contemporary commentators have already consulted the giants of the past before me. There ought to be a mix of the old and the new, and it's sheer chronological snobbery to ignore the greats. Everyone should read Luther on Romans and Candlish on 1 John.

There is a growing snobbery about older classic works such as J. C. Ryle on the Gospels and Matthew Henry's famous commentary. I do not share that disdain. It is true that they ought not to be cited as references in academic works on a text, but they have their uses. I get up early on Sunday morning and, without exception, I will read these works on the passage I have prepared for the day. It is rare that God does not speak to me through these giants of the past.

On a side note, when formulating a sermon, language is important. The use of words is larger than vocabulary. We ought to speak in a classic and yet contemporary way. What I mean is that we should avoid using intentionally antiquarian language, as if that gave our message a superior spirituality, and we ought also to avoid crass street language. Our source material must be filtered. We may think like John Flavel, but we must never speak like him.

There are a number of dangers in commentaries. Some writers are so organized and offer such great models of arranging the text that it is very tempting simply to copy them. John Stott had a tidy mind and an unusually terse style of writing, and it's challenging for me to better his suggestions. There is nothing wrong in copying the suggestions of another, as long as these are acknowledged. Conviction and personal ownership of the message, however, will only come with material that has been worked and reworked by me.

The books that I find least useful are books of sermons. They are fine for devotional and general reading but unhelpful for immediate sermon preparation. I read Lloyd-Jones on both Romans and Ephesians early on in my Christian life, but I would rarely consult them now for sermon material.

In my preparation, I will read about five or six commentaries and take notes as I go along. Preachers will differ with regard to what percentage of the material will have originated in the mind of another, but in my case it would be significant. The material must be sifted through my own mind and become applicable to the specific and very personal context of my congregation. This is where the hard work comes in, because I sense that so many sermons fail at this point. They are half-worked and the ingredients remain raw because they have not been thoroughly baked in the mind and heart of the preacher.

There is no doubt that commentaries which tend towards the exegetical are more useful than those which are more homiletic in character. It's better to get a platform on to which you can take the freshness and immediacy of your own engagement with the text.

Outlining the Message

By this time I will have gathered a very messy printout and a lot of notes gleaned from various commentaries. It is at this point that I will start to look at an outline. The key here is that the outline must be formed by the contours of the text and not the other way around. In recent years, I have moved towards much shorter main headings for the sake of memorability and also to get into the discipline of summary. I am a classic lateral thinker. I really cannot make head or tail of mind maps. Straight lines do it for me. We use PowerPoint very lightly in our services, and so the headings appear as I preach. I never refer to the presentation (which is operated by someone else) and, in fact, I act as if it does not exist. It is a good discipline to display the outline, but the sermon must never stray into being a dispassionate lecture.

It is important to spend a lot of time to get the headings correct. My normal practice is to start off with some working headings, which are usually altered by the end of the process. Alliteration always annoys some listeners, so be very careful when using it. Almost without exception some irrelevant word is used simply because it starts with a particular letter. My people deserve more than three "Ps" and a poem. If I can get balance in the headings, that is a real bonus, but most alliteration is forced, and listening to it is akin to witnessing a train wreck in slow motion.

After I obtain a suitable outline, it is time to hone and slim the sermon. I find that most sermons have too much unnecessary packing. There are a handful of men who can preach effectively for over forty-five minutes, but most of us ought to aim for 30 to 40 minutes. There are, of course, always exceptions. During conventions or conferences, when people have set aside a significant amount of time to engage seriously with the Bible, longer messages are appropriate. It may be personal to me, but I find that I am longer and less focused if my preparation has been lacking or my notes have been shorter.

At this stage in the process, as I work through the sermon, I think of Paul's defense of his message in 2 Corinthians 4:2 (NIV): "we do not use deception, nor do we distort the word of God. On the contrary, by setting forth the truth plainly we commend ourselves to every man's conscience in the sight of God." The key word in this verse is *phanerōsis* which is, according to Strong's definition, "a disclosure, clear display, an outward evidencing of a latent principle, active exhibition". *Phanerōsis* is what a jeweler does when he sets out his jewels for display or sale. There is an intrinsic beauty in the item, but in order to give credit to that glory it should be displayed with skill and consummate care. As pastoral jewelers, we have many tools to help us in our display. It is also helpful to change the image to a meal. The ingredients may well serve the same purpose if liquidized and served as a uniform mash, but the experience is richer by far if care is taken with the presentation.

A key element in presentation is illustration and anecdote. Some people have the bizarre notion that illustrations and stories tend toward superficiality. This is wrong. It is said that Jesus spoke most often using parables and illustrations but that Paul was more objective in his style. If you read even a few lines of Paul you will notice that allusions and illustrations are everywhere—from bodies to buildings and athletics to anchors. I am unusual in that I don't keep a file or store of illustrations. I find that if I write things down, though they seem to be powerful at the time, like the manna of the Exodus they grow old rather quickly. I read widely and this gives me an unending supply of fresh and current material. It may be that I have a quotation or an idea at the very fringes of my memory. In that case, I will use a search engine to get more detail. It is always good to add details, like dates and locations, to your illustrations to give them added authenticity.

Some of the best illustrations come from other preachers. If I have time, I will listen to a sermon from another preacher on the passage that I plan to preach. There are dangers in this, like the temptation to plagiarize, but at the end of the day an audio sermon is an audio book. And you usually find that the man has been raiding the same source of material as you have! Part of my wider preparation is listening to other preachers. I will listen to five or six sermons per week, usually during spare time in the car.

I acknowledge that a celebrity circuit of the famous preachers exists, a group of men who are especially gifted. I think we ought to be relaxed about that and realize that God has given some men more talents than others. We are committed to constant improvement and development of our craft, and one of the best ways of doing this is to watch how the master craftsmen do it. I will also listen to sermons outside my own tradition. The only exception would be that I don't listen to self-consciously liberal preachers who never have anything to say and are usually very poor at saying it.

Applying the Truth

The sermon will not be preached in a vacuum. There is a context in which the message will be heard, and it demands an application to that specific context. When I think about application, a key issue I keep in mind is this: the application must derive naturally from the text. It has been said that preaching follows the familiar pattern of state, explain, and apply. Application points come naturally when we consider the original context (e.g., Romans, written to a thriving city congregation requiring a basic doctrinal outlook). In many ways, it's the application which turns the sermon away from being a mere lecture. We must avoid being mere commentators. Application occurs when I press home the teaching of the passage into the hearts and lives of my hearers. And for application to be truly authentic, I must drill it into my own heart at the same time.

As I think about application, the idea of the bridge is critical. I am always looking for the bridge from the ancient world into our world, from the mouth of God to the streets of the city, town, or village of my church. A sermon which neglects this bridge is an unfinished piece of work and is, in fact, a bridge to nowhere. The key question at the end is always "How shall we then live?" Preaching is teaching, but it is more than that. It is a moment of persuasion; it is a call to action. It is a mistake to assume that application is always practical in the sense that it is to be lived out in the family, work, or church. The force of application may be to stir consciences, to give greater visions of the glory of Christ, or to seek the quickening work of the Holy Spirit.

A question which I always ask myself is, "Where is Christ in this passage?" The key is, of course, that I should only preach Christ from the text when Christ is in the text. The wonderful reality is that He is everywhere, and my task is to shine the spotlight on Him. The Bible is the story of redemption from beginning to end. It begins with Christ in the very first verse of the Bible where we see Him as the Creator who spoke creation into being. And it closes with Him revealing His grace in the very last chapter. A key question to ask is, "Would a Muslim or a secular textual analyst say the same things about this passage as a Christian?" The Bible is not a moral manual but the record of the covenant-keeping God's pledge to save His people through His Son.

Notes

Now I come to the subject of notes. This is the point where the raw material from my study of the text and commentaries is transferred into the finished manuscript. I will do this in one operation, typing the material into a word processor on my computer. In the end, however, it will be a PDF document on my iPad. I will prepare summary notes, never a full manuscript unless I am doing something more academic or formal. It would be rare for me to have more than five pages of size A paper (A4 in the UK) which gives me material for 30 to 40 minutes.

The manuscript, for me, is absolutely fundamental to the whole process, but it should never be the focus of delivering my sermon. The text of Scripture ought to be the focus. There is a clear link between industry in preparation and clarity in preaching. A very common fault with poor preachers is an obsession with the manuscript as opposed to double engagement with the text and the congregation. My aim ought to be that my congregation is not even aware that I have an outline in front of me. It should be one of the hidden pieces of the process. The manuscript is a safety net. I have to be engrossed in the text and engaging the people with my eyes all the time, unless I am referring to or reading from the Bible. Paper or virtual paper is my slave and not my master.

I am always amazed when I hear of the time some preachers take to prepare a sermon. Recently I heard of a preacher who takes thirty hours to prepare each sermon. Preparation time is a difficult question to deal with. My situation calls for two sermons per week, and only in recent years have we built a staff who help to share the load. I still work in a Scottish Presbyterian context where the expectation is sometimes three sermons per week. It is my opinion that that is too much! My job title is that of a pastor-teacher, and it demands that I be out and about among people. Preparing for the pulpit involves a symbiotic relationship with pastoral ministry. Much of my preparation involves listening to the problems and joys of the flock God has given me.

If I define preparation as sitting with pieces of paper, open books, and a switched on computer, then I probably take about six hours to prepare one sermon. The truth is that sermon preparation is ongoing with our general reading and interaction with the changes of life. A relevant comparison is that of a plumber who fixes a faucet in five minutes but charges $150.

It may be argued that years of training and experience went into detecting the specific problem and enabling him to fix it is such a short time. Sermon preparation can never be measured in terms of hours but years.

My sermon is now prepared, and the hour of worship begins. There is a sense, of course, in which sermon preparation goes on to the very last moment. As I mount the steps to the pulpit or podium I am saying and believing, "I believe in the Holy Spirit." I think also of the prayer which the late John Stott prayed at the beginning of every sermon:

> Heavenly Father, we bow in your presence,
> May your Word be our rule,
> Your Spirit our teacher,
> And your greater glory our supreme concern,
> Through Jesus Christ our Lord.

Then, at that moment, when what is called "the romance of preaching" may kick in, I as a preacher stand as a prophet. I open my mouth, and hopefully the breath of God fills the room. If the reaction is, "What a great sermon!" the whole enterprise is damaged. But I look for another reaction, one where the preacher is forgotten, and the cry goes out, "Surely God is in this place."

14 Three Men at a Funeral
(John 19:38-42)

DAVID MEREDITH

Have you ever had an adrenaline buzz at a funeral? If you attend a lot of Christian funerals it may not be as uncommon as some would expect. Make no mistake, death always carries a large element of sadness. We cannot eliminate the sense of loss of earthly relationships when one we have loved is taken from us. It is also a fact that solemn, sad times teach deep truths. After all, the preacher said, "It is better to go to the house of mourning than to go to the house of feasting, for this is the end of all mankind, and the living will lay it to heart" (Eccles. 7:2). Yet there is often a moment when the congregation sings about the resurrection and we realize that the casket in front of us is not the whole story!

> No guilt in life, no fear in death
> This is the power of Christ in me
> From life's first cry to final breath
> Jesus commands my destiny
>
> No power of hell, no scheme of man
> Could ever pluck me from His hand
> Til He returns or calls me home
> Here in the power of Christ I stand

What makes a great funeral? It's the awareness that the dead person lived a productive life after trusting in Christ, and that his or her life has only really begun. So we can go home from a funeral elevated and inspired.

In this passage we read about the funeral that transformed all other funerals, the burial of Jesus. In many ways, it was an ordinary Jewish burial carried out according to "the burial custom of the Jews" (v. 40). But God was about to break this custom because the body would not stay in the grave for long. The Rabbis at that time would struggle to find the protocol for a resurrection after three days.

The Jewish practice then involved a two-stage process. In this case we have a new tomb (v. 41), one hewn out of a rock, with shelving for perhaps three or four bodies. A stone would then be placed over the entrance to prevent tomb robbers. The bodies would decay and after a few years they would be removed and the bones placed in a special box known as an ossuary.

In this passage we can see other features that made the burial far from usual. Look at the two unlikely pall-bearers, Joseph of Arimathea and Nicodemus (vv. 38, 39). Neither of them were blood relations of Jesus. Yet even with them we see God's purpose in that these two men were members of His new family, the Church of God. This is the outworking of what Jesus taught in Matthew 12:49-50: "And stretching out his hand toward his disciples, he said, 'Here are my mother and my brothers! For whoever does the will of my Father in heaven is my brother and sister and mother.'" We can also deduce from their involvement that the Church will often be built up through surprising people, perhaps plucked from obscurity to serve Jesus at a time of need.

In the Gospels we don't read a great deal about the burial of Jesus. It was over-shadowed by the three big events: the trial, the crucifixion, and the resurrection. Yet it is prominent in the teaching of the apostles. Paul said that it is one of the matters of our faith which are "of first importance" … "that Christ died for our sins in accordance with the Scriptures, that he was buried, that he was raised on the third day in accordance with the Scriptures" (1 Cor. 15:3, 4). This is why it is highlighted in the Apostles Creed which says that Jesus "suffered under Pontius Pilate, was crucified, dead and buried; he descended into hell: The third day he rose again from the dead."

Please notice the characteristics of the three men at the funeral that day.

A Previously Unknown Man

In verse 38 we meet a new character in John's account, Joseph of Arimathea. While we don't know the location of Arimathea, we do know some things about Joseph. He was a prominent member of the community, a member of the Sanhedrin (Luke 23:50); he was wealthy (Matt. 27:57), influential and well-known.

In fact, we see here a fulfilled prophecy. Isaiah 53:9 tells us that the suffering servant "made his grave with the wicked and with a rich man in his death, although he had done no violence, and there was no deceit in his mouth." This is how God works. Christ will be vindicated. Although He died as a criminal, He is buried as a monarch. Although He could have been thrown to the dogs, which was what happened to the bodies of crucified criminals, He was carried to a rich man's grave. It is significant that even to the end Jesus owns nothing of His own: He borrowed a boat to preach from, a donkey to ride on into Jerusalem, His clothes were stripped off Him, and now He is buried in a borrowed tomb.

Although Joseph was an unknown man, the most significant thing about him was his secret faith in Christ. Have you noticed the impact that unknown people have in the Bible? At the time of His greatest need Jesus was surrounded by women, by outsiders and people who were perceived to be on the fringe. Where were the apostles? They had fled. Jesus was abandoned and deserted, just as it had been prophesied that men would hide their faces from Him (see Isa. 53:3). We can never presume on our faithfulness tomorrow—status and position in the Church and in the eyes of other people do not guarantee that we will never fail or fall in the future.

Look at Joseph. He had his weaknesses. The fear of the Jews kept him from being open about his faith. Let's be honest about this, we have all been there. Even the biggest of personalities have at times cowered in fear when matters of faith were raised with them. There is something about Jesus that annoys people, and some would say that Joseph was a coward because he did not want to be in the firing line when anger against Jesus presented itself. The wonderful thing is that God often uses cowards.

I think we can apply this to the way we view ourselves and the way we react to believers who are perceived to be weak. The Lord has many weak children in His family, many dull pupils in His school, many raw soldiers in His army, and many lame sheep in His flock. Yet He is committed to them all, and never rejects them. If we deal with our fellow believers like that, we will be blessed. There are many in the church who, like Joseph, are shy and even cowardly. But for all that, like Joseph, they are real and true believers.

But the moment came when Joseph wanted to serve Jesus. Note what he sees: a dead, bleeding body. Look at each time the body is mentioned, in verse 38, twice, and then in verse 40. Notice also the language of death everywhere in this passage: burial customs, tombs and body bags! There was no sign of any miracle from this inert corpse. Are there any clues in the passage as to why Joseph wanted to serve Jesus? No, there are none! But if we look at the parallel passage in Luke 23 we read that Joseph was "looking for the kingdom of God" (v. 51). He now had the faith to know that a kingdom was being birthed at that very moment; his vision was informed by faith and not by sight.

Do we have a similar faith that sees beyond sight? The faith that knows that in the darkest place, even beside the grave, hope can burst through in glorious light?

Joseph uses his influence now. The women would never have got near the authorities simply because of their gender. The time had come for the mask to come off. Joseph becomes bold and takes the body of Jesus away. The alternative was simply awful—those crucified for seditious acts were not buried but were simply left to the elements and to the vultures.

There could be another factor at work here. Jesus had been crucified as a rebel and His body was destined for the rubbish dump. Could it be the case that Pilate gave the body to Joseph because he had examined Jesus and had found Him guiltless? This was not only a snub to the Jewish authorities, whom Pilate hated, but it was a tacit acknowledgment that Jesus was indeed holy and undefiled.

What else do we learn in the passage for our own context? There is the glaring lesson that there are many hidden disciples who have not yet declared their allegiance to Jesus. In Elijah's day there were 7,000 who did not "bow the knee" to Baal. When God has a work to do He always finds people. Are you one of these people?

The culture of the day frowned on handling a dead body, that task was reserved for "Gentile dogs." Joseph no longer cared, so he carried the bleeding body to what he thought would be its last resting place. It's often the strangest and most extreme circumstances that drive us to serve the Lord. When Jesus spoke boldly Joseph remained quiet, but now comes the hour, comes the man.

Joseph reminds me of the daughter of two Ivy League school professors who became a Christian at university in Scotland. Her parents had raised her to be a liberal and fully expected her to embrace their lifestyle of soft drugs, casual relationships, and tolerance towards everything except Christianity. The daughter returned home to New England and managed to be silent for many months until the pressure became too much and her Lord's name was being impugned at a dinner party. There is a time to be silent, but God shows us that there is also a time to speak. The story for that girl did not end well. She was socially ostracized from her old circles, but she came to know a peace with God that surpassed all that she had ever experienced in the past.

I think there is also a point here about being judgmental. We may have a friend in our circles who is always slow to speak. Let's not be quick to judge. We do not know the whole story. It's tough out there, but Jesus knows us better than we know ourselves.

A Developing Man

Joseph was not alone that day. He was accompanied by Nicodemus (v. 39), a man already known to the readers of John. Nicodemus was the man who earlier had visited Jesus at night (see John 3). John's Gospel is full of contrasts. It is clear from what he writes that Joseph is what Nicodemus had once been, shy and retiring.

So what was Nicodemus' contribution to the funeral? Look at verse 39 and notice that he brought large quantities of myrrh and aloes. The quantity was one hundred *litrai*, just short of seventy-five pounds. Just pause for a moment over the amount. You may be interested to know that a large Irish Setter weighs seventy-five pounds! It was a hundred times more than Mary poured over Jesus at Bethany (John 12:3), and remember how the people grumbled about the sheer extravagance then. There are documents that reveal that similar amounts were used in royal burials. It was the quantity reserved for a king.

What's the application here? For a start we have a great example of appropriate and proportional giving. Nicodemus was wealthy and could afford what he gave—and he lovingly gave it. We see also that service is linked to circumstance. Joseph used his influence, but Nicodemus used both money and influence.

Notice also the evidence of development. We see a journey from a clandestine visit to a despised Nazarene (John 3) to Nicodemus becoming a chief mourner at a private but regal funeral. I love the way Matthew Henry writes about it, that "grace which is at first like a bruised reed may afterwards become like a strong cedar and the trembling lamb bold as a lion."[1] I think that God is once again speaking to us about our tendency to judge quickly and harshly. J. C. Ryle reveals pastoral sensitivity when he notes that "we must not condemn others as graceless and godless, because they do not see the whole truth at once, and only reach Christianity by slow degrees."[2] It is a principle of nature that the trees which produce the hardest and strongest wood are often the slowest to grow.

In Christian growth and development there are certain basics like the recognition that we are sinners in need of a Savior. There is the cry for mercy and recognition that Jesus is our only hope in life and in death. But the speed and experience of that growth vary from person to person. We should not judge people by their growth, but realize that life in an adult has the same value as life in a baby. Nicodemus began his spiritual life in the dark (John 3:2), but it developed in the day.

Look also at verse 40: "So *they* took the body of Jesus and bound it." We see here the principle that in the kingdom of God the person who works alone is rare. Both Joseph and Nicodemus

---

1.   Matthew Henry, *Matthew Henry's Commentary on the Whole Bible* (McLean, VA: MacDonald Publishing Company, n.d.), 5:1205.

2.   J. C. Ryle, *Expository Thoughts on the Gospels: John* (Edinburgh: Banner of Truth, 2012), 245.

brought different things to the table of service. Who would have thought three years previously, when they were both sitting at an especially dull meeting of the ruling council, that they would be involved as colleagues in the burial service of the man who would be the Savior of the world?

A Dead Man

The third person here, of course, is Jesus. He is a very unusual third man because He is a corpse. It is probably of no significance that we see a Joseph at His death as well as at His birth, but there is significance in that two unknowns are catapulted by God into the very heart of redemption history.

Notice that with Jesus the reminder of death is never far away. The spices of verse 39 remind us of the gifts of the wise men at His birth. This was a man who was born to die. In the passage you see that this death was neither random nor haphazard. Instead it was tracked by the Scriptures. Look at verses 24, 28, 36, and 37 and the recurrent theme of Scripture being fulfilled. I think we often skim over these references to fulfillment without realizing that we are dealing with the miraculous. Can you explain how such details were foretold over a thousand years earlier? The blogosphere is full of reports of how the writings of Nostradamus are still popular after 400 years, and yet biblical prophecy takes futurology to a whole new level!

John does not hold back in his language concerning death. We see this with his explicit references to blood and water. At the time he wrote his Gospel there were a group of people called Docetists who denied that Jesus really was human. They taught that Jesus simply put on humanity like an actor puts on a costume drama. I think that many people today are practical Docetists. They have a memory of Jesus from their childhood which depicts Him as a blond, angelic figure who hovers over the earth; for them Jesus is a mixture of a Hare Krishna charity collector and Obi wan Kenobi! The church is often complicit in this myth with its other-worldly pietism and lack of engagement with culture. It is relevant also as we engage with our Muslim friends who are shocked by the earthiness and humanity of Jesus.

The death language goes to the very heart of our faith: Jesus had a body (vv. 38, 40), was crucified (v. 41) and was laid in a tomb

(v. 42). We are not talking here about a benign Buddha-like figure who sits cross-legged and smiles. We meet a bleeding man in a grave, life extinct. Yet this is a Jesus to whom we can relate—He is a man who was hungry, who experienced loneliness and misunderstanding, and who knew the pain and reality of death. This is a Jesus who relates to us and who can wholly sympathize with all our pains.

The fact that Jesus died and was buried throws the reality of the resurrection into bold relief. It was from such a base of apparent hopelessness and death that life came, bringing hope with it. The early Church lived in the afterglow of these events and they knew them to be true. In the minds of the early Church the reality of the risen Christ was so real that they were prepared to die for Him.

In the text before us we have a funeral scene that is laden with latent expectation. Most of us have read the book, so we know how it ends. The paradox of the gospel is that His death had more power and efficacy than His life. Jesus did not die as a good example; instead He died as a substitute. His work goes on during His death, indeed His death was the climax of His work.

The passage reveals the purpose of His death. Notice in verse 41 the reference to a garden. John notices gardens quite a lot, such as in his extended account of the events in the Garden of Gethsemane. We know that this sorry story was kicked off by events in the Garden of Eden. Man lost his innocence in a garden, and sin entered into the world with a legacy of morally nuclear proportions; humanity was in meltdown. Yet, as Jesus was laid in a new tomb in a garden, He had already redeemed His people. If we look at Revelation, a book that describes the end of time, we see a city, but in the middle of it is a garden which contains "the tree of life" designed "for the healing of the nations" (Rev. 22:2).

The garden theme is also related to a broader theme of kingship that we can see in the passage. Early readers of John would have been well aware that the kings of Judah were buried in garden tombs (2 Kings 21:18, 26), and even David himself had a garden as his final resting place (Neh. 3:15, 16). Jesus will be revealed as king and it almost feels that there is a constant pressure on John to reveal the kingship of Jesus in spite of the attempts by wicked men to suppress it—notice there is the crown (19:2), the sign (19:21), and now we have the ointments and the garden tomb.

Do you fear death? Jack Kerouac said, "I am young now and can look upon my body and soul with pride. But it will be mangled soon, and later it will begin to disintegrate, and then I shall die, and die conclusively. How can we face such a fact, and not live in fear?"[3] This is the default position of so many today, and yet this passage gives us insight into the nature of death.

Jesus was about to prove that He had removed the sting from death and robbed the grave of victory. Jesus was laid, as it were, in the prison confined by the slab across the tomb (v. 42). Yet there is a sense that things were about to change in a radical way, that death and funerals would never be the same for those whose lives are linked to the life of Jesus. The prison doors were about to be stormed by a force which would be felt through the ages. I love what Bruce Milne writes about the death of Jesus: "He enters into the full reality of death, not merely walking with us right up to the door only to pull back at the final second, leaving us to walk the dark valley on our own. He comes all the way with us right into the grey, after-death world of funeral parlors and the making of arrangements for the disposing of the body, the world of strained faces, hushed voices and tear-stained eyes. He takes his place within the world of the receding past, where death's destructive power is so real and irreversible; dead ... buried ... gone."[4]

This funeral took place on "the day of Preparation." Sabbath was about to come. Sabbath was the day when God rested from His work of creation. In the story we are on the cusp of a new Sabbath, the Lord's Day, when Jesus rose again and created a new world. I'm not sure what your Saturday nights look like but you get the sense that that Saturday night was packed full of expectation. The disciples had been told that He would rise again, but they didn't believe it. If we could see the angels in the

3.   Jack Kerouac, *Atop an Underwood* (New York: Viking Press, 1999), 230.

4.   *The Message of John*. The Bible Speaks Today (Downers Grove, IL: IVP Academic, 1993), 286.

realms of glory during the events of verse 42 we would see them
straining with eagerness to see what would happen next.

Yes, this was the night before Easter. And if we could borrow
a phrase from another season we could say that nobody stirred,
not even a mouse. The picture in verse 42 is that of a quiet grave
after a funeral. Are you familiar with the big Easter hymn, *Christ
arose*? Let me remind you of the last verse and chorus:

> Death cannot keep his prey,
> Jesus, my Savior!
> He tore the bars away,
> Jesus my Lord!
> Up from the grave He arose,
> With a mighty triumph o'er His foes;
> He arose a victor from the dark domain,
> And He lives forever With His saints to reign.
> He arose! He arose!
> Hallelujah! Christ arose!

Yes, these verses speak of a dark domain. But Christ arose from
that dark domain as the victorious king!

15 Blood, Toil, Tears, and Sweat

JOSH MOODY

I am not going to attempt to put everything into this chapter that goes into my preparation. There are very important matters that I am largely leaving out: prayer, for one. I am not sure a sermon can be preached without prayer (or if it can, it most certainly should not be). I am also leaving out the pre-work that goes into planning out my sermon series ahead of time. When I come to the actual week before preaching on Sunday, a lot of the groundwork has been done. I have a pretty good sense of what the book is about as a whole, and how the particular passage I am preaching fits into that, before I even begin my week's work in the text.

This chapter is just a week in my life as a preacher. I am most definitely not saying this is the only way to do it, and in fact, it may not even be how I am doing it in five years' time. I am also not saying it should be slavishly copied, or indeed that the way I do it is particularly unique. It's simply how I will be doing it right now, and perhaps it might be helpful for some to have a little window into this weekly pattern of blood, toil, tears, and sweat.

Monday
My day off. Recover from Sunday. Get over moping if I think my sermon bombed. Get over preening myself if I think my

sermon was angelic. Normalize, breathe, walk, breathe some more.

Tuesday

Right back into preparing the sermon for next Sunday first thing Tuesday morning. (Side note: Tuesdays through Thursdays, I set aside each morning for study and each afternoon for discipleship, leadership, shepherding, and administrative matters.) I ask myself the question, "If I had to preach this sermon right now, or in five minutes, what would I say?" I create a very quick, handwritten outline which attempts to structure a sermon from the passage as if I were preaching it right away. This does several things for me. It gets me into the sermon passage so that I am thinking about it all week. (My brain, like everyone else's, does a lot of subconscious processing, so sometimes my best ideas come in the shower, but that's because I've got the brain thinking about it early in the week.) It also prevents me from coming up with really clever ideas later in the week after I've read a ton of books on the passage, ideas which seem to bear little resemblance to the obvious, straightforward meaning of the passage. I have this quick outline as a sort of *Idiot's Guide* to how to preach the passage, and it anchors me through the week. Sometimes I significantly change it later; sometimes it becomes the basic outline of the actual sermon. But either way, it is not just a starting point; it is an important trajectory which can act as a handrail for the later work. This is all Tuesday morning.

The rest of Tuesday is staff stuff: meetings, conversations, more meetings. Part of my role is shepherding the shepherds. Tuesday, for me, is a big day for doing this. But I do all I can to guard the beginning of Tuesday morning for getting straight into the passage and creating a handwritten outline. (I do this from the original languages, as well as a couple of translations, so I have in my mind the words that the people will actually read as well as the words that were originally written.)

This handwritten outline has at the top of the page an *exegetical* outline, and then at the bottom of the page an *expository* (or sermon) outline. For the exegetical outline, the key here is getting the structure of the passage right, working hard at it until I have an outline that accurately mirrors what the passage was saying then. Then the sermon outline always has *MP* (Main Point) with a simple statement. I try to see if I can make the Main Point include a verb, so that it is actually calling us to do something, believe something, say something, or change something. This is followed by subpoints; an introductory statement; and a statement about relevance, so that I always have actual people in my mind (preaching is *not* teaching the Bible; preaching is teaching the Bible *to people*).

Then right at the top of the expository outline is an answer to the question "hook." Some people will hate the idea that on Tuesday morning I'm already thinking about the hook for Sunday (or think about a hook at all). Bah, humbug, I say. If you want to pretend that it doesn't matter that we get people's attention at the beginning of a sermon, be my guest. But don't read Jesus's (or Paul's) sermons too closely. "What therefore you worship as unknown, this I proclaim to you" (see Acts 17:23). "A certain man had two sons" (Luke 15:11). I have to have a hook. It only needs to be attached to the main point of the sermon, which actually needs to be the main point of the passage; otherwise, I am not doing expositional preaching. But if I am not asking application questions when I am preparing to preach, then I am not preparing to preach, I am preparing to lecture. That will empty my church pretty quickly, and I don't blame them. It's like preparing a really nice meal, but not putting it within reach on the table. The sheep will go somewhere they are fed, and quite rightly, too.

Wednesday

In the morning, I read through a number of commentaries and books on the theme of the passage. These include works that are popular, works that are scholarly, and anywhere in between. I am like a camel sucking up water. I fill up both humps and stuff them as full as I can with as much from reading as widely as I can. I was trained to read fast-ish at university, so it is not that hard for me, sometimes even enjoyable, though at other times it can feel like a chore to wade through things that are either poorly written, or just plain wrong.

This does several things that I find useful. It stops me from preaching downright heresy, which is certainly worth the time. If I cannot find any current evangelical author, or any previous great Christian leader, who agrees with me about what the passage is teaching, then chances are that I am wrong. I *may* not be wrong, but the odds are stacked against me at this point, and I will usually shelve my fanciful idea with a wry grin. Occasionally, I will remain convinced I am right and may chance my arm, *as long as* what I am saying generally agrees with the great Christian creeds and confessions of faith. If it doesn't do that, then I quickly repent, with a brief prayer that if by some odd possibility I am called to be a second Martin Luther, God should make it crystal clear over a long time, and other godly people also should agree with me along the way. So one thing it does, generally speaking, is it keeps me on track.

It also humbles me. I see—particularly by reading *old* books on the passage—that people have thought far more profound thoughts than I have on this passage, and it rattles me and shakes me. It takes me out of my solitary conceit, to use a C.S. Lewis phrase, to dwell in the thought pattern of the communion of pastors and teachers down through the years. Sometimes at this point I will also get useful application insight into the passage too, but that is rare. This is more the nuts and bolts morning.

Thursday

During the morning I will rework the outline. I turn the handwritten outline into a lengthy full outline on a Microsoft Word document on the computer, reworking it as necessary, filling it out. For each subpoint, I work on clarifying the statement, carefully explaining it, finding a helpful illustration for it, and then applying it. Sometimes this takes a long time to do right. I am trying to build a very tightly meshed skeleton for the sermon. There is no flesh yet on the bones, but I want the bones to connect together logically and as an outflow of the main point of the passage. Structure, structure, structure. I spend hours doing this on Thursday morning. I also begin to rack my brain for pithy phrases, or memorable aphorisms, or punchy illustrations, so that when I come to write the manuscript for the sermon, I have a stock of fuel to give the skeleton flesh.

Friday

Friday, the whole of Friday, is my "lock-down-don't-disturb-me-unless-you-are-dying" day. My phone is on "Do Not Disturb." My cell phone is turned off. My outer office door is locked. If I need to walk out of the office down the corridor to get a coffee, I may not greet someone as I walk past them. This is *Friday*. Everyone knows it. My mind is on the sermon. This is important stuff. On Friday I write out a full manuscript, word for word, writing as if I was preaching it. I imagine myself at the pulpit speaking, based upon the outline and the work I have done that week. I try to fine-tune phrases, but I also write at a fair clip, not so fast that I miss stuff, but not so slow that my phrases end up sounding as if they have been written.

Hopefully, and usually, by the end of Friday I have "something". That's usually the phrase I use when my wife asks me how it went. "Well, I've got something." I don't yet know whether it's any good, I don't know whether it is finished, but I have a full manuscript sermon. For a 30-45 minute sermon the manuscript is usually four pages of 10 point Times New Roman. That may seem not much, but that's because though it is a full manuscript, I will come off the manuscript when I am preaching, elaborate some parts, cut out others, depending on what seems to be the need as I am preaching.

Saturday

Saturday morning is often spent at home with the kids. On some Saturday afternoons there are church things. Around 4 p.m. on Saturday afternoon my mind begins to return to Sunday.

I find this break from Friday to Saturday useful. I get back into the office around 4:30 p.m. and take a fresh look at the manuscript. Sometimes I will look at a point and realize I can't say something that I have written. It gives me a little bit of perspective, helps me to cut things or sharpen things since I am no longer quite so connected to it.

I go through the whole sermon, speaking into a camera on my iPad, recording every word, including reading the passage, somewhat (it's bound to be a little artificial) as if I was preaching it. I rarely actually go back and listen to the video-recording after I've done it. But it helps me in a few ways. It times out the sermon so I can get a sense of whether I am going far too long or too short. (A 17-20 minute recording is usually 30-40 minutes preached because of the live dynamic of actually preaching it to people, where I add things in at the moment, or take things out. If I go much over twenty minutes in the video-recording, I think I might have too much material, or begin to beg others involved in the service to be brief.) This also helps me to hear what I have written. That, in turn, can make me cut things out that, when I hear them, I realize I cannot say them. It also gets me back into the sermon. I need to get this sermon by heart, that is in my mind and blood stream, so that I can preach it as a living expression of what is going on inside me as I have wrestled with the text.

I change the manuscript from four pages of letter-size paper to landscape orientation, double column, 14 point Calibri instead of 10 point Times New Roman, and cut them into sheets that will fit snugly in my Bible. I go through the manuscript with a pen: underlining, adding emphases, putting marks I have developed over years that have particular meaning to me, and remind me of the way my brain was working when I was preparing (having grown up with pen and paper rather than a laptop, I still find pen marks "speak" to me in a different way than typewritten words).

Usually this Saturday evening run-through lasts 2-3 hours, so I am done by about 7:30 or 8:00 p.m. Very occasionally, I will begin to go through it and realize that I have a lot of work still to do. That's not normally a good sign, but it can be a necessary evil to have to rework your message. That's probably happened two times in the last ten years.

Sunday

People ask me on Saturday if I'm ready, and I usually say that I'm not ready until I've finished preaching. I am still working on the sermon on Sunday. Currently we have three morning services, and I preach at all three. The first service is at 8:00 a.m. I get up early, not so early that I am physically lethargic, but early enough to get back into the message again. I warm up my voice so I don't stretch the vocal cords and eat a good breakfast. I also take some fruit with me so that I can snack between services. This prevents me from being hungry (and therefore fuzzy), but I'm not "sugar-buzzed" either.

At church I get used to the feeling of the building again (strange to say, but I like to actually walk through the sanctuary/auditorium so that my mind is "in" the right place). I lock myself away in a rather small closet behind the sanctuary, next to where the musicians are warming up. I like to pray, read through my notes, and get my mind ready here. I try to get out to the service a couple of minutes before it begins, particularly the 8:00 a.m. service. I wear one of those microphones that hangs over your ear. I resisted, but after a colleague told me that when John Stott last preached for him, he wore one, I caved in. I don't especially like the way it looks, but I think they are a helpful technology. I glance through my notes one last time during the final hymn or song before I preach.

I usually begin my sermon with some formulaic expression so that I don't have to think of something particularly engaging right away, but can get used to speaking and talking. I like to read the passage because it helps me gauge where people are that morning in their mood or feeling by their response to the Word, and also because reading the Scripture is a big part of what I am doing, and I hate it when it is read badly. In between the services, I hide away and get ready for the next service, but after the last service, I go to the back of the sanctuary and greet people and pastor people as appropriate and needed. That's my pattern right now. In the past I've greeted people in between each service, but I find that can get my mind off the sermon and into particular pastoral needs or joys. If I am also preaching on Sunday evening, which is not normal for me right now, then I do something similar before and after the evening service.

Monday
Shake, rinse, repeat.

16 What Jesus Thinks About Religion

(Revelation 3:14-22)

JOSH MOODY

Friendship has long been considered one of the greatest delights of life. It was the ancient Greeks and Romans who considered the joy of friendship the most wonderful of all human experiences. The Victorians waxed lyrical on the subject of friendship. Modern life in the West, however, seems to have created a situation where genuine friendship is becoming comparatively rare. Evidence of this is not hard to find. Men, in particular, seem these days to find it nearly impossible to have real, deep friends.

We could suggest various reasons why this is so. It seems to have something to do with modern *Western* life. Outside the West, friendship is showing no sign of abating, while in the West the very predominance of counselors and self-help books seem to function as surrogate friends, in at least some, if by no means all, instances. Here in our fast-paced American society who, after all, has *time* for friendship? Or the emotional energy required? And how many people are there left who spend enough of their lives in one town to develop real, deep friendships?

It is still an ideal in our lives, but an ideal that recedes over the horizon of possibility with each new demand made upon us, each new geographical relocation, each new wound we pick up from an attempted quick-fix relationship.

Other more pressing matters take up our attention, matters like economic survival, family, study, work, things like getting through the 5pm to 7pm daily-crisis-hour of family life.

All of which makes it good to know that when we come to the subject of religion, we can gladly leave our emotional vulnerability behind. We don't really need to engage with God personally, at a deep friendship level; we just need to go through the motions, to enact the ritual. In fact, the church itself is an institution which has as its ideal the establishment of such a stable edifice that the vulnerability of spiritual engagement is no longer necessary. We don't need to cry out to God for funds; we have the money in an investment fund in the bank. It doesn't matter if we lose a person or two from church; after all, there are still plenty more. And God Himself can be helpfully kept at arm's distance, outside the parameter of our emotional and vulnerable center, necessary yet not engaged.

One of the preeminent historians of the church, J. H. Merle d'Aubigné, summarized that it was exactly this haughtiness of self-reliance that led the Reformation, which began so well, to become embroiled in worldly politics. And it was exactly this issue which was facing the church in Laodicea.

If you read all seven letters to the churches of Asia you will discover the different situations and needs of each church and the Lord Jesus' remedy for each. To the Ephesians, who had lost their first love, Christ calls them to remember. To Smyrna, facing martyrdom, Christ calls them to bravery. To Pergamum, corrupted by doctrinal compromise, Christ calls them to disciplined consistency. To Thyatira, facing moral compromise, Christ calls them to purity. To Sardis, sleepy Sardis, Christ calls them to "Wake up," to put their trust not in their incomplete deeds but in Him. To Philadelphia, commended, Christ urges them to continue to hold on to the Word. Now, finally in Laodicea, we have a church that needs nothing!

"For you say, I am rich, I have prospered, and I need nothing" (v. 17). They were fine, thank you very much. It was nice of Jesus to have written them a personal letter, but they had a perfectly good organization. They didn't need money! They didn't need Him!

But what Jesus is saying in this letter is that religion which shuts Him out is useless. For, He says, He is necessary, first, even for the wealthy; second, even for the beautiful; and third, even for the healthy.

Wealthy or Poor?

Religion which shuts Jesus out is useless, because Jesus is necessary even for the wealthy.

Now let's get a sense of how horrified Jesus is! He even has to say this: "I know your works: you are neither cold nor hot. Would that you were either cold or hot! So, because you are lukewarm, and neither hot nor cold, I will spit you out of my mouth" (vv. 15-16). But they think they're wealthy, "I have prospered" (v. 17), when in fact they are not. They need to get "gold refined by fire" from Jesus (v. 18). Put these pieces together and we get the picture of what was going on in Laodicea.

Laodicea was a remarkably rich city. It was a banking center in which the famous Cicero cashed his bills of exchange. Its wealth was based on a number of different factors, as we will see. One of these factors was its location. It was at the crossroads of several important trading routes. Ramsay calls it "a knot on the road-system." Here, of course, it had every opportunity for advancing in financial wealth by trading. So attractive was its wealth that there are records of rabbis complaining of the Jewish diaspora being drawn to Laodicea for its baths, gymnasiums, and general good time.

Despite this, however, it had one great vulnerability: its water supply. Its location being chosen for the road system, not for water, it had to pipe in its water from the surrounding Lycus Valley. There were two other cities in the Lycus Valley, both receiving degrees of attention in our New Testament. One was called Hierapolis, the other Colossae. In Hierapolis, there were steaming hot waters renowned for their healing properties. In Colossae, there was cold water, fresh and renewing to the taste. In Laodicea, the water was piped in, and it arrived lukewarm and initially, before settling, useless for anything apart from an emetic—a medicine to make you vomit.

The Laodiceans think they are wealthy, but Jesus is pointing out their vulnerability. They had wealth—who could deny it?

They also had tepid, stagnant, putrid water. The translation in verse 16, "I will spit you out of my mouth," is a rather polite phrasing. Jesus is saying, "I am about to vomit you out of my mouth." That tepid, lukewarm, deposit-encrusted water which makes you vomit if you don't treat it first, well that's exactly how you make me feel. How I wish you were either hot, like the bubbling, beautiful waters at Hierapolis, or cold, like the refreshing springs at Colossae. Instead, you think you're so perfect that you really make me sick.

This is the only time such an emotion is predicated of God in the Bible. He is not angry. He is not disappointed. He is disgusted. But there is grace. "I will spit you out of my mouth." He says "I will"—that is, "about to." It hasn't happened yet. There's a space, there is room for a change of heart for the church at Laodicea. There is still time to repent.

The Laodiceans must realize that they need to buy from Jesus "gold refined by fire" (v. 18). They may have riches, but there are riches that they do not have and desperately need.

Clothed or Naked?

Second, not only are they really poor, they are also really naked. Here we see that religion which shuts Jesus out is useless, because He is necessary even for the beautiful.

From verse 17 we learn that they think they need nothing, "not realizing that you are wretched, pitiable, poor, blind, and naked." Jesus counsels them—how gentle and friendly is that word—he counsels them to buy from Him "white garments so that you may clothe yourself and the shame of your nakedness may not be seen" (v. 18).

Not only was Laodicea famous for its wealth in general, in particular it had an international trade in textiles. One garment became so widely known that at the much later Council of Chalcedon, in A.D. 451, Laodicea was simply referred to by the name of the garment, the *trimata*. Yet, beautifully dressed as they were, the church in Laodicea was really naked. Nakedness in biblical phraseology is often connected to shamefulness. While in the Garden of Eden, Adam and Eve were both naked and felt no shame (Gen. 2:25). Since the Fall, however, nakedness has evoked images of wretchedness, and being given clothes, approval and blessing. Joseph was granted new clothes by Pharaoh when he was advanced to his position of vice-regent over Egypt (Gen. 41:42). And the prophet Isaiah walked naked for three and a half years as a sign of the coming judgment upon Israel through Assyria (Isa. 20:1-3).

The Laodiceans are to buy clothes from Jesus. That does not mean that such blessings are not a free gift from Jesus. He is, rather, pointing out once more their superficial self-reliance. *Buy*, that is, go to the market. They were proud of being a market town. They thought they were the great commercial buyers and sellers at a profit, yet it was they who needed to buy, to receive, from Jesus.

The World Series of baseball happens every year. Perhaps not as popular as before—a Gallup poll suggests that baseball ranks third behind basketball and American football as the public's favorite sport to watch—it's nonetheless a significant event in the yearly calendar.

It is as though Jesus says, "You think you've got the World Series completely sown up and you're going to win it yet again, but actually it's you who need to learn just how to pitch at all. You can't even get the thing over the plate." Laodicea was a great textile center, yet it was the Laodiceans who had to import clothes from Jesus!

Seeing or Blind?

The Laodiceans are not only really poor and really naked, they are also really blind; they just don't see it. And so we see in the third place that religion which shuts out Jesus is useless, because He is necessary even for the healthy. They not only needed clothing from Jesus, they also needed "salve to anoint [their] eyes so that [they] may see" (v. 18).

Once more the irony is thick. Laodicea was a medical center with a specialization in ophthalmology. And it was they who needed to import "salve" to put on their eyes! It is possible that a certain reputed ancient formula for improving eye problems, called "Phrygian Powder", was made locally. Certainly, the medical school at Laodicea was founded by a person who was mentored by a specialist in eye care. They've got the eyesight thing all sorted. Jesus tells them to get some from Him because

203

they are not seeing straight, or even seeing at all. You are "blind," and you need some salve so that you can see!

What was going on? Why did they seem so respectable, organized, sorted, wealthy, well-clothed, balanced, and yet were really pitiful, poor, naked, and wretched? I don't think they would have realized it. This, of all the letters, would have come as a shock. They were doing just fine, or so they thought. In fact they *were* neither cold nor hot; they were avoiding those dangerous extremes. They would have gotten to verse 15 when the letter was read out, and everyone would have been nodding and saying, "Yes, quite so, we are neither hot nor cold, thank goodness, praise the Lord," and suddenly Jesus points out the issue. Yes, neither cold nor hot—you're lukewarm like that tepid water that makes you throw up.

But what was the issue?

There are hints here, but you've got to pick them out carefully. Note, verse 14, how Jesus introduces Himself: "the words of the Amen, the faithful and true witness, the beginning of God's creation." The *Amen* is Hebrew, while the phrase "faithful and true witness" is an expansion for the non-Hebrew speakers in the congregation. God is the God of truth; He is *the truth*, the God of Amen. John is probably picking up the divine epithet in Isaiah 65:16. He is God—the God of Amen—the real and true God, this is Jesus. "The Amen, the faithful and true witness" and, note, "the beginning of God's creation." It is the *beginning* of creation, not the first thing created, but the active principle of creation, the source, the originator, the preeminent "uncreated principle of creation" as one commentator puts it.

This sounds very much like Colossians 1:15 and following, where Jesus is exalted in similar terms as the beginning of all, the uncreated principle of creation, the God, the I AM, the ruler.

Colossae was down the road, about ten miles or so, from Laodicea. They were in constant communication; in fact, it's possible that the pastor in Laodicea at that time was drawn from the congregation in Colossae, at least one commentator speculates so. At any rate they were close. They knew each other well, and it's likely that the same doctrinal issues which earlier troubled the Colossians were now impinging on the Laodiceans, though in a somewhat different form no doubt. In Colossae, there was a troubling tendency to give way to a syncretized form of Christianity whereby Jesus became merely one among many of the angelic powers of God mediating creation. Instead, Jesus is powerfully proclaimed as God Himself, the beginning of creation (Col. 1:15).

Here, less doctrinal, more practical, the Laodiceans were marginalizing Jesus. But Jesus is *The Amen*, He is God, and He is absolutely necessary for all spiritual prosperity, wealth, true wealth, clothing, true clothing, seeing, true seeing.

Their material prosperity combined with hearsay of aberrant teaching down the road combined to give the church at Laodicea a feeling, a nice lukewarm feeling, that they could do it without Jesus. God was quite enough. But Jesus is The Amen, and it is *from* Him—the original is quite emphatic—*from Him personally* that they must do business. They must "buy" gold, clothes, and eye-salve because religion which shuts out Jesus is useless. It's just an emetic.

Now we can hear with clarity those famous words of Jesus captured in Holman Hunt's *The Light of the World*. "Behold," Jesus says, "I stand at the door and knock. If anyone hears my voice and opens the door, I will come in to him and eat with him, *and he with me.*"

This, too, is laced in local significance. The Laodiceans were so rich that, after the recent earthquake, it was their boast that they alone of all the cities of Asia had rebuilt without imperial aid. Just recently they had re-laid a magnificent triple gate to the city. Now they could keep out whom they chose. With the Roman abuse of the ancient hospitality practice of billeting officials at great expense to the ruin of the more wealthy inhabitants, that gate was good news for the Laodiceans. Jesus, though, is standing at it. He is not forcing His entry. He is knocking. He is not only knocking, He is calling, "If anyone hears my voice." And the meal of hospitality for which He is seeking entry is a meal of friendship: "I will come in and eat with him, *and he with me.*"

Of course, what's striking about these words is that they are written to a church, to Christians. "Behold I stand at the door and knock. If anyone hears my voice and opens the door, I will come in to him and eat with him, and he with me."

What are we doing to keep Jesus at arm's length? Are we frightened He will change us? Are we afraid He will abuse our vulnerability?

Will you open the door of your heart to Jesus today, perhaps for the first time, or once more? What will happen when you do? "I will come in," Jesus has promised. It will be so. "I will come in to him and eat with him and he with me." What will happen will be a re-established friendship between you and The Amen, the Lord Jesus Christ.

We don't need Jesus as our friend! We have church! We have money! We have need of nothing! That was the boast of the Laodiceans.

But without Jesus you have nothing. Only with Him, and being friends—yes, friends—with Him will you get to sit on the throne of destiny, of authority in the age to come. Death is the final reality that even a blind person sees. "He who has an ear let him hear what the Spirit says to the churches." Open the door of your heart to Jesus today.

Who knows, maybe even you need a friend in heaven.

17 Spirit-filled Sitzfleisch
The Prayerful Art of Sermonizing

DOUGLAS SEAN O'DONNELL

When I was an intern at College Church in Wheaton, Pastor David Helm was in charge of ministry training. The first time the interns gathered for our weekly training, Helm began by asking us to recite the books of the Bible. After "Genesis" and "Exodus" were named, I called out "Deuteronomy." The correction came swiftly, "Leviticus," and on we moved. The simple drill was to remind us Bible/Theology majors that we needeed to know our Bibles, and that knowing our Bibles starts with knowing some of the basic details about them—like the Table of Contents. I still have trouble knowing the correct biblical ordering of books, but that elementary exercise helped me to learn that returning to the basics is not to be neglected.

A second exercise Helm had us do was take a pencil and pad of paper and go across the street to the front lawn of Wheaton College's campus to spend thirty minutes writing down everything we saw. He didn't tell us why he was wasting our time with such a stupid exercise (my thought at the time), but already humiliated by mixing up Leviticus and Deuteronomy I shut my trap and followed orders.

That exercise in observation was life-changing. I saw for the first time how little I saw. Being forced to write down things like "two squirrels are chasing each other," and "a cardinal flew above my head," and "a boy is chasing a girl who is out of his league" showed me what Helm intended to show us: that stopping to make observations of the obvious is an important attribute of the effective preacher.

What I was taught that day is what I now call Spirit-filled *Sitzfleisch*. *Sitzfleisch* is a German word comprised of the words *sitzen* (to sit) and *fleisch* (flesh). To preach God's Word well it takes "sitting flesh," that is, the ability to stay glued to a chair—for at least thirty minutes!—in order to see what God's Word says. I add the adjective "Spirit-filled" before *Sitzfleisch* to emphasize that the art of observation of the holy canon requires the illumination of the Holy Spirit. In another article I wrote that touched on this theme, I wrote then what I commend to you now:

> We are used to hearing the phrase "Spirit-filled preaching," which emphasizes the Spirit spontaneously assisting the preacher in the act of preaching. I take no issue with Spirit-filled preaching so long as it is properly defined and acted out. Let us "give room" for the Spirit in the pulpit. But let us also "give room" for the Spirit in the study. Why not ask the Spirit to give you the desire to sit and study? Why not ask the Spirit to open your eyes to see the text's truths, implications, and applications? Why not ask the Spirit to inspire you to study the text in community—with other pastors, interns, commentators? Why not ask the Spirit to broaden your mind with the reading of the best books of poetry, novels, and theology? Why not ask the Spirit to make you a pastor-scholar, someone who lives and works by the discipline of Spirit-filled *Sitzfleisch*?[1]

A Week in the Life

Monday: Sit, Mark-up, Outline

My week of sermon preparation begins with Spirit-filled *Sitzfleisch*. I sit with the text open on Monday morning as I might stand with it open on Sunday morning. Sit, read, sit, pray, sit, think, sit, write, sit, edit, sit, kneel, sit, stand, preach—is my weekly workout routine.

---

1. Douglas Sean O'Donnell, "As One Approved: Passing the Preacher's Test," in Craig Brian Larson, ed., *Interpretation and Application* (Peabody, MA: Hendrickson, 2012), 3-14.

After I walk my son Simeon to school, I return to my chair in the living room to start the sitting. Other than a periodic mumbling to myself (and an occasional squirrel and cardinal outside the window), all is quiet in the world. The day before, I print out my next sermon's text on an otherwise blank piece of paper. Sometimes I print the Greek or Hebrew of the text beneath it. Most often, it is just my native tongue (God bless Mr. Wycliffe and Mr. Tyndale!). My Monday morning goal is to have a homiletical outline.[2] To reach that goal, I take half a day simply to observe the text. I look for the skeletal structure, which may or may not in turn be my sermon's outline. I draw lines from verses or phrases and write down questions next to them. (I will later explore answers to those questions by myself, with friends, and with commentators, who are also my friends.) Mostly, I jot down observations. This includes underlining key words, circling potential important phrases, and thinking through possible applications. It also includes taking into consideration the context of the book and canon. If it is an Old Testament text, it also includes asking how the person and work of Christ relate to this passage. I scribble on the edges the word "Christ?" with a possible cross-reference or two.

What the prominent New Testament scholar Adolf Schlatter said of the science of scholarship—that it is "first observation, second observation, third observation,"[3] I say of preaching. Good preaching is derived from pleasurable yet painstaking observation of God's Word.

My Monday afternoons are reserved for administrative, shepherding, and mentoring tasks. However, my weekly Monday meeting with my pastoral intern includes the two of us repeating what I did that morning. My intern first (a) lists observations, (b) asks questions, and (c) takes a shot at a sermon outline. I then follow with my observations, questions, and outline. This practice has proved very helpful for me. Two sets of eyes are

---

2. The art of exegesis to me is purely a homiletical exercise. I am looking to get this text into a sermon. Some might disagree with my cut-out-the-middle-man approach. So be it.

3. As noted and translated by John Piper, in John Piper and D. A. Carson, *The Pastor as Scholar and the Scholar as Pastor: Reflections on Life and Ministry* (Wheaton: Crossway, 2011), 28.

better than one, and other people usually have other skills that can help illuminate the text. For example, my current intern is better than I am with the biblical languages.

Tuesday: Filling-in the Outline

Speaking of the biblical languages, I usually read through the text in the original Greek or stumble through the Hebrew. I have had one year of Hebrew and two of Greek. Every morning after my prayer and Psalm reading, however, I spend at least ten minutes reviewing vocabulary and listening to New Testament texts (I use John D. Schwandt, *The Audio Greek New Testament* and Jonathan T. Pennington, *Readings in the Greek New Testament*). Moreover, I have friends who help. For example, Dr. Michael Graves of Wheaton College is a close friend. If I have questions about the Hebrew, he helps. Did I befriend Mike only to have him help with Hebrew? Well . . . no, of course not. Find a good language guy, buy him lunch monthly, have the family over for the holidays, then steal his mind! If you are not good with languages, as I am *not* (save the Queen's English, mind you), you must take matters into your own hands. Befriend those lonely language scholars. (Just kidding, Mike.) Listen to vocabulary while you run at the YMCA (I do!). Take ten minutes a day at least to brush up and grow up.

Tuesday is my "get a little help from my friends" day. I take my sermon outline and I fill it in with insights from excellent commentaries. To me, commentaries don't merely help with difficult issues, correct my interpretations, and add exegetical insights, they trigger thoughts. Put differently, they open up my exegetical imagination!

In the April 2011 issue of *Themelios*, Murray J. Harris reviewed J. Ramsey Michael's commentary on the Gospel of John. In a brief aside Harris said of recent commentaries "what an embarrassment of riches we now have!"[4] I couldn't agree more. For a preacher to neglect commentaries altogether is the height of sloth and stupidity. For a preacher to use only one or two is still reclining on the La-Z-Boy of laziness. I use between five and thirty commentaries a week. Call me crazy? That's fine.

---

4. *Themelios* 36:1 (April 2011): 102-103.

I'd rather be called crazy than lazy. My logic is this: If I can gain insights from my intern on Monday, who is a Bible student at the local college, can't I also (and moreover!) gain insights from my commentator buddies on Tuesday, who are usually Bible professors at the most prestigious colleges, universities, and seminaries? Hanging out with commentators in the study or at Starbucks is the world's greatest Bible study. Don't neglect attending.

What I do is this. I fill in my sermon outline with insights from commentators and/or insights from me, often triggered by a commentator. You'd be surprised at all that can be said on a particular pericope. After a day of doing this, my outline is so full, I will have to decide—when I start to write my manuscript—what will go into the sermon and what will sadly remain on the cutting-room floor (or in a footnote that I shall at least appreciate with a smile).

Wednesday: Day Off

Wednesday is my day off. I do absolutely nothing except write books and articles.[5] Since it is my day off, I have lots of time to write articles like the one you are reading and throw in something on the "Wednesday" section of this article so it looks like I'm a "redeeming-the-time" machine.

What I have for you is a word of warning: don't procrastinate. Sermon-prep procrastinators are the lowliest forms of life. (You might laugh at that line, but I don't.) John Piper wrote, "Lazy people cannot be leaders."[6] I'll add to that, "Procrastinators cannot be preachers." I know that we shepherd people who have real physical, emotional, and spiritual needs. I know that we have technological temptations—phones, e-mails, texts, blog reading, blog posting, web surfing, etc. But I also know that our calling requires us to sit and study the Scriptures. Listen, sermon preparation is sacred time. It is as sacred as prayer, burying the dead, baptizing your firstborn, and kissing your wife with Song

---

5. "A leader does not see the pressure of work as a curse but as a glory. He does not desire to fritter away his life in excess leisure. He loves to be productive." John Piper, *The Marks of a Spiritual Leader* (Minneapolis, MN: Desiring God Foundation, 2011), 28.

6. ibid., 27.

of Solomon kisses. Yet, sadly, too few pastors are in the habit of getting to this sacred duty and delight early in the week. The foolish preacher procrastinates. Don't play the fool. I won't pity you, and neither will your congregation. By the "grace of God" that is in you (1 Cor. 15:10) and God's "energy that ... powerfully works within" you (Col. 1:29), work hard, toil, abound "in the work of the Lord, knowing that in the Lord your labor is not in vain" (1 Cor. 15:58).

Thursday–Saturday: Writing the Manuscript
Mary Oliver begins her poem, *Logos*:

> Why wonder about the loaves and the fishes?
> If you say the right words, the wine expands.
> If you say them with love
> and the felt ferocity of that love,
> the fish explode into many.[7]

Each week I am tasked, as you are, to use words to speak about God's Word. It is a noble task. It is a high calling. Those two convictions, among others, sustain me when I come to writing and delivering the Sunday sermon. Each Sunday I am preparing to give a State of the Union speech regarding our union with God and our union with other believers. I'm not sure I believe that the sermon is the highest art form, but I do believe that it is the God-designed forum for communicating the most important truths in the universe. A high view of preaching, with a humble view of the preacher, goes a long way to producing a solid sermon.

I manuscript because this charge to communicate God's Word matters. I read that manuscript in the pulpit for the same reason. If you don't do the second, I'll leave that to your freedom in Christ. If you don't do the first, I'll now reprimand you. Sit down please.

A Jonathan Edwards scholar once shared with me how Edwards' early sermons were meticulously written out, while his latter ones were less so. From that change he deduced that it had nothing to do with laziness or a switch in methodology

---

7. Mary Oliver, "Logos," in *Why I Wake Early* (Boston: Beacon Press, 2004), 40.

(i.e., that he became a preach-without-notes preacher), but *rather* because after decades of preaching he actually knew what to say. I advise younger preachers to manuscript until they can actually trust that what they are going to say about God's Word is both accurate and edifying.

On Thursday morning, if not earlier in the week, I begin writing my sermon. I shoot for 4,000 words and usually hit 5,400 with 1,000 words falling on the editing-room floor. For me, 4,400 words amounts to a thirty-five minute sermon. I don't know the total tally of hours for each sermon, but I would guess I average about an hour a minute (thirty-five hours). If that number sounds high, it might be. Perhaps I'm exaggerating to earn your respect. Or, perhaps I have just un-earned it with that boast. Either way, I spend more time than any sane pastor with a wife and five children should. Don't pity me. Don't emulate me. Just pray for my wife.

With my filled-in homiletical outline on the left of my desk, my opened Bible on the right, and my hands on the keyboard of my laptop, I begin at the beginning—with the introduction. I was told by one of my mentors not to do this and to save the introduction for last. I'm sure that would save time and make sure the introduction always fits the exegesis, but I simply have a hard time saving the first thing for last. Trust me, I have issues. However, to my defense, by Thursday, I know all the exegesis, many of the illustrations and applications, and thus my introduction tends to fit well. I rarely have to go back and re-write it or scrap it completely. Introductions are important. They should attract your listener's attention, introduce the text's theme(s), and invite curiosity. The key to a good introduction is constant change: no two introductions should sound the same. In a typical month, for example, the first sermon might start with a personal story, the second with a famous line from great literature, the third with a list of probing questions, and the fourth with a one-liner about how there is no need for an introduction when Jesus tells stories like this (!) ... and off we jump right into the Parable of the Prodigal Son.

My sermon outline also intentionally provides variety. One week it might be structured based on the exegetical structure of the text, the next on the key applications: e.g., two lessons on the four soils of the Parable of the Sower. The preacher should be like a good baseball pitcher. While you don't want to throw your congregation curveballs, you certainly don't want to throw them your 95 mph fastball each and every week. Don't be so predictable.

Speaking of illustrations (I hope that baseball one worked on my mostly male readers), I limit my illustrations to between zero and two per sermon. I won't defend my school of thought other than to say I find observations and applications of the Bible text so utterly interesting that sometimes leaving the text for some extra-biblical illustration irks me. Why pour milk on top of your filet? Hey, that's a pretty good illustration (!) and it is also a good illustration of many of the illustrations I use—witty one-line word-pictures. Jesus liked that stuff too.

Exegesis, outline, applications, and illustrations are all part of the art form. We have to be good at all of them for the sermon to sing on Sunday. If you have no skills at exegesis, that's okay, there are other jobs out there. Check out Monster.com today. Exegesis is foundational. If you don't know how to properly handle the Word, get out of the pulpit until you do. Attend some Charles Simeon Trust workshops. Read *How to Read the Bible for All It's Worth.*[8] Study for three years under Greg Beale.

Most preachers I know, however, don't struggle with the exegesis as much as they do with the outline, applications, and illustrations. Or more broadly, they struggle with making the sermon manuscript good. I do have some advice here. You need to create an environment that promotes good writing. Good runners come from Kenya because they come from a culture of long-distance running. They run to get food for the family. They run to get water from the well. (I believe the high altitudes help too.) Great basketball players come from inner-city playgrounds because that is the place where speed, strength, and skills are formed on an hourly basis. Ways to hone your sermon-writing skills are by reading about and listening to good preaching. But

---

8. Besides Gordon D. Fee and Douglas Stuart, *How to Read the Bible for All Its Worth,* 3rd ed. (Grand Rapids: Zondervan, 2003), see Dan McCartney and Charles Clayton, *Let the Reader Understand: A Guide to Interpreting and Applying the Bible,* 2nd ed. (Phillipsburg, NJ: P&R, 2002) and Graeme Goldsworthy, *Gospel-Centered Hermeneutics: Foundations and Principles of Evangelical Biblical Interpretation* (Downers Grove, IL: InterVarsity, 2010).

there is more to it than that. You must surround yourself with other skilled players. I digest books on writing and rhetoric as part of my regular diet. I also read good writers, Christian and non-Christian, classics and contemporary. If you are writing a sermon each week, I find it helps to actually know how to write (insert laughter). Read great literature and listen to skilled orators not merely to gain information but also to shape the structure, cadence, and vocabulary of your own sermons.

In Conclusion

After the first sermon I preached at the first church I served as an associate pastor, a seminary-trained congregant came up to me to compliment me on the body of the sermon and to encourage me to work on my conclusion. He was right. That conclusion bombed. And I wish I could say now, fourteen years later, that my conclusions are as golden as the beloved's arms in Solomon's Song. Alas, they remain my Achilles' heel. Thus, I only have four words of advice. First, read someone else on how to give powerful, tear-jerking conclusions. Second, a simple summary of the sermon's points, or a brief story that summarizes those same points or at least the last one, seems to work well enough. Third, never introduce your conclusion with the phrase, "In conclusion." Fourth, if all else fails, pause abruptly, lower your head, and end with an unrehearsed long, earnest prayer.

Shall we pray?

18 A Sovereign, Scriptural Plan
(Matthew 26:47-56)

DOUGLAS SEAN O'DONNELL

Have you ever received an encouraging note from a friend that is so uplifting that it's humbling? I received one this past October for pastor's appreciation month. Below is a portion of it:

> My heart really *overflows* with appreciation when I think of you. In your vision casting for New Covenant Church ... my love for the church was rekindled. In your consistent pointing to Jesus and marveling at Him in each sermon, my apathetic thought that "my best years with the Lord were behind me" has been drowned by ever increasing love for my Lord! When I think back to the hunger in my soul during college to hear more about Jesus in church, and then I think about how I have been fed on three years of Christ-exalting preaching under your pulpit – I AM THANKFUL!

> I come on Sundays filled with anticipation for understanding the Word better and loving Jesus more. I am grateful for how well you know the passage you preach and the people you are preaching to! You anticipate our questions and confusions, and trace out how we can apply it. I am grateful for the clarity and beauty you preach with—no jargon, no tactics, no posturing. You hold out the Word to us in a way that unveils its truth and beauty and power. I always feel a sinking feeling inside me when I realize you are wrapping up. I am never ready for you to end.

I thank God for calling and equipping you—and for building us up through you![1]

What is the purpose of a Sunday morning sermon? My philosophy is simple. It is to *declare the excellencies of Jesus Christ*. The language is borrowed from the apostle Peter. In 1 Peter 2:9, the Spirit-inspired apostle writes to the church, "But you are a chosen race, a royal priesthood, a holy nation, a people for his own possession, that you may proclaim the excellencies of him who called you out of darkness into his marvelous light."

Throughout the Gospel of Matthew Jesus is seen as a heroic figure. As the tragedy of Golgotha, however, comes into better focus in Gethsemane, we see Jesus as both the hero and the victim, or more accurately phrased: the hero by becoming the victim. In what Dorothy Sayers called "the greatest drama ever staged,"[2] we see a hero unlike any hero and yet so likeable. He is so fascinating, captivating, and even alluring. He is someone I find easy to marvel at in each sermon.

I invite you to join me in my marveling at Him. For that's what Matthew (again and as always) wants us to do. In this text he highlights the light of Jesus Christ by contrasting Him with the darkness of old and new Israel. By "old Israel" I mean the religious rulers ("the chief priests and elders of the people" mentioned in verse 47 and "the high priest" referenced via his servant in verse 51) and the crowd, those "with swords and clubs" who come to arrest Jesus. By "new Israel" I mean the church, embryonic in the Twelve, and thus including "all the disciples" mentioned in verse 56 as well as Peter and Judas singled out in verses 51 and 48-49 respectfully (or not so respectfully). There are six groups/characters in this drama—(1) the chief priest and elders, (2) the crowd, (3) Judas, (4) Peter, (5) all the disciples, and (6) Jesus—and only one looks like the "light of the world" (John 8:12; 9:5; cf. Matt. 5:14). Other than Jesus, a great darkness covers the characters. Yes, set against the black failure

---

1. This wonderful letter is from Moriah Sharp, October 30, 2011.
2. Dorothy Sayers, *Creed or Chaos?* (New York: Harcourt, Brace, and Co., 1949), 5. The hero/victim imagery is also hers.

of old Israel (the Jews) and new Israel (the church) the white light of true Israel (Jesus) shines.

Failure of Old Israel (Jews) and New Israel (Church)

Before we get to that light, let's first look at the darkness of old and new Israel. As was just noted, the character of Christ is set apart by contrasting Him with the other characters. The first contrast is that of the Jews. Representative of the whole people is the "great crowd" sent "from the chief priests and the elders *of the people*." The crowd comes out at night to arrest Jesus. Behind it all, however, is the religious establishment, the highest ranking member being the high priest. The high priest's servant is there. He is the chap who has some cosmetic surgery done to him in verse 51. He is there because his boss sent him. We learn this boss's name in verse 57. It's Caiaphas. Jesus will soon stand on trial before him, where after our Lord will talk about "the Son of Man [being] seated at the right hand of Power and coming on the clouds of heaven" (v. 64), Caiaphas will tear his robe, cry out "blasphemy," and call for the verdict which he gets: "They answered, 'He deserves death'" (vv. 65-66).

Jesus "came to his own, and his own people did not receive him" (John 1:11). That is the dark reality we see in our text and the next and the next and the next. It is the crowd, with the prodding of their leaders, that will cry out "Crucify, crucify!" And here it is the crowd with their swords and clubs—expecting a fight from the temple table turner?—who are there to do the will of the cowardly clergy. One wonders what happened to the crowd. The people were as pro-Jesus as we are all pro-life. What turned their vote in the opposite direction? Last time I looked in Matthew "the crowd" was "astonished at his teaching" (22:33) and spreading "their cloaks on the road" when Jesus rode into town (21:8). Now they are armed "with swords and clubs" treating Him like he is an insurrectionist or terrorist. It makes no sense to Jesus: "Have you come out as against a robber, with swords and clubs to capture me? Day after day I sat in the temple teaching [unarmed in broad daylight in a sedentary position for days], and you did not seize me" (v. 55). It should make no sense to us. Sin so often is senseless.

Old Israel rejects their Messiah. But so does new Israel—the twelve apostles. Verse 56 ends the scene with this dark drapery pulled across the stage: "Then all the disciples left him and fled." Those who at "the *beginning* of the Gospel . . . 'left' (*aphienai*) their nets to follow Jesus (4:20); now near the *end* they 'leave' (*aphienai*, the same verb) to find safety."[3] Jesus is forsaken by His fleeing followers. "Like the scapegoat on the Day of Atonement, Jesus will have to go to His destiny alone."[4] The solitude of Jesus in Gethsemane somehow gets more solitary.

The Lost Sheep

But before all the sheep scatter, Matthew's camera lens closes in on two significant sheep—a lost one (Peter) and a black one (Judas). We'll leave Judas for last, for in this case the last shall be last. First, look with me at Peter. I say "Peter" based on John's version of story. I know that Matthew might be up to something important by not telling us the name of the man who "drew his sword and struck the servant of the high priest and cut off his ear" (v. 51), but it is not realistic for those who have four Gospels before them to pretend that we don't know that Peter was the swordsman and Malchus was the slave. John's record— "Then Simon Peter, having a sword, drew it and struck the high priest's servant and cut off his right ear. (The servant's name was Malchus)" (John 18:10)—makes that difficult to do! Now, Luke adds that Jesus healed the man's ear (Luke 22:51). I'll leave that detail alone. We'll leave the ear on the ground as Matthew does. No need to borrow all our information from other Gospels.

So Peter was the swordsman. Okay then, first things first: What was Peter doing with a sword in the first place? It is "unexpected and unexplained."[5] Perhaps it was for self-defense.[6] Perhaps it

---

3.   Frederick Dale Bruner, *The Churchbook: Matthew 13–28*, 2nd and rev. ed. (Grand Rapids: Eerdmans, 2004), 677. Bruner cites Raymond E. Brown, *The Death of the Messiah: From Gethsemane to the Grave; A Commentary on the Passion Narratives in the Four Gospels*, 2 vols. (New York: Doubleday, 1994), 1:287.

4.   Grant R. Osborne, *Matthew*, Exegetical Commentary on the New Testament (Grand Rapids: Zondervan, 2010), 987.

5.   W. D. Davies and Dale C. Allison Jr., *A Critical and Exegetical Commentary on the Gospel according to Saint Matthew*, International Critical Commentary, 3 vols. (Edinburgh: T&T Clark, 1988–1997), 3:511.

6.   Raymond E. Brown, *The Death of the Messiah*, 1:268–9.

was normal (cf. Luke 22:36-38): the rough and tumble fishermen of Galilee were always packing heat. Who knows? I don't. I also don't know why—viewing the odds—Peter would have raised his sword in the first place. Did he really expect to win the battle? Perhaps he was simply keeping his word, "Even if I must die with you, I will not deny you!" (Matt. 26:35). Or, perhaps he thought Jesus would be forced—like Jesus was when Peter began to sink in sink the water—to lend a supernatural hand.

Now before we lower Jesus's hammer on Peter's sword, let's at least note that Peter was one brave soldier. We are not told that Andrew or Thomas or Bartholomew drew their weapons, or that Philip or Matthew or Thaddaeus tried to shield Jesus. What were they all doing? Shaking in their boots? Lacing up their running shoes? I like to imagine the sons of thunder (James and John) saying, "Lord, shall we strike with the sword?" (Luke 22:49) ten seconds before they were hiding behind the biggest olive tree. In Matthew, Peter alone was courageous. He was always the most courageous. He was the only one to get out of the boat to walk on water. He was the only one to boldly confess Jesus as the Christ. And he was the only one to enter into the courtyard of Caiaphas' house. That took courage! The Caiaphas' courtyard bit especially took courage, for don't you think Malchus might be there? He works there. And don't you think Malchus might like a chance to go toe to toe with Peter without Jesus around to stop the fight?

Peter's courage aside, Jesus isn't so pleased with courageous Cephas. Our Lord's last pre-Easter teaching in Matthew is reserved for Peter, and it is not a pat on the back but a sword to the heart (cf. Rev. 2:12, 16). It's a sharp rebuke:

> Then Jesus said to him, "Put your sword back into its place. For all who take the sword will perish by the sword. Do you think that I cannot appeal to my Father, and he will at once send me more than twelve legions of angels?" (vv. 52-53)

Matthew vaguely describes the swordsman as "one of those who were *with Jesus*" (v. 51), but Jesus is saying that the one who is really *with me* is not for this. Jesus' sword has two edges. First, Peter either underestimates or seeks to misappropriate Jesus' power, for our Lord says to him, "Do you think that I cannot appeal to my Father, and he will at once send me more than twelve legions of angels?" (v. 53). Does Jesus believe in angels? Oh yes. Does Jesus believe in His own guardian angel? Oh no. Rather, He believes in His own guardian *angels*! In the first century, the Roman army had about twenty-five legions. A legion was comprised of 5,600 soldiers.[7] Jesus claimed that He had immediate access ("at once") to "more than twelve legions of angels" (v. 53). That is an enormous angelic army!

And when you think of angels don't think of the cute, cubby, Precious Moment's version. Rather, think about the angel who was sent to lead the Israelites out of Egypt (Num. 20:16), and the angel who helped blot out "the Amorites and the Hittites and the Perizzites and the Canaanites, the Hivites and the Jebusites" (Exod. 23:23), and the angel who "struck down 185,000 in the camp of the Assyrians" (2 Kings 19:35), and the angel who protected Shadrach, Meshach, and Abednego in the fiery furnace (Dan. 3:28), and the angel who saved Daniel by shutting "the lions' mouths" (Dan. 6:22), and the angel who "seized the dragon, that ancient serpent, who is the devil and Satan, and bound him for a thousand years, and threw him into the pit, and shut it and sealed it over him ..." (Rev. 20:1-3). Those are just six angels in Jesus' arsenal. Think what 70,000—72,000 angels like that might do to the mob of mere mortals here! Oh, Jesus has the power. He makes that quite clear. Who needs Peter's sword when you have the angels from the Lord, or, to paraphrase Jerome, "Who needs defense from twelve apostles on earth when one has twelve legions of angels in heaven?"[8]

First, Peter underestimates Jesus's power, or at the very least he misunderstands the timing of that power. Second, Peter still (!) misunderstands the mission and thus the means of the mission, for our Lord says to him, "Put your sword back into its place. For all who take the sword will perish by the sword" (v. 52). If you want to know what Jesus thinks about Christians bombing abortion clinics or crusading against the Muslims, wonder no more. Perhaps there is even something symbolic about the servant's *ear*

---

7. Ulrich Luz, *Matthew 21–28*, Hermeneia (Minneapolis: Fortress, 2005), 4:420. Other commentators understand a legion to be comprised of 6,000 men.

8. St. Jerome, *Commentary on Matthew*, Fathers of the Church, vol. 117, trans. Thomas P. Scheck (Washington DC: Catholic University of America, 2008), 304.

being cut off,[9] for where Christians have used violence to promote (or protect?) Christianity those regions of the world are somehow least receptive to the gospel. Having no ears, they cannot hear!

So here it is as if Jesus says, "Listen Peter, I don't care if the servant of the high priest in Jerusalem uses a sword to do his master's will. The servants of this high priest in heaven will not use such means." It is not that Jesus is merely advocating again His own law of nonresistance—"do not resist the one who is evil" (Matt. 5:39). That is an under-reading of the text. And it is not that Jesus is advocating pacifism. That is an over-reading of the text. Jesus is pro-government—"render to Caesar the things that are Caesar's" (22:21)—and one of the things that is Caesar's is the wielding of the sword for the promotion of peace and justice, for the punishment of wrong doing, and for the prevention of riots, lootings, and anarchy. Read Romans 13:1-7 (cf. 1 Pet. 2:13-17). Note also here in Matthew that Jesus doesn't say, "What's with the sword? Throw that weapon away! Christians aren't part of the NRA (National Rifle Association)!" No, instead, he tells Peter to put his "sword back into its place" (v. 52). There is a place for the sword. That place is self-defense. That place is just war. That place is in the hands of a legitimate and properly functioning government with its legitimate and properly functioning armed forces and police force.

Jesus' mission is at the center of His rebuke. His mission is the cross. Peter, stop resisting the cross of Christ. Put down your sword. Perhaps Peter is not personally named by Matthew because the evangelist wants all disciples of Jesus—then and now and forever—to heed Jesus' warning. If the message is the cross, the means ought never to be the sword. *Sword* and *swords* are used six times in our text, but Jesus desires that His church use it zero times. The sword is never to be used in propagating the gospel. Never. A violent church is a dead church. A cutting-off-the-ears church is a stabbed-in-the-heart church.

The Black Sheep

Finally, we come to Judas. I wish we could color this page black for effect. For Judas, you see and you already know, is one black

---

9.   Bruner, *The Churchbook*, 671.

sheep. But he is a cool cat too. He somehow got a hearing with the top dogs of the day, and then actually got them to give him some cash for one kiss. Now, it's the kiss itself which makes Judas' pitch-black heart somehow blacker. Look with me again at verses 47-50, and tremble before this darkness:

> While he [Jesus] was still speaking, Judas came, one of the twelve, and with him a great crowd with swords and clubs, from the chief priests and the elders of the people. Now the betrayer had given them a sign, saying, "The one I will kiss is the man; seize him." And he came up to Jesus at once and said, "Greetings, Rabbi!" And he kissed him. Jesus said to him, "Friend, do what you came to do." Then they came up and laid hands on Jesus and seized him.

Notice that Judas is called "one of the twelve" in verse 47 and yet "the betrayer" in verse 48. Those two titles are there to heighten the irony and showcase the diabolic nature of his crime. We are to say with our arms raised in shock and protest, "One of the twelve would betray him?"

Next notice what Judas says and does to Jesus. He *says*, "Greetings, Rabbi" (v. 49). Why not point to Jesus from a safe distance and whisper to the guard next to him, "Yeah, that's the guy"? But to come face to face with Jesus and then say to him, "Greetings, Rabbi" (v. 49) which can also be translated, "Hello there, Rabbi!" or worse, "Rejoice, Rabbi" or even "Shalom, Rabbi,"[10] while two seconds before you have said to the crowd, "The one I kiss is the man; grab him!" (v. 48, Bruner's translation)[11] is just plain wicked. The "rabbi" bit is bad enough. Jesus is *not* his teacher anymore. Whatever Judas learned from Jesus—about money, honesty, etc.—he has unlearned.[12]

If the false greeting is not enough, what Judas *does* to Jesus is doubly wicked. "Judas twists a greeting of friendship ... into

---

10. See ibid., 669.

11. ibid., 668.

12. As Davies and Allison Jr. note: Not only is Jesus "forsaken and left alone, but his teaching seems without effect: betrayal, violence, and cowardice characterize those who have paid him most heed". *A Critical and Exegetical Commentary on the Gospel according to Saint Matthew*, 3:517.

a death sign."[13] He gives Jesus a kiss.[14] Was it a kiss on the forehead, like a mother would give a sick child? Was it a kiss on the cheek like men in many parts of the world then and today give as a sign of comradeship, peace, wellbeing, even safety? Or was it kiss on the lips, also a traditional sign of friendship, but certainly a more intimate one? In Giotto's famous fresco of the scene, Judas kisses Jesus on the lips with his arms around Jesus' shoulders. It's a very intimate pose. In that painting, circling Jesus and Judas, there is a violent battle brewing. The artist depicts all this motion and commotion. Meanwhile, at the center, there is this still-life. Giotto has somehow painted a pause in the action for us to see Judas' affectionate evil—his unholy kiss of death.[15]

In Luke's version, after Judas kisses Jesus, Jesus says, "Judas, would you betray the Son of Man with a kiss?" (Luke 22:48). There is a sense of surprise in His voice. And there should be a sense of surprise also in our eyes. A kiss, Judas? Really? How insincere! What wickedness, "inner decadence,"[16] and "false friendship."[17] Hypocrite of hypocrites! It may have been dark, and Judas somehow needed to signal to the armed crowd the marked man, but this (a kiss?) … this is the darkest darkness!

But then there is Jesus. What does Jesus say to all this? It is the shortest speech He will give: "Friend, do what you came to do" (v. 50). By calling him "friend" is Jesus mocking him? He might be.[18] Jesus is not opposed to egging on His enemies. But here,

---

13. Donald Senior, *The Passion of Jesus in the Gospel of Matthew* (Collegeville, MN: Liturgical Press, 1985), 84.

14. This was a kiss like Joab's kiss of Amasa, where 2 Samuel 20:9-10 tells us, "And Joab said to Amasa, 'Is it well with you, my brother?' And Joab took Amasa by the beard with his right hand to kiss him. But Amasa did not observe the sword that was in Joab's hand. So Joab struck him with it in the stomach and spilled his entrails to the ground without striking a second blow, and he died."

15. The commentary is mine. The painting is found in Luz, *Matthew 21–28*, 4:415 (figure 28).

16. Bruner, *The Churchbook*, 668-9.

17. Origen, "Commentary on Matthew 101," quoted in *Matthew 14–28*, ed. Manlio Simonetti, Ancient Christian Commentary on Scripture, NT Ib (Downers Grove, IL: InterVarsity, 2001), 261.

18. "Matthew has already used it [the word "friend"] in 20:13 and 22:12, in the first text as a distancing, condescending address, in the second with a threatening undertone". Luz, *Matthew 21–28*, 3:418.

I don't think that is the case. Rather, I think the word "friend" is sincere and sad, as in the sense, "Do you really want to go through with this after all we have been through together?"[19] Jesus still loves this "one of the twelve" He hand-picked. Jesus must and does love His enemy. Does He wish that He, like the father of the prodigal son, might embrace Judas with the kiss of forgiveness, reconciliation, love? Yes. But no, Judas' kiss lingers on our Lord's lips reminding Him of all the betrayals and infidelities He has come to give His life for, even our betrayals and infidelities.

We All Like Sheep

Total depravity is what is depicted here. I have said before that the Gospels—as a genre—don't define or explain a doctrine, they show it to us. For example, in Matthew's Gospel, *faith* looks like the Roman centurion coming to Jesus, believing that Jesus can cure his servant from a distance and with a word. What then does the doctrine of *total depravity* look like? Or, less Calvinistic but no less Pauline: What does Paul's indictment—"None is righteous, no, not one ... for all have sinned and fall short of the glory of God" (Rom. 3:10, 23)—look like? It looks like our text. Whether we call it "total depravity" or "total undependability,"[20] what is clearly illustrated in our text is sheep after sheep going astray while the Lamb of God is led away to the slaughter (Isa. 53:6-7). God is about to place the "iniquity of us all ... on him" (Isa. 53:6b). *All* have gone astray ... *all* our sin on Him. Thank you, Jesus!

From the trial scenes to the crucifixion itself, don't miss that everybody (but Jesus!) sins and falls short of the glory of God—Jews, Gentiles, and even inner-circle disciples.[21] There

---

19. N. T. Wright, *Matthew for Everyone*, 2 vols. (Louisville: Westminster John Knox, 2002), 2:164. The first half of the sentence is Wright's, the second half is mine.

20. Bruner, *The Churchbook*, 665.

21. "For the crucifixion to have taken place, the cooperation of three simultaneous forces was needed ... the treachery of Judas, who was a Christian; the hatred of Annas, who was a Jew; and the indifference of Pilate, who was a Gentile." Dominic M. Crossan, "Anti-Semitism and the Gospel," *Theological Studies* 26 (1965): 189, quoted in Bruner, *The Churchbook*, 665-66. The description of Judas as a "Christian" obviously belongs in quotation marks. His discipleship proved to be a sham.

are the "big and little disciples (Peter and Judas), big and little Israel (Sanhedrin and people), and big and little Rome (Pilate and soldiers)" and at the cross itself again Gentile and Jew (the disciples still hiding) stroll by to shake their heads at Jesus, the colossal failure of a Christ.[22] Ah, but then as it is now, "against this awful backdrop of infidelity, Jesus' fidelity looms high and lonely, and that is the point: amid all human failure, there is one who is *totally dependable*."[23]

Fulfillment by True Israel (Jesus)

The portrait Matthew has painted for us is that of darkness and light. We have looked into the darkness: at the picture of the failure of old Israel (the Jews) and new Israel (the church). Next we look into the light: at the picture of the fulfillment of true Israel (Jesus).

Each week I'm indebted to Bible commentators. Studying the Bible on my own has much benefit. Studying the Bible in community, however, has a far greater benefit. Reading alongside and interacting with commentators is the ultimate Bible study. I attend it every week. This week, I'm especially grateful to William Barclay. Barclay's two points on this passage will be my two subpoints for the second half of this sermon. Thank you, William. The two points are as follows: (1) Jesus's death was *by His own choice.* (2) Jesus chose to die because He knew that it was *the purpose of God.*[24]

That second point hits on the fulfillment of Scripture theme, which is the more obvious theme. The first point, however, hits on this less obvious but no less important theme of Jesus's authority throughout His betrayal. Let us see this first point first.

By His Own Choice

To find this theme of Jesus's authority, it is helpful to read through the whole passage again, with the question in mind, "Who's in charge?" The answer that comes to the surface again

---

22. Bruner, *The Churchbook*, 666. Bruner summaries: "One of the purposes of the Trial Stories in the Passion Narrative is to teach the sinfulness of *all* strata of the human race" (668).

23. ibid., 666.

24. William Barclay, *The Gospel of Matthew*, 2 vols. rev. ed. (Philadelphia: Westminster, 1975), 2:351.

and again is Jesus. Let me show you what I have seen and what you too should see.

Look again and more carefully this time at verse 47, "While he [Jesus] was still speaking, Judas came ...." Stop there. That's an interesting way to start a scene and phrase a sentence. Another commentator, one of my best commentator friends—Bruner not Barclay—quotes one of his best commentator friends—Gnilka—(we are all in this together) saying, "The power of Jesus' Word is pictured here: it is as though Judas was *drawn* here by the speech of Jesus."[25]

Well, I don't know if I fully agree with that observation. But I also don't fully disagree. Perhaps that's right. What is certainly right is that the power of Jesus' word is on display throughout our text. Other than a few words from Judas—only two to Jesus (v. 49)—the rest of the time it is Jesus who doles out the commands and corrections: Jesus to Judas, "Friend, do what you came to do" (v. 50); Jesus to Peter, "Put your sword back into its place" (v. 52); and Jesus to the crowd, "Have you come out as against a robber, with swords and clubs to capture me?" (v. 55a) ... shame on you. If you just look at Jesus' short speeches here and ask the question, "Who's in charge?" The answer is obvious. Jesus is in charge.

Now come again to verses 48-50, and see three signs of Jesus' authority demonstrated in His intentional inactivity. First, notice that Jesus didn't resist the kiss. He submitted Himself to that shameless act.[26] He could have recoiled and stepped back. But He didn't. Second, notice that Jesus didn't resist arrest. The end of verse 50 reads, "Then they [the crowd] came up and laid hands on Jesus and seized him." Throughout this Gospel only Jesus laid His hands on others ... to heal them. But here He allows the sick in soul to lay their hands on Him. Why? Well, to heal them in a far different way. Lo, He goes "into the hands of sinners" (cf. 17:22; 26:45) to open wide His hands for the salvation of sinners. Jesus has the power to fight. He couldn't make that point clearer in verse 53. With one whistle the heavenly hosts are at His disposal. But He stops the angels' surge as He stops

---

25. Gnilka, 2:417, emphasis added and quoted in Bruner, *The Churchbook*, 667.

26. Chrysostom, "The Gospel of Matthew (Homily 83.2)," quoted in *Matthew 14–28*, 260.

Peter's sword because He is here using His power and authority to freely and willingly give up His power and authority.

Jesus never needed to journey to Jerusalem for the Passover. Having come, He could have played by the religious leaders' rules. What's with "his deliberate policy of magnificent defiance"?[27] Easy on the table turning, easy on the Son of Man language, easy on the Christ claims, and easy on the riding into town like King David! Even here in Gethsemane, why not slip away into the dark or literally run for the hills when you first see an army of torches and lanterns marching up the hill? You see, on this Good Friday (it is after midnight now) Jesus has chosen to give the world its greatest good. Every step of the way to Calvary the light gets brighter and brighter and clearer and clearer: "Jesus died, not because men killed him, but because He chose to die."[28]

The Purpose of God

Jesus's death was *by His own choice*. That is our first sub-point. Our second is: Jesus chose to die because He knew that it was *the purpose of God*. Barclay writes, "He took this way [—that is, not the way of violent revolt, but the way of sacrificial love—] because it was the very thing that had been foretold by the prophets."[29] In verses 52-54, Jesus said:

> Put your sword back into its place. For all who take the sword will perish by the sword. Do you think that I cannot appeal to my Father, and he will at once send me more than twelve legions of angels? But how then should the Scriptures be fulfilled, that it must be so?

Jesus reiterates that point of purpose in verses 55-56:

> At that hour Jesus said to the crowds, "Have you come out as against a robber, with swords and clubs to capture me? Day after day I sat in the temple teaching, and you did not seize me. But all this has taken place that the Scriptures of the prophets might be fulfilled."

---

27. William Barclay, *The Gospel of Matthew*, 2:351.

28. ibid.

29. ibid.

As we come now to the end of Matthew's Gospel we are reminded of how it began. In chapters 1–4, we heard that familiar phrase, "this took place to fulfill what the Lord had spoken by the prophet ...." There Matthew tells us of the fulfillments; here Jesus does. There from Jesus's birth (1:21) to His baptism (3:15) the Scriptures cited are specific; here there is this broadening inclusiveness. It's as if Jesus says, "Take all that the prophets wrote—convergence all their sayings together—and you've got me and my passion narrative."[30] What Jesus said in 5:17—"Do not think that I have come to abolish the Law or the Prophets; I have not come to abolish them but to fulfill them"—he is now acting out. What Paul would write later about Jesus, Jesus would have applauded: that "all the promises of God find their Yes in him" (2 Cor. 1:20a). The Son of Man of Daniel (Dan. 7:13-14)? Yes. The New Covenant of Jeremiah (Jer. 31:31)? Yes. The Suffering Servant of Isaiah (Isa. 52:13–53:12)? Yes. The forsaken and mocked king of Psalm 22? Yes.

Jesus resolves to go to the cross because He knows it is the will of God. He knows it is the will of God because He knows His Bible. And His Bible speaks of Him—the Messiah—and His sufferings as the climax of the script.[31]

That's a Lot of Information

At a staff meeting, the pastoral staff was discussing the length of sermons related to the average attention-span. (We determined that we are all very proud of our congregation.) One of my colleagues asked me if I ever had someone tell me that my sermons were too long. I said, "Yes, I have." At the first church I pastored full-time, after a forty-minute sermon, I had a slick businessman tell me, "If you can't say it in twenty-minutes, then you don't know what you're selling." Or, it was something to that effect. I also had an older gentleman sometimes come up to me afterwards, with a bewildered look on his face and say, "Thank you, Pastor, for that sermon." Then he would pause and give his kind rebuke, "That ... was a lot of information."

---

30. On Matthew's "fulfillment formula" and its relation to the prophets, see Senior, *The Passion of Jesus in the Gospel of Matthew*, 88 n. 61.

31. "Jesus believed in a special form of the Bible—a crucio-christocentric Bible," or "passio-christocentric, a Suffering-Christ-Centered Bible". Bruner, *The Churchbook*, 674-5.

This sermon will end up being about forty minutes and there has been a lot of information. What shall we do with all this information? Let's marvel at Jesus—that's always a good application. Let's love Jesus more—that's always another good application. But the one application I want you to leave with today has to do with seeing the story of Scripture unfold in the person of Jesus. Too often we remove the story from the Bible and collapse "the gospel ... into the abstract, de-storified points in the Plan of Salvation."[32] God is holy. You are a sinner. God loved you so much He sent Jesus. Believe. That's true, but that's not how the Gospels present the gospel, or how Jesus shares it. Jesus roots His whole ministry in the whole story of Israel—its prophets, priests, and kings, its saints and sinners and Scriptures. As Scot McKnight notes, "The Story of Jesus Christ, then, isn't a story that came out of nowhere like the Book of Mormon, and it isn't a timeless set of ideas, as with Plato's philosophical writings. The story of Jesus Christ is locked into one people, one history, and one Scripture: it makes sense only as it follows a complete Story of Israel."[33]

So, can we share the gospel without sharing the story of Scripture? How would Jesus answer that question? I think He would say, "No." How would Paul? "No," likewise. In what is the clearest definition of the gospel in the New Testament (cf. Rom. 1:1-5),[34] he writes:

> Now I would remind you, brothers, of the gospel I preached to you, which you received, in which you stand, and by which you are being saved, if you hold fast to the word I preached to you – unless you believed in vain. For I delivered to you as of first importance what I also received: that Christ died for our sins in accordance with the Scriptures, that he was buried, that he was

---

32. Scot McKnight, *The King Jesus Gospel: The Original Good News Revisited* (Grand Rapids: Zondervan, 2011), 51.

33. ibid., 50.

34. See McKnight's excellent summary of Roman 1:1-5 (ibid., 60). cf. John Chapman, *Know and Tell the Gospel: Help for the Reluctant Evangelist* (London: St. Matthias, 1981), 18-28; John Stott, *Romans: God's Good News for the World* (Downers Grove, IL: InterVarsity, 1994), 46-54.

raised on the third day in accordance with the Scriptures, and that he appeared to Cephas, then to the twelve (1 Cor. 15:1-5).[35]

To Paul, as it was to Jesus, the question, "How important is our knowledge of the Old Testament?" is as important a question as, "How important is evangelism?" Without Jesus there is no gospel. Without the Old Testament there is no gospel. Without Jesus fulfilling the Old Testament there is no gospel. What good news do we herald? What light do we bring to the dark world? That Jesus died for our sins, rose again from the dead to grant us eternal life, and will come again in power to make everything right ... *just like the Hebrew Bible said.* Our gospel is "the saving Story of Israel ... lived out by [true Israel] Jesus, who lived, died, was buried, and was exalted to God's right hand," and who will soon come in glory to establish His forever kingdom.[36] So, in light of that Light: repent, believe, be baptized and receive the forgiveness of sins, the Holy Spirit, and life everlasting. That is our application for today. That is our application for everyday. Because that is the good news of Jesus Christ.

I don't know if I preach with clarity and beauty, as one person once claimed not so long ago. If so, I'll let God get all the glory for the gift. What I do know is that I try, Sunday after Sunday, to gospel the Gospel of Matthew, knowing that the more people understand the full story the more likely they are to marvel, as I do, at Jesus.

---

35. Cf. these words from the Nicene Creed: "Who, for us men and for our salvation, came down from heaven, and was incarnate by the Holy Spirit of the virgin Mary, and was made man; and was crucified also for us under Pontius Pilate; He suffered and was buried; and the third day He rose again, *according to the Scriptures. . .*" as well as those earlier (AD 190) from Irenaeus: "this faith: in one God . . . in one Christ Jesus . . . and in the Holy Spirit, *who made known through the prophets the plan of salvation,* and the coming, and the birth from a virgin, and the passion, and the resurrection from the dead, and the bodily ascension into heaven of the beloved Christ Jesus, our Lord, and his future appearing from heaven in the glory of the Father to sum up all things and to raise anew all flesh of the whole human race". *Against Heresies*, 1.10.1, emphasis mine, quoted in McKnight, *The King Jesus Gospel*, 66.

36. Ibid., 160.

19   How I Prepare

Richard D. Phillips

The subject of sermon preparation is of great interest to young pastors and theological students since their calling involves the regular preparation of sermons. Virtually every week I prepare at least one sermon and often two. Needless to say, I follow a system designed to enable me to do my best on a consistent basis. Moreover, there is a spirituality to sermon preparation that is just as essential as during sermon delivery. Sermon preparation is an act of worship, spiritually enriching the preacher and enabling him to serve Christ and His people.

I organize my sermon preparation into four steps. Although I did not derive my approach from his writing, I find that it corresponds closely with what Alistair Begg has outlined in his excellent booklet, *Preaching for God's Glory*.[1] Begg breaks down sermon preparation in these terms: Think Yourself Empty, Read Yourself Full, Write Yourself Clear, and Pray Yourself Hot. Since I cannot improve on that language, and since I often think of it during my own preparation, let me explain how this approach informs my sermon preparation.

Think Yourself Empty
This step refers to the preacher's personal study of and meditation on the preaching text. Usually on Monday (which

---

1.   Alistair Begg, *Preaching for God's Glory* (Wheaton, IL: Crossway, 2011).

is ostensibly my day off), but not later than Tuesday, I study the text in order to understand what it says and how it says it. Since my Greek is relatively serviceable, if it is a New Testament text I will study it carefully in the original language, using what helps I require for more difficult passages. I prefer to study and meditate on the original text so that I have the grammar and syntax clearly before me. If the text is in Hebrew, especially if it is a longer passage, I will probably only translate key verses, although I will certainly look through the whole passage in the original language. I consider the use of the Greek and Hebrew to be extremely valuable, since much may be lost in even our good translations.

Study of the text takes place in an attitude of prayer. "Lord, show me the message. Unfold the logic of this text. Let me grasp the key thought. Enable me, Lord, to understand this passage so that I may teach it to your people." By meditating on the text, I let it speak to me. What is being declared? What is being commanded? What is promised? What is revealed about God? About man? About life and salvation? Of particular importance for me is to grasp the overriding purpose. What is the Holy Spirit saying in this passage? The preacher is to play a prophetic role in the life of the church, and this requires him to deliver sermons with a clear and compelling point. Expository preaching means to display what is there; so the first step in sermon preparation is to study what is in the text in order to understand it deeply and clearly.

In my view, this first step of study and meditation is the most vital part of sermon preparation. There is simply no substitute for the preacher wrestling with the text (or the text with him!) so that he has a clear sense of the point, the teaching, and the organization of the passage. This study should yield a working outline of the sermon. This outline will normally have an introduction, the main points, the subordinate points, and the conclusion. It occasionally happens that I do not feel confident about the introduction or conclusion at this point, in which case I will wait for my reading to help me decide. If I think that I have a good introduction or conclusion at this point, I will often write this out right away, knowing that it may be subjected to severe editing later.

Read Yourself Full

I am often asked how many commentaries I read in sermon preparation. The answer is as many as I can manage. Most weeks I read more than twenty commentaries, which amounts to every competent volume that I have been able to purchase on the book. To this end, my secretary provides me with a weekly file that includes Xerox copies of all the commentaries on my text, so that I may have them available to read throughout the week. I am frequently seen reading commentary Xeroxes while my car is being fixed, while waiting between meetings, at the doctor's office, etc. As one who preaches full-time, sermon preparation study occupies a large part of my life. I often hear other preachers say that they read only four to six commentaries in sermon preparation. I cannot imagine reading so little, when I am set apart for the ministry of God's Word. I admit that my zeal for study is related to my awareness that my sermons are going to be published for other pastors to read. But even if my sermons were not going to be published, I would want to read as much as possible in preparation. As Begg's label suggests, I want to fill myself up with the writings of wise, godly, and insightful scholars on the text that I am to preach.

Notice that the commentary reading takes place after study and meditation have already yielded a detailed sermon outline. Occasionally, this reading will lead to revisions in my outline, but the commentaries do not as a rule provide me with my sermon. Rather, they help me think through the points that I am preaching. I would be perfectly able to preach my sermon without the commentaries, based on my sermon outline, and on many occasions I have needed to do this. But to offer my best in preaching God's Word week-to-week, I need to study so as to gain insights into the text, into the doctrines proclaimed, into applications that should be made to various hearers, and to its connection with the person and work of Christ.

My approach to commentary study involves a careful notation system. Starting with my sermon outline, points 1, 2, and 3, for instance, each of which has subpoints a, b, and c, I will mark the commentary pages that speak to these items. I keep a leather working notebook that has all my sermon preparations in them. Page after page has the sermon outline, with notations made after each point or subpoint as to the location of valuable comments found in the books I have read. This notation system plays a helpful role in my sermon writing.

Inevitably, there will be a handful of commentaries that are most consistently useful in preaching a certain book. Others, especially those by authors with a lower view of Scripture, will not be helpful as often. Yet, I find that even the worst commentary turns out to be useful enough at times to justify the effort in reading it. A question will be raised or an argument made that I hadn't thought of. Whether I agree with it or not, it stimulates my thinking and enables me to bring deeper insight into the text and its application.

Write Yourself Clear

The commentary-reading phase of sermon preparation usually takes two days. By now, it is Thursday or Friday, depending on my pastoral obligations during the week. The time has come to write the sermon. By this do I mean the writing of a complete manuscript? In my case, the answer is *yes*. Not only do I write a complete manuscript for the sermon, but I recommend this practice to most others. I say this for two reasons. First, very few preachers can handle the text carefully in their preaching without having carefully written out their sermon. I find that extemporaneous sermons often fail to treat the text carefully, and I suspect that one reason is that it demands a level of detail that few can attain without careful notes. Second, writing out a manuscript aids greatly in the organization of the sermon. I find this to be true especially for young preachers. A written manuscript forces each point to have a clear beginning, middle and end, along with a transition to the next point. Writing requires discipline, and sermons should be subjected to the discipline of careful organization and presentation.

Does this mean that I actually preach from the manuscript during the sermon? I find that many pastors will write out a manuscript but then reduce it to notes for the actual sermon (Martyn Lloyd-Jones purportedly did this for many years). The reason for this would seem to be in order to free the preacher from note-dependency during sermon delivery. In my case, I do bring the manuscript into the pulpit and preach from it. This is a far cry from reading a manuscript. As I will argue in the next section, the process of prayer and editing allows me to become very familiar with the manuscript so that I can preach it with little apparent dependency. I am surprised, in fact, at how often people marvel that I can preach so carefully without any notes at all, showing that they are not even aware that I have a manuscript before me. While there are some preachers whose particular gifts run in the direction of extemporaneous preaching, my opinion is that young preachers especially can improve the clarity and depth of their preaching by preparing and preaching from a sermon manuscript. Having a manuscript does not inhibit me from departing from it as led by the Spirit during sermon delivery, but it does inhibit me from having a disorganized or unclear sermon.

When I start to write my sermon, I usually have the introduction already written out. This probably occurred at some point in steps one or two. Having before me my sermon outline, I now write it out working through the outline starting with point one. By now I have read myself full, so I have much to say about each point. I also have notations from my reading that I now go back to for reference. There may be an extremely helpful quotation that will allow me to express my point in a particularly helpful way. (This, by the way, is the point of quotations—particularly apt ways of expressing the point that cannot be improved upon.) When I have made my last point, I transition to the conclusion in order to finish the text. I may or may not write the sermon in a single setting, and it is not particularly important if I do or not.

At this point it may be helpful to answer some particular questions.

What is the proper role of illustrations? In my view, illustrations should be used either to make the teaching more clear or to drive home the application. In a great deal of preaching today, the illustration "carries the freight" of the sermon. This should not be the case. The point of the sermon is to deliver the Word of God—proclaiming, explaining, and applying it—not to tell clever and heart-warming stories. An illustration-laden sermon is likely to make the preacher popular but is less likely to make his hearers godly. For this reason, I do not regard illustrations as necessary to the sermon, although they are often very helpful. Contrary to much practice today, the key to good preaching is not the ability to craft or find great illustrations but rather to mine the text of God's Word so as to present its riches to the church. The point of illustrations is to polish the gem of God's Word, as it were, and to present it in a way that is compelling and clear. For this reason, illustrations are usually best used in applying the passage through the experience of others or a comparison that brings home the application to the heart.

Where are good sermon illustrations to be found? Different preachers possess differing gifts when it comes to illustrations. Some are masters at seeing useful illustrations in everyday life. Others are adept at presenting their own personal experiences in a compelling way. I counsel moderation in the latter approach, lest your preaching be limited by your own narrow life experiences and perspective. I would argue that the best illustrations come from 1) the Bible and 2) reading. A biblical illustration is particularly useful since it teaches more of the Scriptures and helps hearers to connect one portion of the Bible to another. When I say that illustrations should come from reading, I do not mean only from commentaries, much less from sermon illustration books (which I find to be rarely useful—although I own them all!). Rather, good preachers read a great deal from a wide variety of sources and find illustrations for their preaching in them. To this end, I have a file for each sermon series that I am preaching where I put useful illustrations when I read them. If I find a good story that will make a useful sermon illustration, I ask myself, "Which passage does this fit?" Into that file the illustration goes, to be pulled out during sermon preparation that week.

How do I approach applications? In general, I try to apply each main point during the sermon as I go along. The exception to this procedure is when the exposition is more technical than normal, in which case I find it helpful to hold the applications to the end. Normally, however, I proclaim, explain, and apply each point as it comes in the sermon. It is a good practice to think of different kinds of people hearing the sermon. The place to start is by asking if there is a particular target group in the text itself. Is Jesus rebuking legalists? Then legalists must be rebuked. Is the prophet challenging the greedy rich? Then the greedy rich must be challenged. I try to keep three categories of people always in mind: believers generally; those who are downcast and discouraged by sin or by trials; and unbelievers. Christians should always gain practical instruction from the text. The downcast should always have their spirits raised. And unbelievers must always hear the message of salvation through Jesus Christ.

How do I practice Christ-centered preaching? This subject is worthy of its own chapter. Perhaps it should be first addressed in terms of what it is not. Christ-centered preaching does not mean that every sermon must be focused on the doctrine of justification. Christ-centered preaching does not forbid the application of biblical commands or reproofs. Nor does Christ-centered preaching require the sermon to conclude in a less-than-plausible attempt to connect details in the text to Jesus. Christ-centered preaching means that the context in which every text is preached is the redemptive achievement of God through the saving work of His Son. Does the text teach me about God? Then Jesus Christ is the truest revelation of that attribute. Does the text reveal the evil of sin? Then Jesus Christ is the only remedy for sin. Does the text show wisdom for life? Jesus is the sum of that wisdom. Paul said, "because of [God] you are in Christ Jesus, who became to us wisdom from God, righteousness and sanctification and redemption" (1 Cor. 1:30). So it is for every sermon: its message of wisdom, righteousness, sanctification, and redemption is a message centered on the person and work of Christ. From this perspective, the preacher finds little difficulty in ensuring that every sermon clearly proclaims salvation for sinners through faith in Jesus Christ.

Pray Yourself Hot

Hopefully my sermon manuscript has been written by Friday morning or at least Friday afternoon. This will allow me prayerfully to edit the material. I combine editing with prayer because both are essential in completing the sermon.

Editing a sermon manuscript is essential to excellent preaching. It is amazing to me how often, after years of weekly preaching, I still find gross redundancies or unclear points in the first draft of my sermon. Editing not only allows the preacher to remove grammatical and other errors, but also to review the structure of the sermon. Does an application need to be held until later in the message? Is the doctrine clearly and accurately explained? Is there an insight that can be added to deepen the teaching of the text?

In my approach, editing plays several vital functions. One has to do with the sermon length. My first draft is invariably too long and must be cut down. Since I know after many years of preaching that I will average four minutes per manuscript page, I know how much has to go. Another point is to remove dubious material. Preachers must not fall in love with their own writing but must subject their material to rigorous cutting. My own approach is this: if it even occurs to me to remove material, then I always remove it. Any real doubt as to the value of a paragraph or a couple of sentences means that there really is no doubt. In this way, like a sculptor finishing his work, each edit produces a more polished, clean, clear, and useful sermon for my congregation. I prefer to get in at least three or four edits of each sermon between the first draft and the actual preaching: one on Friday night, two on Saturday, and a final edit early on Sunday morning (or afternoon, for the evening sermon).

A third purpose of editing is to write the sermon on my mind and heart. The reason I do not appear to be note-dependent while preaching is that I have gone over the material in such detail that I merely glance at a paragraph and I know what is in it. Prayerful editing uploads the sermon into my mind so that, if I had to, I could adequately preach the sermon without my notes. Not long ago I was preaching in another church when I mishandled my notes and sent them flying into the first couple of pews. Having no choice, I plowed ahead and found that while I missed some details that I would have wanted to include, I was able to preach essentially the very sermon written on my manuscript.

Fourth, sermon-editing is a rich context for praying over the sermon. To be sure, the preacher should pray over his material apart from editing. But sermon-editing sets the message before the preacher, which he in turn sets before the Lord. The preacher should pray for his delivery and for the sermon's reception in the pews. I pray for my sermon up until the very moment that I enter the pulpit. My final prayer each week is that recommended by Charles Spurgeon: "Lord, I believe in the Holy Spirit! Send now your Spirit!"

The question is often asked me, "How long do you take in preparing your sermons?" My honest answer is that the entire week is given to sermon preparation. It should be obvious that the sermon preparation approach I have cited involves quite a few hours. But more than that, the preacher should spend his days and nights in continuous meditation on the sermon—its glorious message, the challenge of explaining it clearly and potently, and the need for effective application. This is the life of the preacher, not merely a working process that occupies a few hours. Having thought himself empty, read himself full, written himself clear, and prayed himself hot, the preacher appears not merely as a craftsman with a sermon. He stands a man with a message, passionately declaring divine truths to needy hearts, speaking from God through His Word to His people for the building of His church.

20 The Man of God and the Word of God
(1 Kings 13:1-34)

RICHARD D. PHILLIPS

The background for the story of the man of God from Judah is the rebellion launched by Jeroboam against Rehoboam, the son of Solomon who had come to the throne after his father's death. Solomon's otherwise glorious record is greatly marred by the fact that he was led into idolatry by the many foreign wives he married. In judgment for this, God raised up Jeroboam as a rival, and when Solomon died the kingdom was torn in two, with Jeroboam ruling the ten northern tribes and Rehoboam the two tribes of Judah and Benjamin in the south.

Jeroboam, however, did not serve the Lord; instead he erected golden calves for the people to worship, one set in Dan (in the far north) and another in Bethel, not far from Judah. Jeroboam's unbelieving logic is explained in 1 Kings 12:27: "If this people go up to offer sacrifices in the temple of the LORD at Jerusalem, then the heart of this people will turn again to their lord, to Rehoboam king of Judah, and they will kill me and return to Rehoboam king of Judah."

The Man of God and the Word of God

First Kings 13:1-2 tells of this man God sent to reprove the king for his idolatry: "A man of God came out of Judah by the word of the LORD to Bethel. Jeroboam was standing by the altar to make offerings. And the man cried against the altar by the word of the

LORD and said, 'O altar, altar, thus says the LORD: "Behold, a son shall be born to the house of David, Josiah by name, and he shall sacrifice on you the priests of the high places who make offerings on you, and human bones shall be burned on you.""'

That same day the man of God gave a sign: "This is the sign that the LORD has spoken: 'Behold, the altar shall be torn down, and the ashes that are on it shall be poured out'" (v. 3).

Jeroboam did not take this very well, and he signaled for the man of God to be arrested. "Seize him!" he cried, "And his hand, which he stretched out against him, dried up, so that he could not draw it back to himself" (v. 4). Verse 5 tells us that the altar was also split in two and the ashes poured out, just as the man of God had said. Here we have an excellent example of God defending his faithful servant who stands fast against the wicked. At the king's request, the man of God prayed for him and he was healed. The king then offered him a meal and a gift, but the man of God answered that he could not, "for so was it commanded me by the word of the LORD, saying, 'You shall neither eat bread nor drink water nor return by the way that you came.' So he went another way and did not return by the way that he came to Bethel" (vv. 9-10).

So far this is an interesting and edifying story, yet if we stop here we miss the real significance of this chapter. The story takes a twist when another prophet, from nearby in Bethel, sets out to meet the man of God. This new angle in the story picks up in verse 14, where the prophet from Bethel encounters the prophet from Judah:

> And he went after the man of God and found him sitting under an oak. And he said to him, "Are you the man of God who came from Judah?" And he said, "I am." Then he said to him, "Come home with me and eat bread." And he said, "I may not return with you, or go in with you, neither will I eat bread nor drink water with you in this place, for it was said to me by the word of the LORD, 'You shall neither eat bread nor drink water there, nor return by the way that you came.'" And he said to him, "I also am a prophet as you are, and an angel spoke to me by the word of the LORD, saying, 'Bring him back with you into your house that he may eat bread and drink water.'" But he lied to him (vv. 14-18).

Things have gotten complicated, as they often do. The man of God had received a revelation from God and now this man, claiming also to be a prophet, tells him that he has a new word from God given through an angel. How is he to handle this? The story concludes:

> So he went back with him and ate bread in his house and drank water. And as they sat at the table, the word of the LORD came to the prophet who had brought him back. And he cried to the man of God who came from Judah, "Thus says the LORD, 'Because you have disobeyed the word of the LORD and have not kept the command that the LORD your God commanded you, but have come back and have eaten bread and drunk water in the place of which he said to you, "Eat no bread and drink no water," your body shall not come to the tomb of your fathers'" (vv. 19-22).

Here is this poor prophet. He has served God courageously and well. He has stood up to the wicked king and waged war in the power of the Lord. He has refused to be deterred from his path, has withstood the temptation to be co-opted by the king, and has gone the way God had told him. Then, along comes this man claiming to also be a prophet and asserting a claim to divine warrant. He tells him that there is an easier way, that an angel has told him he could rest and relax. The only problem is that this contradicts the earlier revelation the man of God has received from the Lord. And for listening to this new and contradictory word, the man is in fact struck down by the Lord.

You see the point being made in this passage, namely the authority of God's Word and the great peril of disobedience. To really understand this we need to go back to the book of Deuteronomy, the book of God's covenant that served as Israel's charter as God's nation in the Promised Land. Deuteronomy greatly stresses the importance of obeying God's Word, which at that time came largely through prophets. There was a vital need, therefore, to safeguard the people against false prophets. In Deuteronomy 13, God gave them a way to test a purported prophet:

> If a prophet or a dreamer of dreams arises among you and gives you a sign or a wonder, and the sign or wonder that he tells you

> comes to pass, and if he says, "Let us go after other gods," which you have not known, "and let us serve them," you shall not listen to the words of that prophet or that dreamer of dreams. For the LORD your God is testing you, to know whether you love the LORD your God with all your heart and with all your soul (vv. 1-3).

How was a prophet to be known? First of all, the things a prophet foretold must come to pass. But even that was not enough. The prophet must not lead the people in worship of other gods. When a false prophet appeared, even one who could predict the future, God was testing the people to see if they were devoted to Him and to His Word. What this shows is the binding and authoritative character of God's prior revelation. Once God has spoken, any new word claiming to come to God must conform to that prior word, or else it must be rejected as false. In the face of a false prophet, the people were to follow and revere the Lord, and they were to do so by holding fast to the Word he had previously revealed: "Keep his commands and obey him; serve him and hold fast to him" (v. 4 NIV). We see now what the apostle Paul was getting at in Galatians 1:8-9:

> But even if we or an angel from heaven should preach to you a gospel contrary to the one we preached to you, let him be accursed. As we have said before, so now I say again: If anyone is preaching to you a gospel contrary to the one you received, let him be accursed.

This poor man of God received a purported word from the Lord that contradicted prior revelation from God. His error was in failing to test the word of a prophet as God had prescribed. His story tells us how seriously God takes our fidelity to His Word, for this man of God, so faithful in his confrontation against Jeroboam, was struck down by the Lord for his failure to hold fast God's revealed Word.

Sola Scriptura

As we think about 1 Kings 13, it is important for us to remember the Protestant Reformation and in particular to reflect upon the great Reformation principle of *sola scriptura*—Scripture alone. This passage helps us to articulate exactly what we mean by that.

Sola Scriptura does not mean that Christians should only read the Bible, or that nothing of value can be received outside the Bible. Something that strikes you if you read the Protestant Reformers is how well versed they were in the theological writings of others, both from the medieval era and the ancient church fathers, as well as of the classical philosophers, who of course were not even Christians. The Reformers were very learned and widely read men. Yet they took their stand on the principle articulated in this passage, namely that God's Word differs in precisely this, that it holds authority over all other sources. God's inspired Word in the Bible stands against and above all other sources of truth, judging and ruling over the hearts of God's people. They trembled at the thought that they might make the error of this poor man of God from Judah, that they might place the word of mere man above or beside that of God, and be rightly judged for doing so. Martin Luther said this:

> We must make a great difference between God's Word and the word of man. A man's word is a little sound, that flies into the air, and soon vanishes; but the Word of God is greater than heaven and earth, yea, greater than death and hell, for it forms part of the power of God, and endures everlastingly.[1]

In Luther's day, like today, there were many who respected the Bible while denying to its unique and ultimate authority. The Roman Catholic Church, then as now, taught that Scripture and church tradition are equal in authority, with the result that the human teachings of the church serve to interpret the teachings of Scripture. In this way, tradition and ecclesial authority were elevated above the Bible. It is especially this that *sola scriptura* denies; the Reformers steadfastly denied that any human authority stands above or beside the Scripture. John Calvin put it this way:

> There is no authority in the church of God but what is received from Him. If then we admit of a doctrine, it must not be borrowed from the authority or wisdom of men, but we must know that it came from God. This is a notable point; for God

---

1. Martin Luther: *That Doctrines of Men Are to be Rejected* quoted in James Montgomery Boice, *Foundations of the Christian Faith* (Downers Grove, IL: IVP Academic, 1986), 69.

will prove thereby whether we be His people or not. He is our King indeed, because we have no laws nor ordinances except from Him.[2]

This is a conviction that the Church in our generation needs to recover. There are always two voices calling out to us, two messages ringing in our ears—the true and the false, that of God and that of the world. If we are not, therefore, heeding the true Word of God then we are, by default, listening to other voices, to false words from worldly prophets. Our passage shows that the man of God must be a man of the Word of God, or else he will inevitably be a man of the world, with a deadly result.

There is increasing evidence that this is what is happening in many evangelical churches. Biblical preaching is down and with it is a lack of biblical literacy among God's people. When I speak of biblical preaching, I mean that preaching that has as its goal simply the proclamation and explanation and application of a portion of Scripture. When people ask me what I aim for in preaching, I answer with just this: I want them to believe and understand and apply the Bible. Surveys show, however, that this is not a widely held view, and that the result is a widespread lack of biblical knowledge. An astonishing number of evangelicals do not know the Ten Commandments, cannot give a reasonably coherent definition of the doctrine of justification, and in many cases cannot name the four Gospels. According to one recent study, you are more likely to agree that "God helps those who help themselves," and that "there is no absolute truth," if you are an evangelical than if you are not.

If the Bible is not being preached, then what is? To an alarming degree, the vacuum is being filled by the message of the world. In a recent essay, David Wells wrote, "The church is awash in strategies borrowed from psychology and business that, it is hoped, will make up for the apparent insufficiency of the Word and ensure more success in this post-modern culture."[3] What difference does

---

2.   John Calvin, *The Mystery of Godliness and Other Select Sermons* (Morgan, PA: Soli Deo Gloria Publications, 1999), 132.

3.   David F. Wells, Foreword to *Whatever Happened to the Reformation*, Gary Johnson & Fowler White, eds. (Phillipsburg, NJ: Presbyterian and Reformed, 2001), xix.

that make, you may ask? The difference is that instead of a gospel of salvation that comes from God—one that delivers us from the bondage and guilt of sin to acceptance with God and a new life by the power of His Spirit—we have substituted a therapeutic gospel in which our problem is unhappiness and insecurity and in which salvation is found in health, wealth, and happiness. Instead of the Son of God dying for us on the cross which we embrace in self-denying faith, such a gospel requires only that we gain high self-esteem and learn some skills that will help us be nice to others. Wells summarizes the shift:

> Theology becomes therapy .... The biblical interest in righteousness is replaced by a search for happiness, holiness by wholeness, truth by feeling, ethics by feeling good about one's self. The world shrinks to the range of personal circumstances; the community of faith shrinks to a circle of personal friends. The past recedes. The Church recedes. The world recedes. All that remains is the self.[4]

That is the death the church is experiencing today, the lion that will tear us limb from limb like this man of God from Judah. If we want to be saved by God, if we want to be God's people, receiving God's blessings in salvation, then it is to God's voice that we must tune our hearts, His Word alone that must become our guide once more.

The Threat of Novelty
Our passage in 1 Kings presents a particular polemic that has to do with the new against the old. The man of God received a new word that purported to be from God. His mistake was in listening to the new word without ensuring its conformity to the old word already received from God. This points out the *priority* of the Word of God. Prior revelation from God is binding and authoritative, and any new word must be judged by it, not the other way around.

But we love novelty in theology, we love a new word seemingly from the Lord, particularly when it tells us what we already want to do and believe. Perhaps this too was the man of God's

---

4.   David F. Wells, *No Place for Truth Or Whatever Happened to Evangelical Theology* (Grand Rapids: Eerdmans, 1994), 183.

weakness. Why was he so ready to believe this false prophecy? Perhaps because it was exactly what he was hoping to hear. He was hungry and tired, and here was an opportunity to let down his guard. So, too, is ours a time that embraces new words, new theologies, new perspectives. We hear this all the time now: "We need to get away from the old, puritanical, restrictive way of looking at things ... we need a new approach that fits the new way of things." All the time we hear that the new is better— "New Generation Tide" is a better detergent than the old Tide; new model cars are more desirable than the old junkers; new computers are faster than the old obsolete model that came out last month. Surely, then, new approaches to spiritual matters are better than the stuffy old gospel, the boring old-style Bible Christianity that was the rock of our fathers.

I hear one particular phrase all the time today: "We believe that God has fresh light to break forth from the Scriptures." That is almost the motto of our day. You see that phrase in magazines and as a header in academic catalogs. I suppose it is true, for the Scriptures are not done speaking to us. But people who say this seem never to mention the Deuteronomic principle of prophecy—that all new light must correspond with the old light or else it is not light at all but darkness masquerading as light, even as Satan masquerades as an angel of light.

Again, we hear all the time the famous quotation "All truth is God's truth." I suppose that too cannot be refuted. But all *claims* to truth are not God's truth. The false prophet from Bethel was not speaking God's truth, though he *claimed* to be. I find that this saying tends to be mainly used to support the validity of non-biblical sources. People say "all truth is God's truth" when they want us to buy into secular psychology or new-age practice or secular church-growth methods.

All truth may be God's truth, but let us not forget that the Bible alone is the very Word of God, the very God-breathed Scriptures that are distinctive in providing us the sure and binding revelation from God. No other source bears this credential and binds the conscience with this authority. Failure to remember this will surely have us believing claims to truth that are not truth, will have us sitting down at tables with prophets like that nice gentleman from

Bethel who speak words of death into our unsuspecting but also unfaithful ears.

People say we need new formulations of doctrine for a new age. Things are so different now, they say, from the sixteenth century and its Reformation, from the seventeenth century when great doctrinal statements like the Westminster Confession of Faith were written. But to this I reply, "What really is different?" When it comes to the great matters of faith and salvation, of God in heaven and man on earth, what really has changed in the last 2,000 years since Jesus ascended into heaven? Is man's situation before God any different? Is God less holy? Are we less sinful? Are we less in peril for the guilt of our sins? Is the challenge of godly living and godly dying really different today than 500 years ago? In the face of the complaint that ours is an outdated creed, this is our reply: "Jesus Christ is the same yesterday and today and forever" (Heb. 13:8). A.W. Tozer wrote, "One of the most popular current errors, and the one out of which springs most of the noisy, blustering religious activity in evangelical circles, is the notion that as times change the church must change with them."[5] In contrast, our wisdom is that of Jeremiah 6:16 NIV, which says, "Stand at the crossroads and look; ask for the ancient paths, ask where the good way is, and walk in it, and you will find rest for your souls."

I cannot help but observe what a contemporary figure this man of God from Judah is. If there is a better portrait of the evangelical movement today than this, I don't know it. He had been courageous in serving the Lord, just as evangelicals were courageous in opposing an unbelieving culture. He refused to be swayed by Jeroboam's threats, just as evangelicals stood boldly before the taunts of arrogant and atheistic twentieth century modernity.

Perhaps he was thinking about what a great servant he had been, in the very way evangelicals have smugly patted ourselves on the back; perhaps he was newly confident in his ability to

---

5. A.W. Tozer, *Renewed Day by Day: A Daily Devotional* (Camp Hill, PA: Christian Publications, 1980), entry for February 7. See also D. Martyn Lloyd-Jones, *Old Testament Evangelistic Sermons* (Edinburgh: Banner of Truth, 1996), xvi.

live out the "victorious Christian life." Yet when a message from one who wore the clothing of a friend came to him, even a message that flatly contradicted the Word of God he had received, he was easily overtaken and destroyed. So also is the evangelical movement today being destroyed by its willingness to hear and follow patently unbiblical messages and methods simply because they were heard on Christian radio or sold in a Christian bookstore or hawked by a man sporting a fish symbol on his bumper. Having so courageously stared modernity in the face, we are being taken in by the smoother but equally deadly postmodern attacks on the gospel.

The Sufficiency of Scripture

As we look back on the Reformation, a great movement of faith in the Word of God by the people of God, we do so in an age when the Church needs reformation once again. And if it is going to happen again, it is going to be according to the same principles and convictions as before. This episode in 1 Kings clearly sets forth the *authority* and the *priority* of God's Word. But there is one more matter about which we must be convinced, and that is the *sufficiency* of God's Word for God's work in the church.

The former senior minister of Tenth Presbyterian Church in Philadelphia, James M. Boice, made this one of his great emphases. In his last book to be published he wrote this:

> Do we believe that God has given us what we need in this book? Or do we suppose that we have to supplement the Bible with human things? Do we need sociological techniques to do evangelism, pop psychology for Christian growth, extra-biblical signs or miracles for guidance or political tools for achieving social progress and reform?

> It is possible to believe that the Bible is the inerrant Word of God, the only infallible rule of faith and practice, and yet to neglect it and effectually repudiate it just because we think that it is not sufficient for today's tasks and that other things need to be brought in to accomplish what is needed.[6]

---

6. James M. Boice, *Whatever Happened to the Gospel of Grace?* (Wheaton: Crossway, 2001), 72.

One of the places where Boice turned for support is Psalm 19, where God Himself more than commends the Bible's sufficiency in the life of His people. Written by King David, it says this:

> The law of the LORD is perfect, reviving the soul.
> The statutes of the LORD are trustworthy, making wise the simple.
> The precepts of the LORD are right, giving joy to the heart.
> The commands of the LORD are radiant, giving light to the eyes.
> The fear of the LORD is pure, enduring forever.
> The ordinances of the LORD are sure and altogether righteous.
> They are more precious than gold, than much pure gold; they are sweeter than honey, than honey from the comb.
> By them is your servant warned; in keeping them there is great reward (Ps. 19:7-11 NIV).

What else could be commended to this superlative degree? What else that can be placed in the hands of man is described as *perfect, trustworthy, right, radiant, pure*, and *sure*? And what else has such power—*reviving the soul, making wise the simple, giving joy to the heart and light to the eyes, enduring forever in righteousness*? Surely these things commend the sufficiency of God's Word and thus make biblical preaching and teaching the first priority for all who would serve Him.

Here We Stand

Sola scriptura is known as the formal principle of the Reformation. It is this conviction that gives form to all else, that leads us to the Bible alone as the arbiter of truth. Not surprisingly, perhaps the defining moment of the Protestant Reformation is one that put this principle into action. It happened in 1521, early in the Reformation, when Martin Luther was called to stand before the Emperor and the church authorities at the Council of Worms. With the threat of execution by public burning lingering in the air, Luther was confronted for his teaching, which opposed the false teachings of the Roman Catholic Church. Luther's books were piled on a table, to which the accuser pointed, demanding, "Will you recant of these?" Luther had anticipated this confrontation with a sleepless night of fervent prayer. He assured his accuser that he was prepared to recant of anything he had written, if he could be corrected by the Bible. Brushing this aside, the churchman cried, "Do you or do you not repudiate your books and the errors which they contain?" Luther then gave the immortal reply, "Unless I am convinced by Scripture and plain reason—I do not accept the authority of popes and councils, for they have contradicted each other—my conscience is captive to the Word of God, I cannot and I will not recant anything, for to go against conscience is neither right nor safe. God help me. Amen."[7] Then, committing himself irrevocably to God's Word, Luther gave his final response, "Here I stand, I can do no other."

Do we care that much about truth? Until we are willing to stand, to sacrifice, if need be, to die for truth, there will be no Reformation today. Unless we are ready to affirm that the book we hold contains the very words of God revealed to us plainly, we will have no boldness in the truth. Paul assures us, "All Scripture is God-breathed and is useful for teaching, rebuking, correcting and training in righteousness, so that the man of God may be thoroughly equipped for every good work" (2 Tim. 3:16-17 NIV). Let us, then, believe that "the Word of God in the hand of God is quite sufficient to do the work of God."[8] Only that confidence will enable us to be the church God intends us to be, with His power and with true relevance for a lost and dying world.

Jesus prayed to the Father, "Sanctify them in the truth; your word is truth" (John 17:17). To Pilate he stated, "For this purpose I was born and for this purpose I have come into the world—to bear witness to the truth. Everyone who is of the truth listens to my voice" (John 18:37). May God help us there to stand, with our Lord Jesus, beside the saints of old, upon the Word of God. And may God thereby grant reformation to His church.

---

7. Roland H. Bainton, *The Reformation of the Sixteenth Century* (Boston: Beacon, 1952), 60-61.

8. Wells, *Whatever Happened to the Reformation*, xxii-xxiii.

Christian Focus Publications

Our mission statement –

STAYING FAITHFUL

In dependence upon God we seek to impact the world through literature faithful to His infallible Word, the Bible. Our aim is to ensure that the Lord Jesus Christ is presented as the only hope to obtain forgiveness of sin, live a useful life and look forward to heaven with Him.

Our books are published in four imprints:

CHRISTIAN FOCUS

Popular works including biographies, commentaries, basic doctrine and Christian living.

CHRISTIAN HERITAGE

Books representing some of the best material from the rich heritage of the church.

MENTOR

Books written at a level suitable for Bible College and seminary students, pastors, and other serious readers. The imprint includes commentaries, doctrinal studies, examination of current issues and church history.

CF4•K

Children's books for quality Bible teaching and for all age groups: Sunday school curriculum, puzzle and activity books; personal and family devotional titles, biographies and inspirational stories – because you are never too young to know Jesus!

Christian Focus Publications Ltd,
Geanies House, Fearn, Ross-shire,
IV20 1TW, Scotland, United Kingdom.
www.christianfocus.com